WARCRAFT®

THE SUNWELL TRILOGY™

Volume 2

Shadows of Ice

Written by
Richard A. Knaak

Illustrated by
Jae-Hwan Kim

BLIZZARD® ENTERTAINMENT

HISTORY OF THE WORLD OF

The world of Azeroth has long been plagued by the misuse of magic. Originally, only dragons and night elves were able to practice the mystic arts, though eventually, even humans began to wield the unstable energy. Unfortunately, the unrestrained spell casting eventually caught the attention of a malevolent, extra-dimensional force known as the Burning Legion.

The Burning Legion's first attempt to invade Azeroth, known as the War of the Ancients, was only thwarted after many lives were lost and the world's sole continent was shattered. With their second attempt, the Burning Legion used the orcs from the world of Draenor as their pawns.

Twisted and corrupted by the Burning Legion's influence, the orcs invaded Azeroth through the Dark Portal. After many ferocious battles, this Second War ended with the orcs' defeat and imprisonment. Still determined to conquer Azeroth, the Burning Legion created one of its most twisted servants, the Lich King, to weaken Azeroth's defenders.

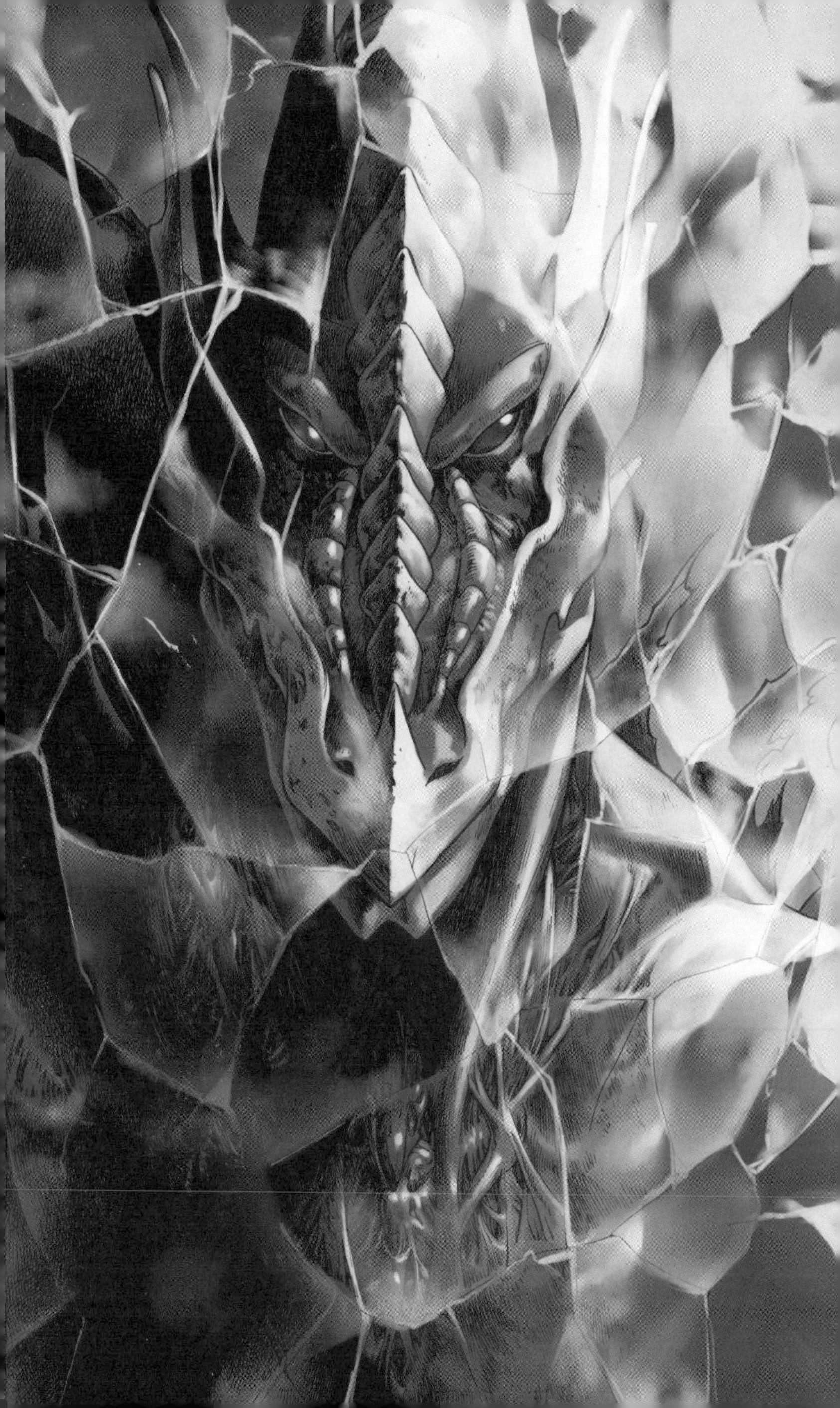

Warcraft: The Sunwell Trilogy Vol. 2
Written by Richard A. Knaak
Illustrated by Jae-Hwan Kim

Lettering and Layout - Rob Steen
Copy Editor - Peter Ahlstrom and Hope Donovan
Production Artists - James Dashiell and Jason Milligan
Artist Liaison - Eddie Yu
Cover Artist - Jae-Hwan Kim
Cover Design - James Lee

Editor - Rob Tokar
Digital Imaging Manager - Chris Buford
Production Manager - Jennifer Miller
Managing Editor - Lindsey Johnston
Editorial Director - Jeremy Ross
VP of Production - Ron Klamert
Publisher and E.I.C. - Mike Kiley
President and C.O.O. - John Parker
C.E.O. and Chief Creative Officer - Stuart Levy

BLIZZARD ENTERTAINMENT

Senior Vice President,
Story and Franchise Development - Lydia Bottegoni
Director, Creative Development - Ralph Sanchez
Lead Editor, Publishing - Robert Simpson
Senior Editor - Cate Gary
Associate Copy Editor - Allison Monahan
Producer - Brianne M Loftis
Vice President, Global Consumer Products - Matt Beecher
Senior Manager, Global Licensing - Byron Parnell
Special Thanks - Sean Copeland, Evelyn Fredericksen, Phillip Hillenbrand,
Christi Kugler, Alix Nicholaeff, Justin Parker

This book contains material originally published by TOKYOPOP Inc.

First Blizzard Entertainment printing: October 2018

ISBN: 978-1-9456-8319-0

10 9 8 7 6 5 4 3 2 1

Printed in China

The Lich King spread a plague of death and terror across Azeroth that was meant to snuff out human civilization. All those who died from the dreaded plague would arise as the undead, and their spirits would be bound to the Lich King's iron will forever.

The army of the dead swept across the land, and Quel'Thalas, the glorious homeland of the high elves which had stood for thousands of years, was devastated. The undead Scourge then moved south to Dalaran, and then to Kalimdor, home of the night elves.

Though the undead Scourge was stopped at Kalimdor, they had transformed Lordaeron and Quel'Thalas into toxic Plaguelands. Grieving for the loss of their homeland, most of the high elves have adopted a new name and a new mission. Calling themselves "blood elves," they now seek out and siphon magic from any available source, including demons.

Meanwhile, half of the undead forces staged a coup for control over the undead Scourge. Eventually, the banshee Sylvanas Windrunner and her rebel undead--known as the Forsaken--claimed the ruined capital city of Lordaeron as their own and vowed to drive the Scourge from the land.

Currently the Lich King resides in Northrend; he is rumored to be rebuilding the Icecrown Citadel. His trusted lieutenant, Kel'Thuzad, commands the Scourge in the Plaguelands. Sylvanas and her rebel Forsaken hold only the Tirisfal Glades, a small portion of the war-torn kingdom, while the humans, orcs, and night elves are

WarCraft
The Sunwell Trilogy

The story thus far . . .

Kalecgos, a young blue dragon, was sent by his master to investigate a strange surge of magical power. Before he could reach his destination, Kalec was shot down by the dragon hunter known as Harkyn Grymstone. Grymstone was a twisted, bitter dwarf who lost his loved ones in a dragon attack. He and his ragged band of hunters were only too happy to serve those who would enable them to slay all the dragons they could find.

Transforming into a humanoid form to escape the hunters' nets, a wounded Kalec was aided by Anveena, a kind, innocent maiden who lived nearby. Kalec tried to warn Anveena away, but she seemed unconcerned about the pursuing hunters. Even more remarkably, the young woman seemed unfazed by Kalec's true nature, though most people's reaction to meeting a dragon would be to flee or try to kill it.

Anveena's parents were equally welcoming to Kalec, and they maintained their friendly dispositions even when Grymstone kicked down their door. Kalec and Anveena used a hidden escape tunnel under the house to avoid the hunting party,

BUT THEY WERE DISCOVERED AND FORCED TO FLEE. KALEC TRANSFORMED BACK INTO A DRAGON AND FLEW AWAY WITH ANVEENA, BUT HIS WOUNDS AND GRYMSTONE'S ATTACKS DROVE HIM FROM THE SKY ONCE AGAIN.

UNABLE TO CONTROL HIS DESCENT, KALEC CRASHED INTO A NEARBY LAKE. ANVEENA SWAM TO SHORE AND FEARED THE WORST UNTIL SHE FOUND KALEC LYING AT THE WATER'S EDGE. LUCKILY, THE YOUNG DRAGON WAS ABLE TO TRANSFORM AGAIN AND WASH ASHORE BEFORE HIS BULKIER DRAGON FORM CAUSED HIM TO DROWN.

RETURNING TO ANVEENA'S HOME, KALEC AND ANVEENA FOUND ONLY BURNING WRECKAGE...AND THE UNDEAD SCOURGE. FIGHTING THE SHAMBLING CORPSES, KALEC AND ANVEENA WERE EASILY CAPTURED BY THE RENEGADE ELF KNOWN AS DAR'KHAN. DAR'KHAN PLACED PAIN-INDUCING MYSTICAL COLLARS AROUND KALEC AND ANVEENA'S NECKS, AND OFFERED THEM RELATIVELY PAINLESS DEATHS IN EXCHANGE FOR INFORMATION ABOUT THE SUNWELL.

Kalecgos
A young blue dragon. Though trapped i humanoid form by a mystical collar Dar'Kha placed around his neck, Kalec retains man of his magical talents, including the ability t create a sword out of nothingness.

THE SUNWELL WAS A POOL OF MYSTICAL ENERGY THAT WAS THE ESSENCE OF THE HIGH ELVES' LIVES. LOCATED IN THE ELVEN KINGDOM OF QUEL'THALAS, THIS SOURCE OF MAGIC WAS AS

IMPORTANT TO THE ELVES AS EATING OR BREATHING. THEY USED ITS VAST POWER TO BUILD THEIR CITIES, MOLD THE LANDSCAPE AND MAKE WHATEVER THEY DESIRED. UNFORTUNATELY, DAR'KHAN DESIRED MUCH MORE THAN THE REST OF HIS BRETHREN, LEADING HIM TO AN UNHOLY PACT WITH ARTHAS, THE CORRUPTED HUMAN KNIGHT WHO BECAME THE LICH KING.

DAR'KHAN ENABLED THE UNDEAD SCOURGE TO BYPASS QUEL'THALAS'S FABLED DEFENSES WHILE HE DRAINED THE SUNWELL'S ENERGIES. WHILE HIS PROUD HOME WAS OVERRUN BY VICIOUS, ZOMBIFIED CORPSES, AND DAR'KHAN FOUGHT HIS FELLOW ELVEN SORCERERS FOR CONTROL OF THE WELL, SOMETHING WENT HORRIBLY WRONG. THE SUNWELL'S POWER EXPLODED SPECTACULARLY, RAVAGING WHAT LITTLE REMAINED

Anveena
A caring, innocent young maiden. Anveena helped a wounded Kalecgos escape from dragon hunters, though her home and parents were destroyed.

untouched by the Scourge.

Dar'Khan was saved by the power of his dark lord, and sent across the continent in search of the Sunwell's escaped magic . . . which would seem to be the same power that Kalec's master sensed. Dar'Khan tried torturing Kalec for information, but he was interrupted by the arrival of Tyrygosa, a female blue dragon who is also Kalec's intended. Together, Tyri and Kalec managed to wipe out Dar'Khan's undead servants and drive the elf away . . . but they could not remove the collars he placed on his two captives.

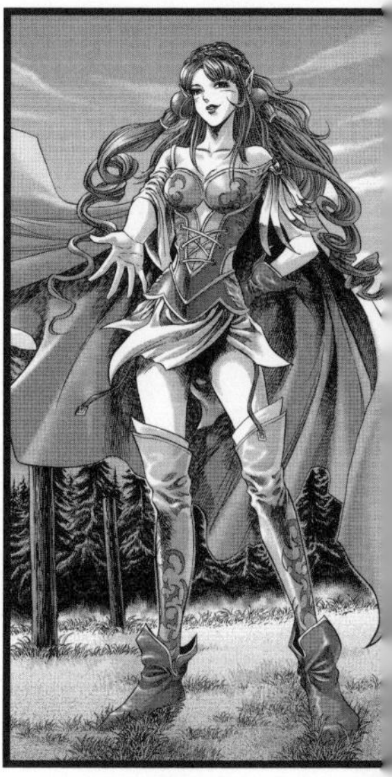

Tyrygosa
A female blue dragon and Kalec's intended. When forced to assume a humanoid shape, she refuses to look merely human. In her words, "At le[ast] elves are aesthetically pleasing."

Sifting through the shattered timbers of Anveena's home in search of her parents, the trio instead discovered a strange egg, which housed an even stranger winged serpent. Anveena named him Raac (for the noise he makes) and Kalec and Tyri suspected that the bizarre creature might have something to do with the Sunwell energy that attracted them and Dar'Khan.

Since Kalec's collar prevented him from transforming, Tyri carried her companions to the town of Tarren Mill in search of Borel, a man who Anveena's parents spoke of often. Though she never met him, she believed he might be able to help them remove Dar'Khan's collars. The group

Jorad Mace

A human paladin whose loyalty was sworn to Arthas . . . before Arthas betrayed his father, his homeland and his species. Mace is continually haunted by his terrible loss.

ATTRACTED A LOT OF ATTENTION IN THE SMALL TOWN, INCLUDING THAT OF JORAD MACE. MACE RECOGNIZED BOREL'S NAME, THOUGH HE WAS MORE INTERESTED IN HELPING ANVEENA ESCAPE THE TOWN THAN AIDING KALEC AND TYRI AGAINST A SURPRISE ATTACK BY HARKYN GRYMSTONE AND HIS FELLOW DRAGON HUNTERS.

GRYMSTONE HAD THE DRAGONS CORNERED WHEN HE SUDDENLY FOUND THAT HE, TOO, WAS SURROUNDED BY THE UNDEAD SCOURGE AND DAR'KHAN. DAR'KHAN REVEALED THAT HE HAD DISGUISED HIMSELF AS A HUMAN PRINCE TO PROVIDE THE VENGEFUL DWARF WITH THE RESOURCES NEEDED TO KILL ANY DRAGONS THAT MIGHT BE DRAWN TO THE AREA BY THE SUNWELL'S POWER. AS DAR'KHAN PREPARED TO TAKE RAAC FROM ANVEENA, A SURPRISE ATTACK FROM JORAD MACE HELPED THE DRAGONS AND DRAGON HUNTERS TURN THE TIDE.

WITH THEIR COMBINED EFFORTS, THE UNDEAD WERE WIPED OUT AND DAR'KHAN WAS CONSUMED IN A BLAST OF TYRI'S DRAGON FIRE.

When Mace informed the others that they might find Borel on Aerie Peak, an apologetic Harkyn Grymstone advised them to seek his cousin, Loggi, who lives in the mountains near there.

Hoping that Loggi might be able to remove the magical collars, Kalec, Anveena, Tyri, and Jorad Mace search not only for the dwarf, but also for the mysterious Borel, who may know more about the Sunwell than anyone. However, reaching Aerie Peak may be harder than imagined, even with a dragon to fly them there . . .

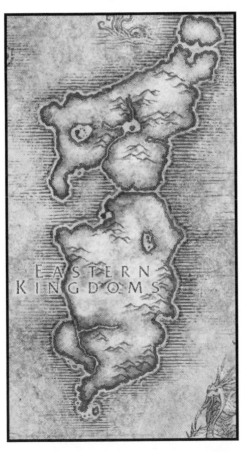

CHAPTER ONE

Terror on the Mountain

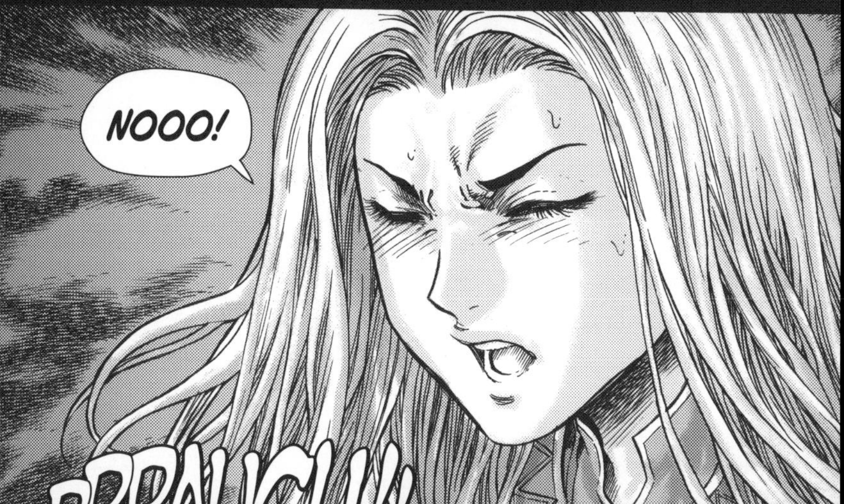
NOOO!
RRRAUGH!!

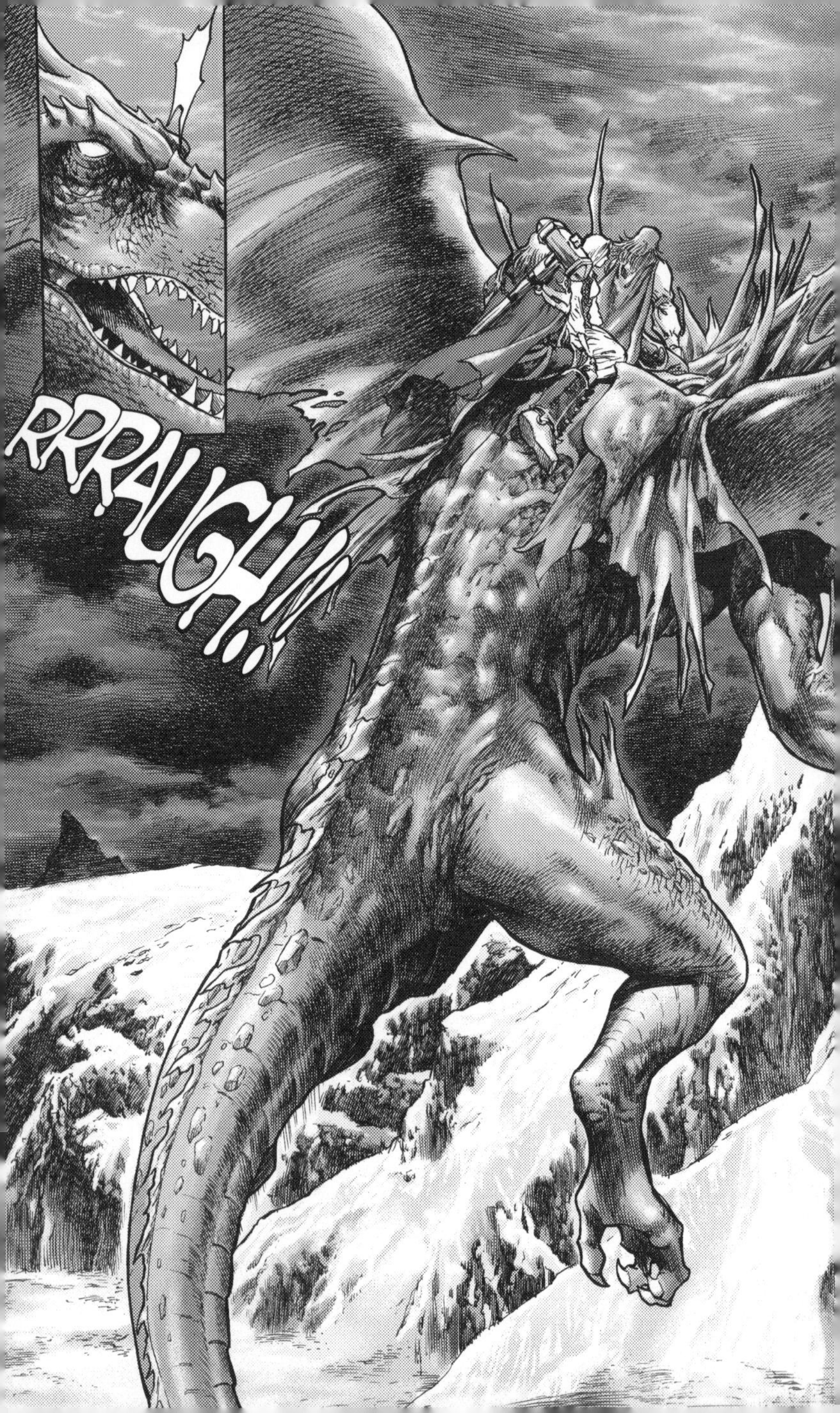
RRRRAUGH!!

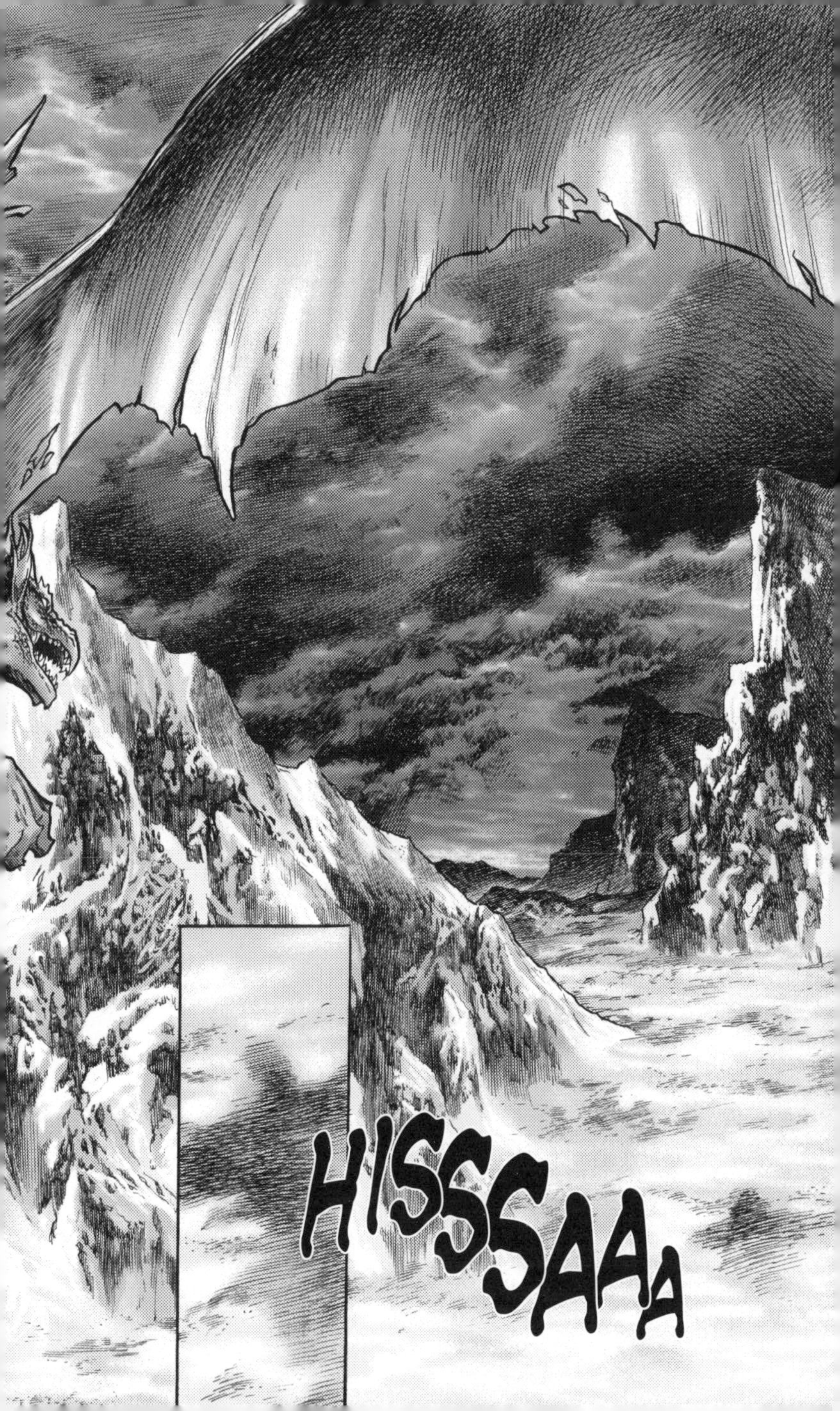
HISSSAAA

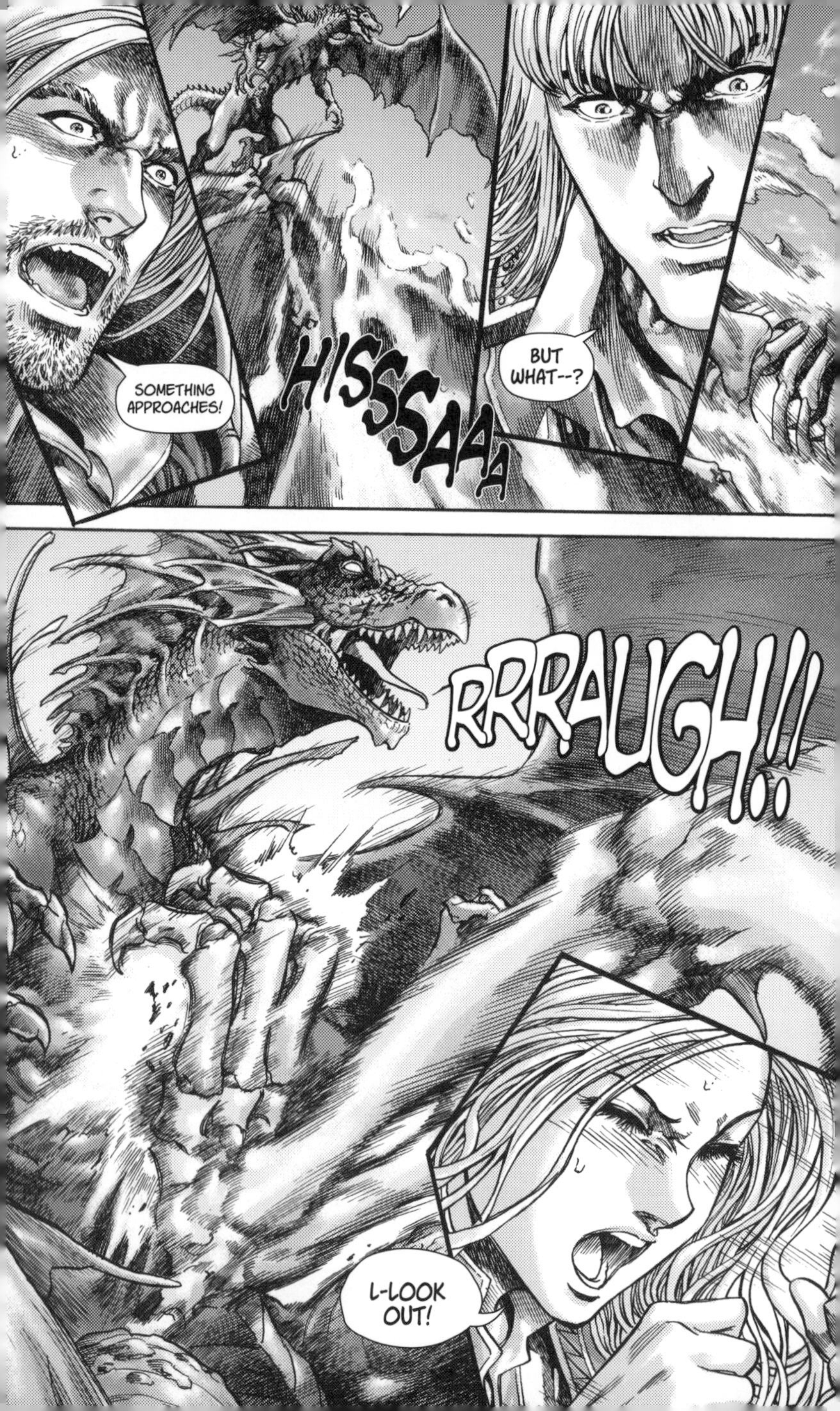
SOMETHING APPROACHES!
HISSSAAA
BUT WHAT--?
RRRAUGH!!!
L-LOOK OUT!

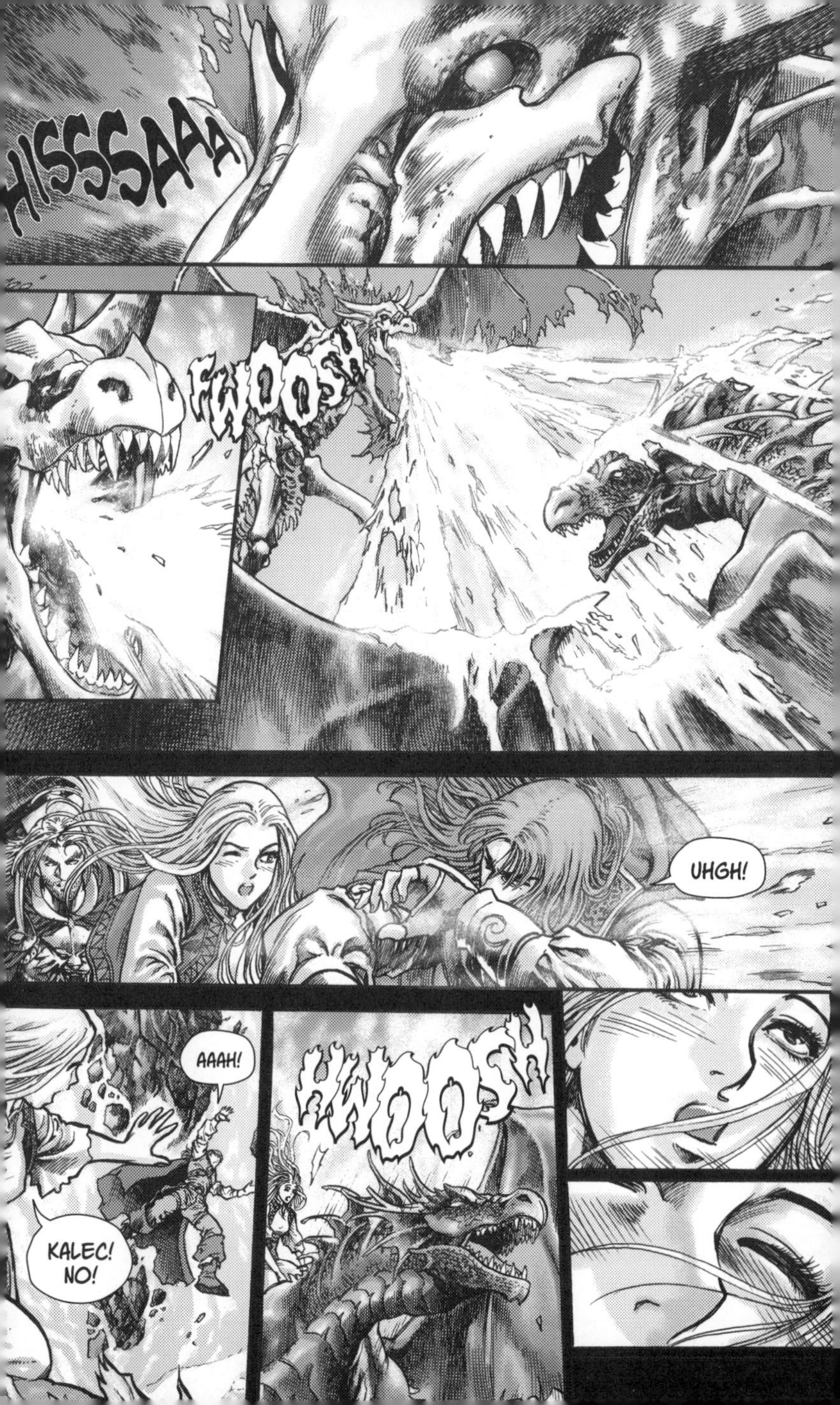
HISSSAAA
FWOOSH
UHGH!
AAAH!
KALEC! NO!
WHOOSH

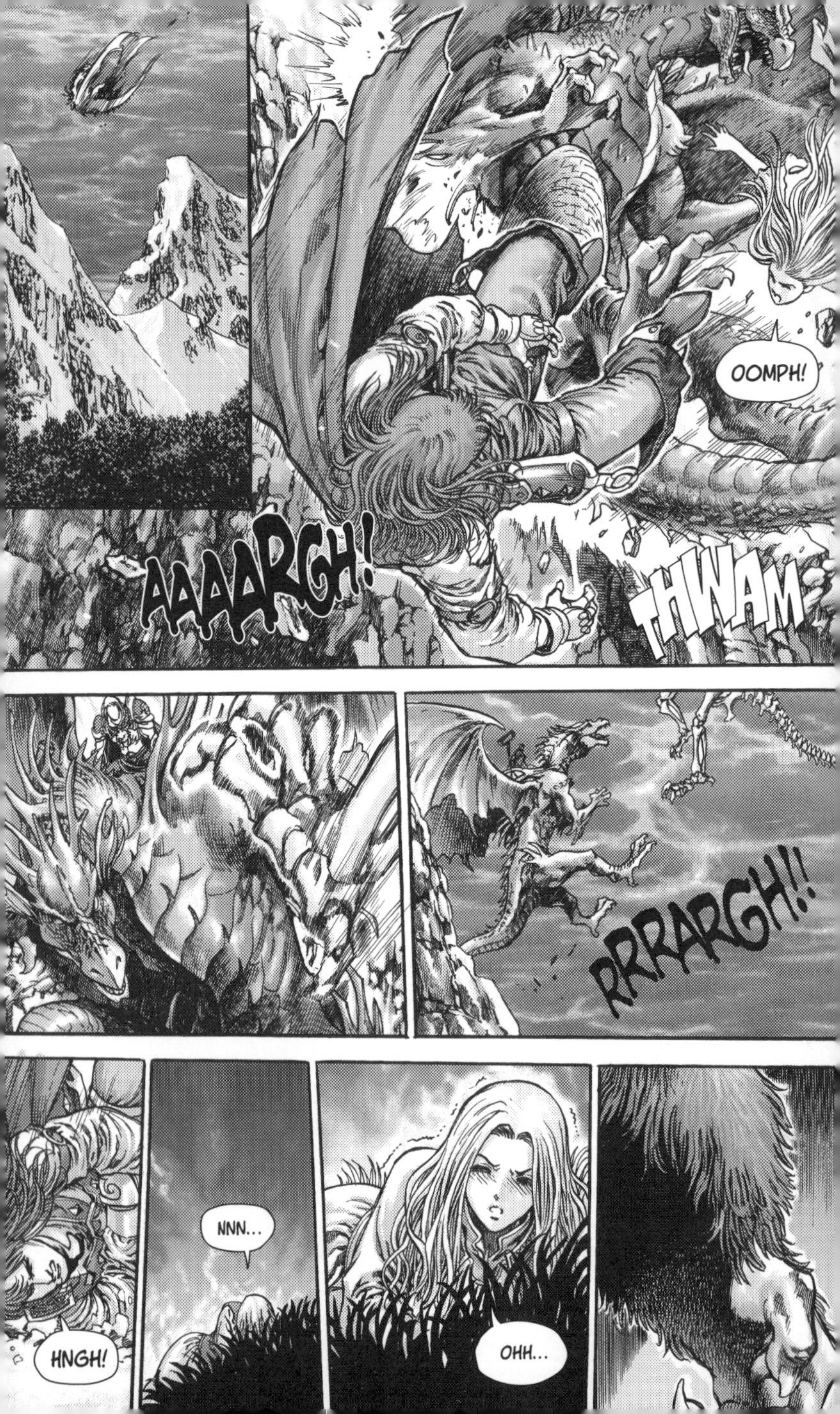
OOMPH!
AAAARGH!
THWAM
RRRARGH!!
HNGH!
NNN...
OHH...

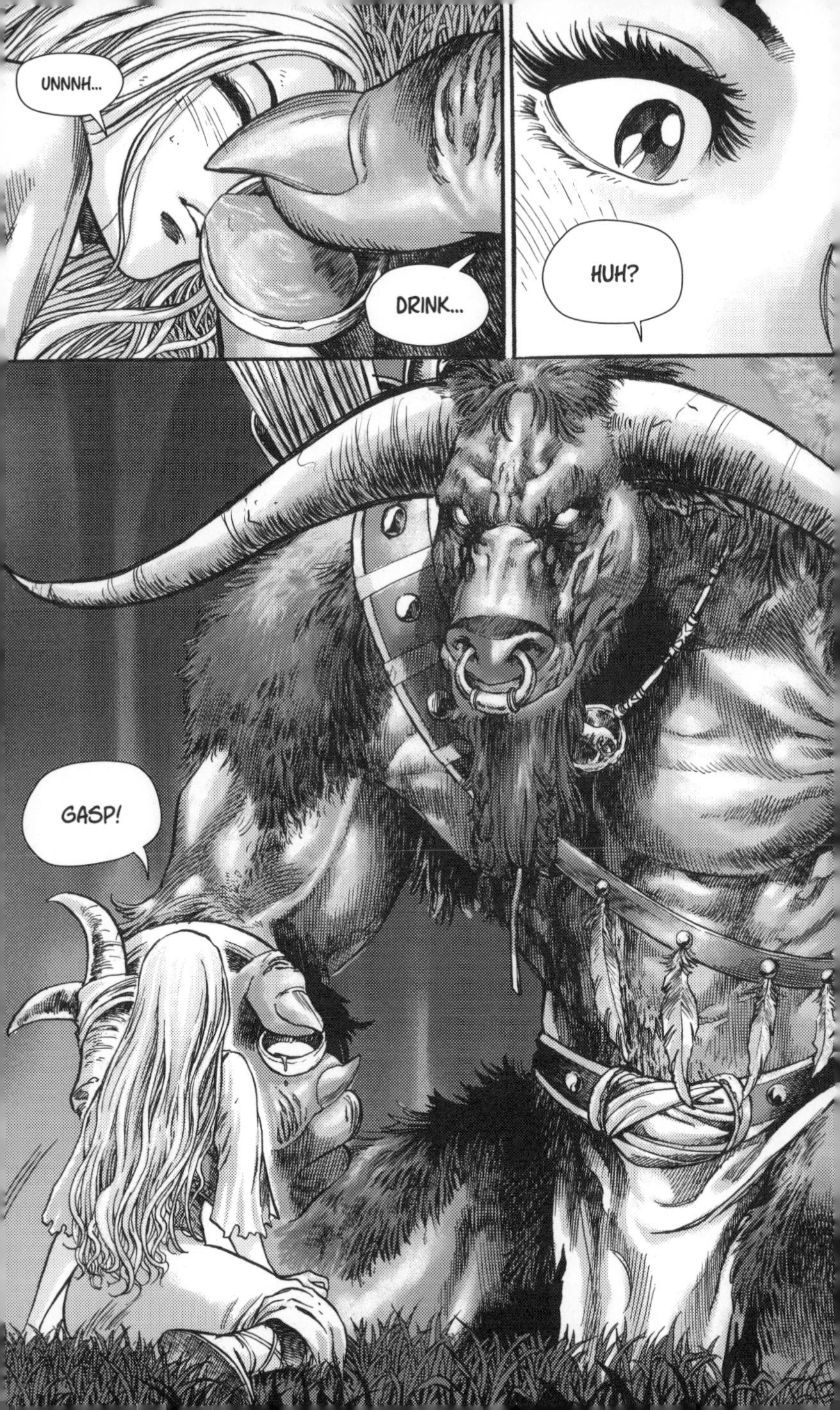
UNNNH...
DRINK...
HUH?
GASP!

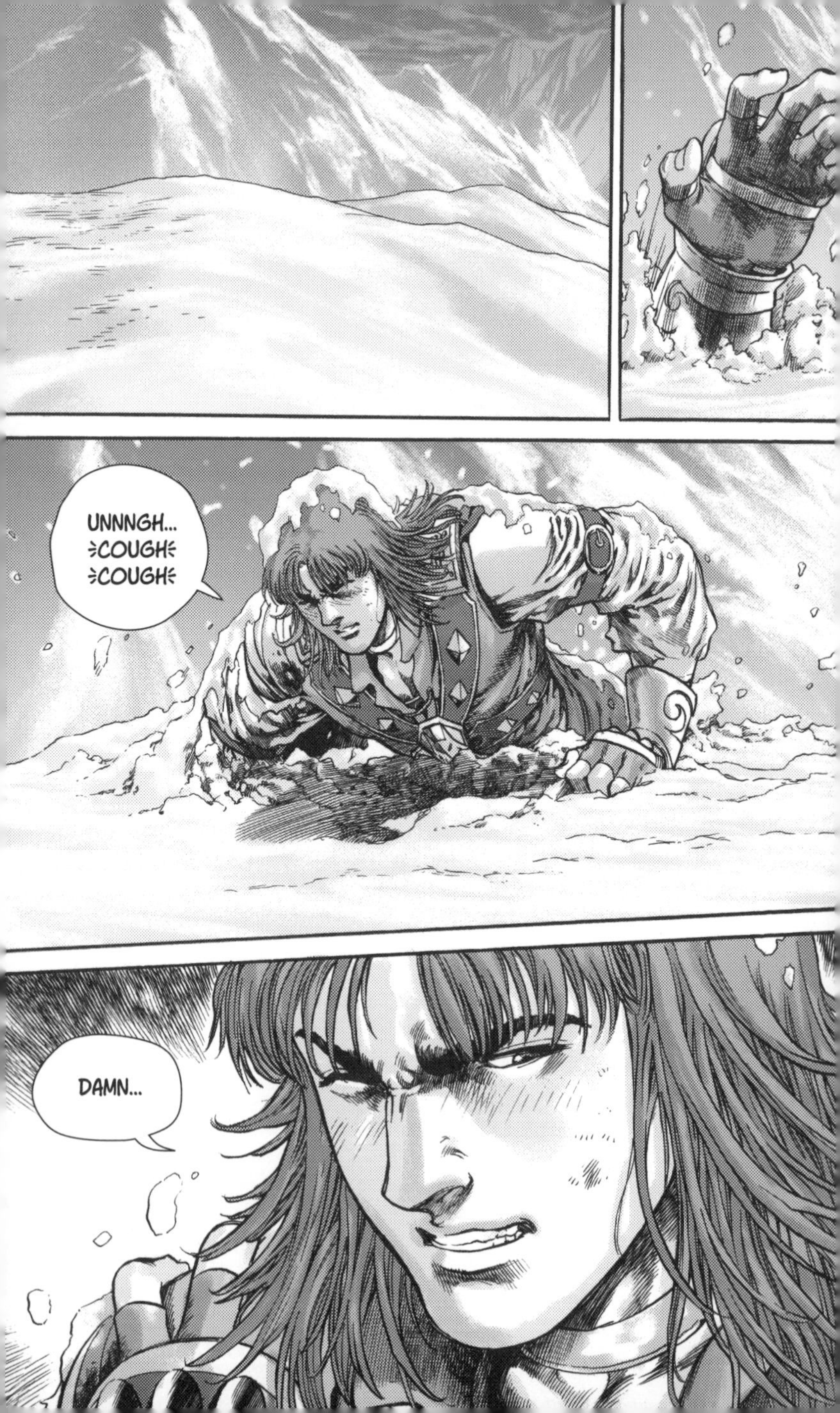
UNNNGH... ⪡COUGH⪢ ⪡COUGH⪢
DAMN...

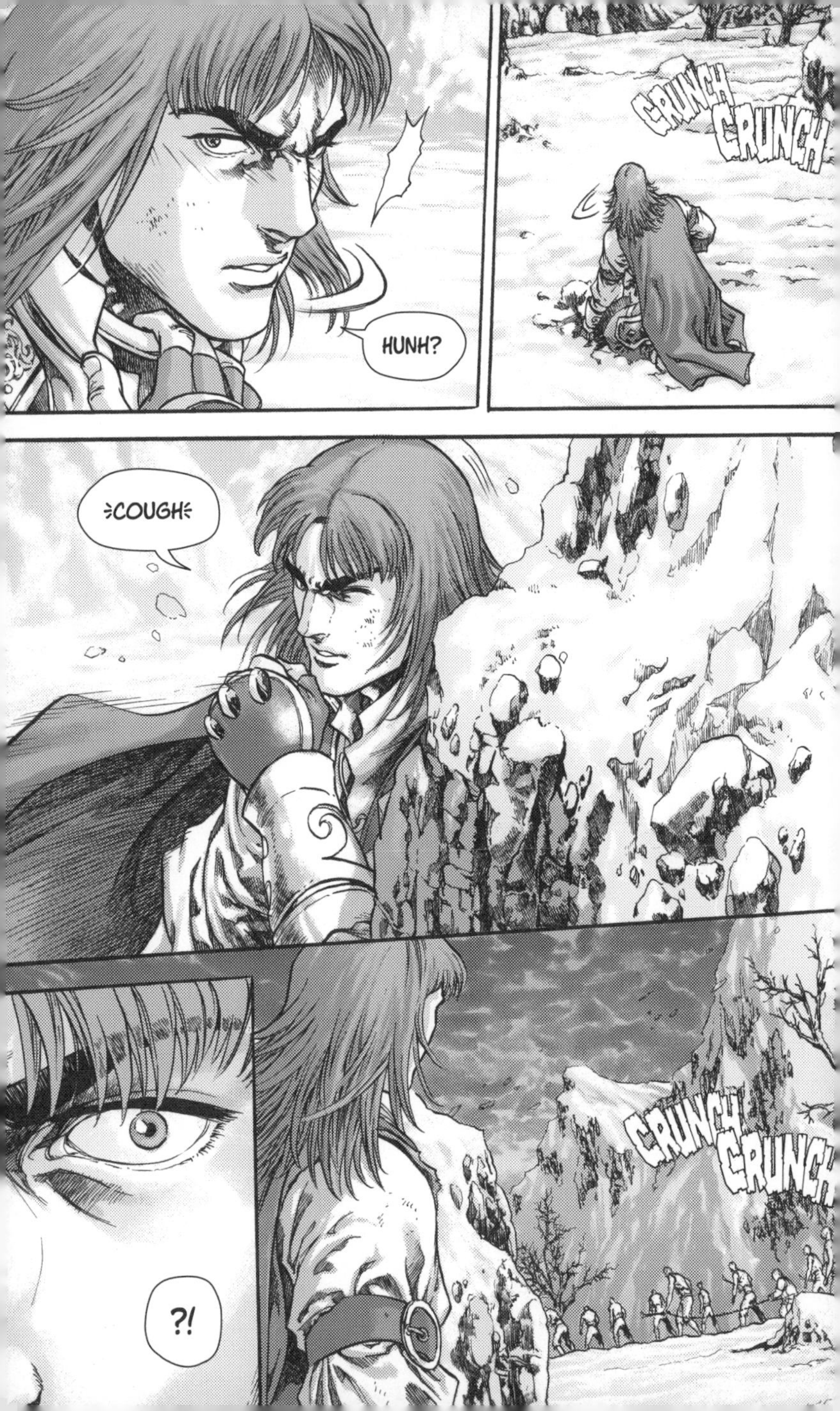
HUNH?
CRUNCH CRUNCH
COUGH
?!
CRUNCH CRUNCH

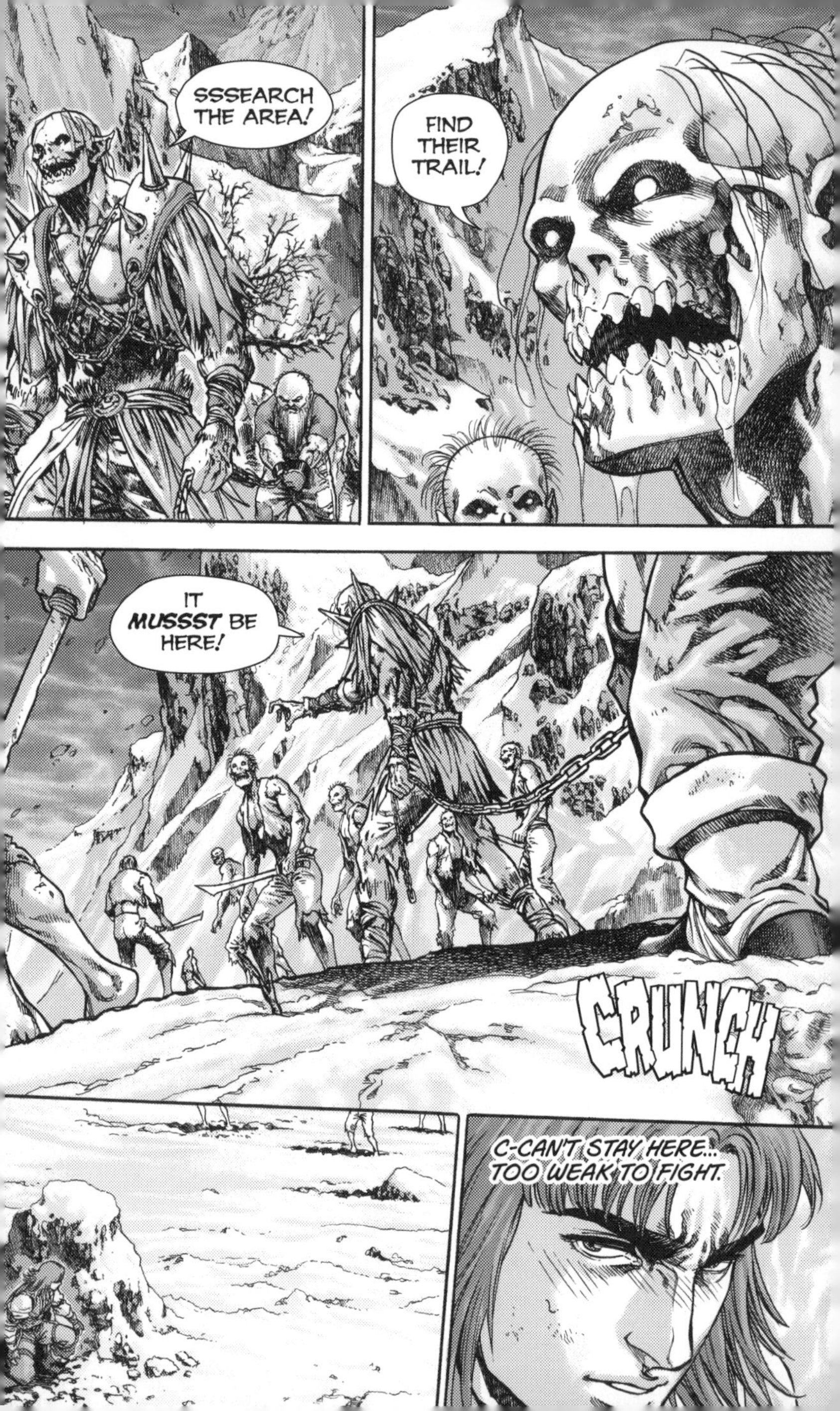
SSSEARCH THE AREA!
FIND THEIR TRAIL!
IT *MUSSST* BE HERE!
CRUNCH
C-CAN'T STAY HERE... TOO WEAK TO FIGHT.

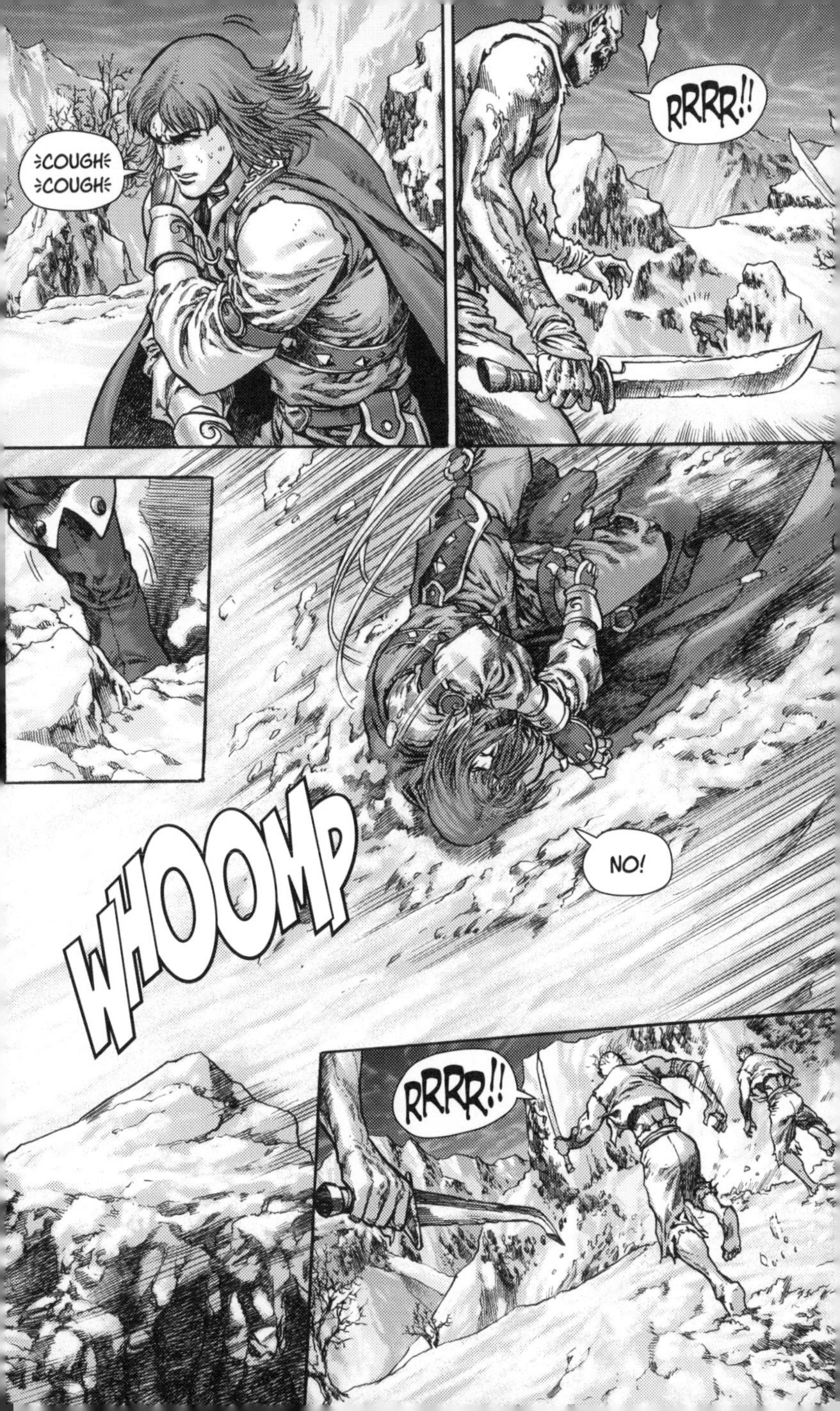

COUGH
COUGH
RRRR!!
WHOOMP
NO!
RRRR!!

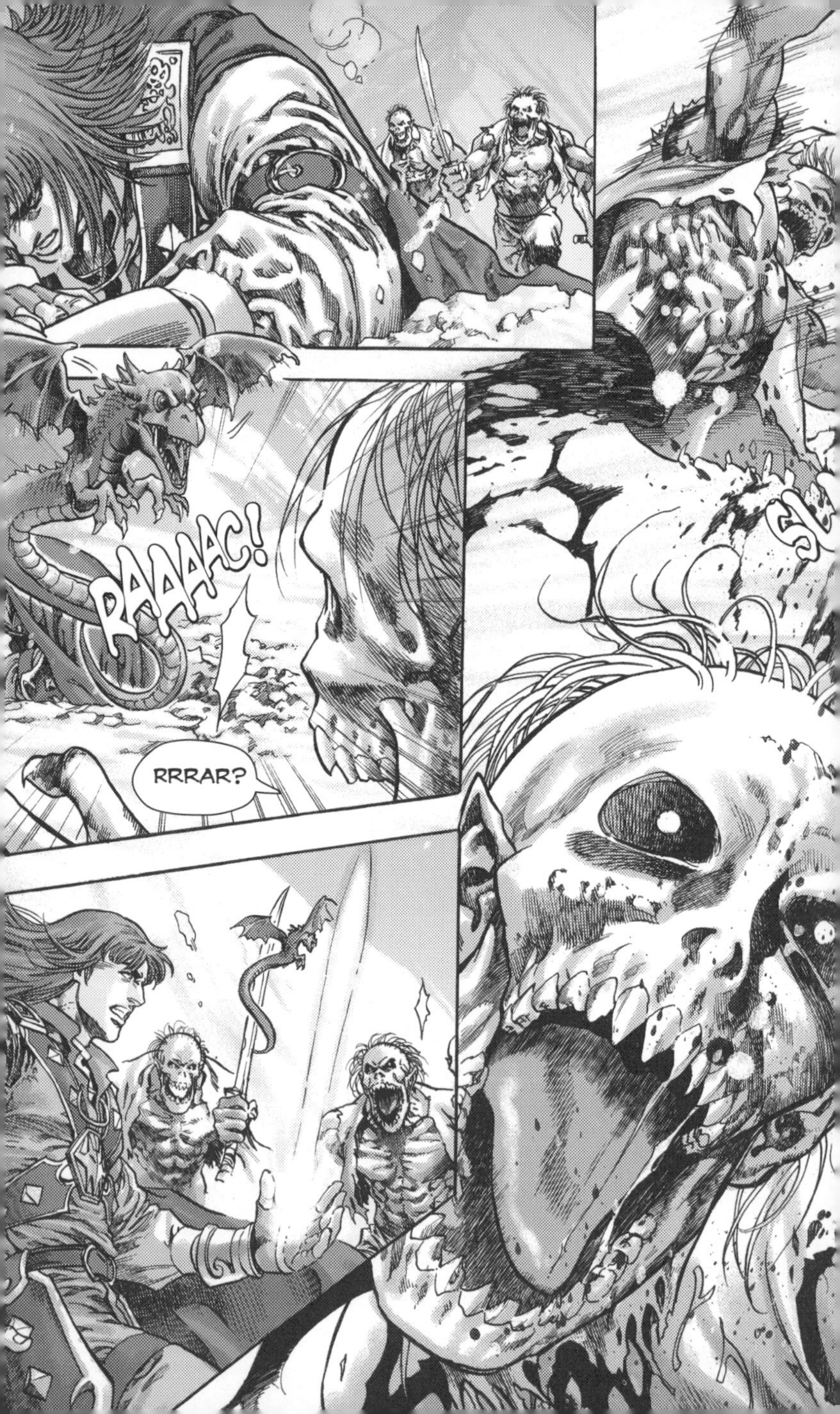
RAAAAC!
RRRAR?

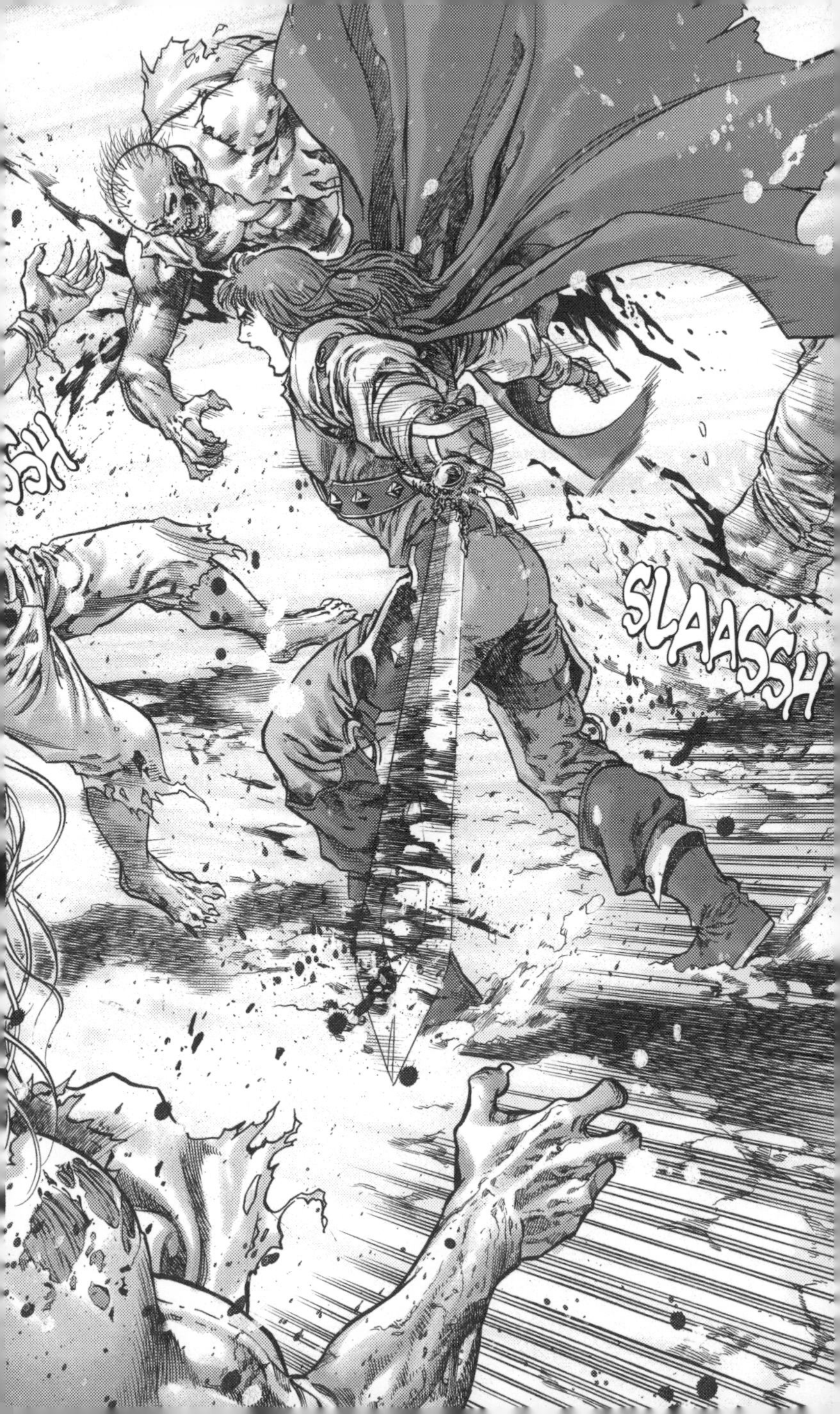
SLAASSH

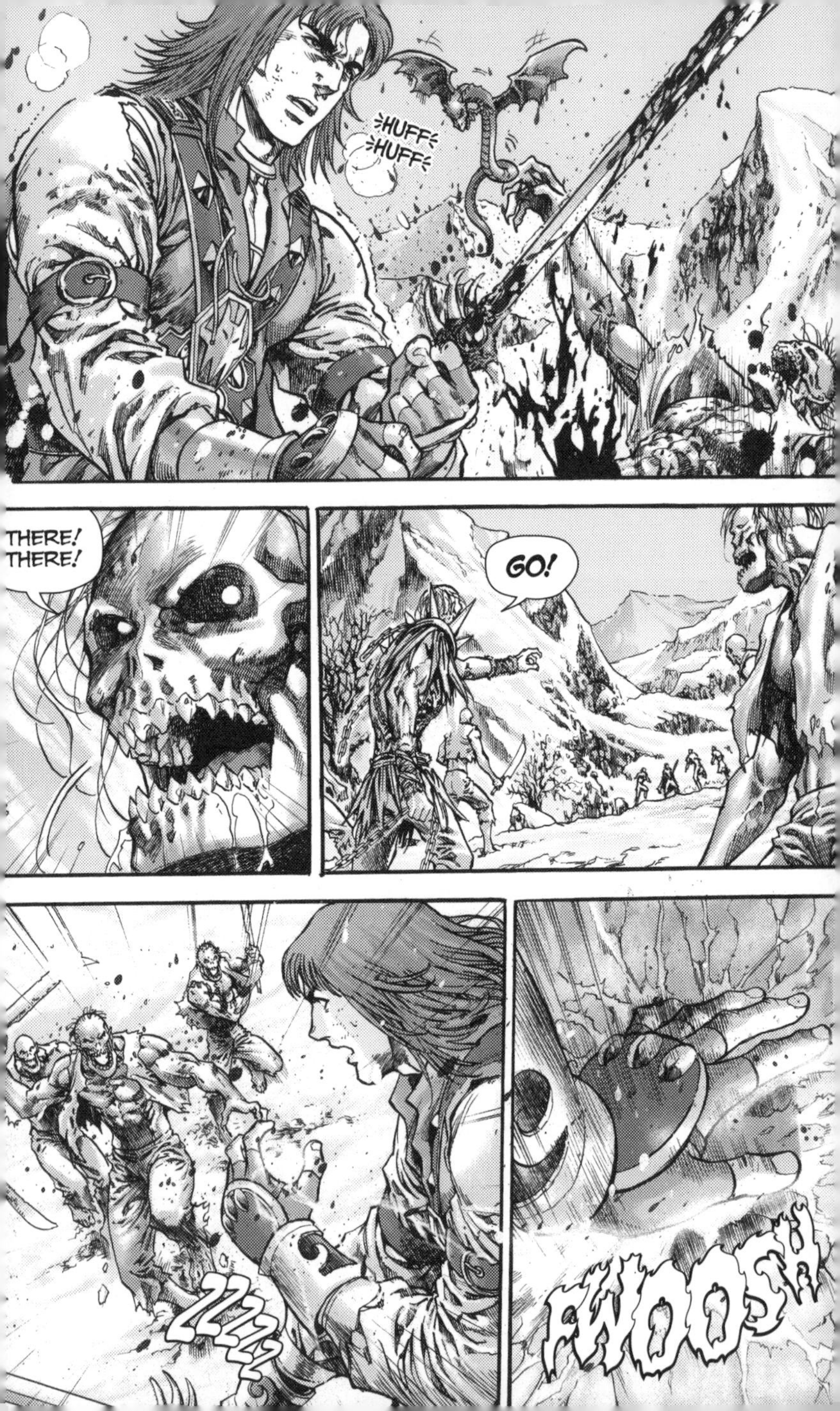
HUFF
HUFF
THERE! THERE!
GO!
ZZZZZ
FWOOSH

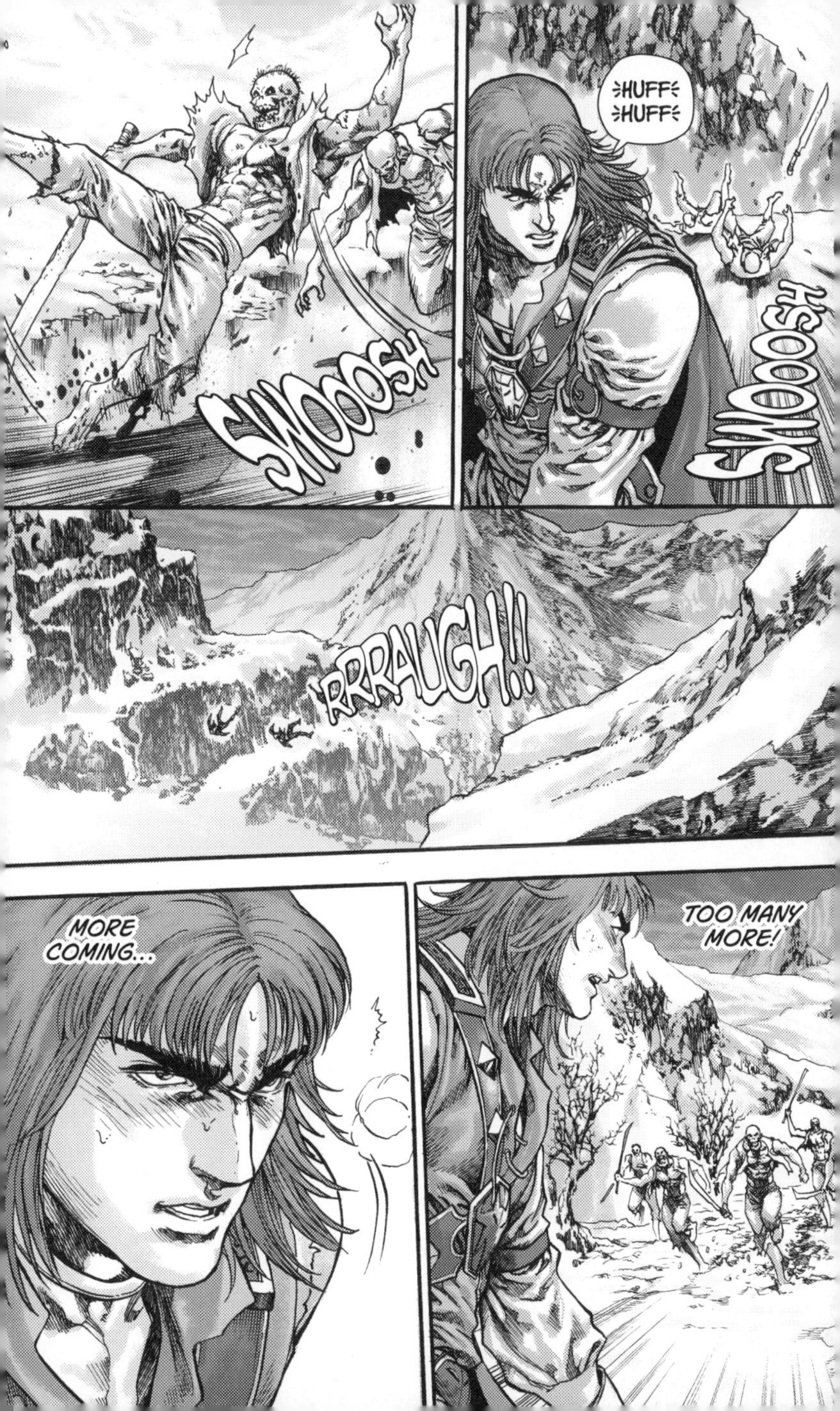
SWOOOSH
HUFF HUFF
SWOOOSH
RRRAUGH!!
MORE COMING...
TOO MANY MORE!

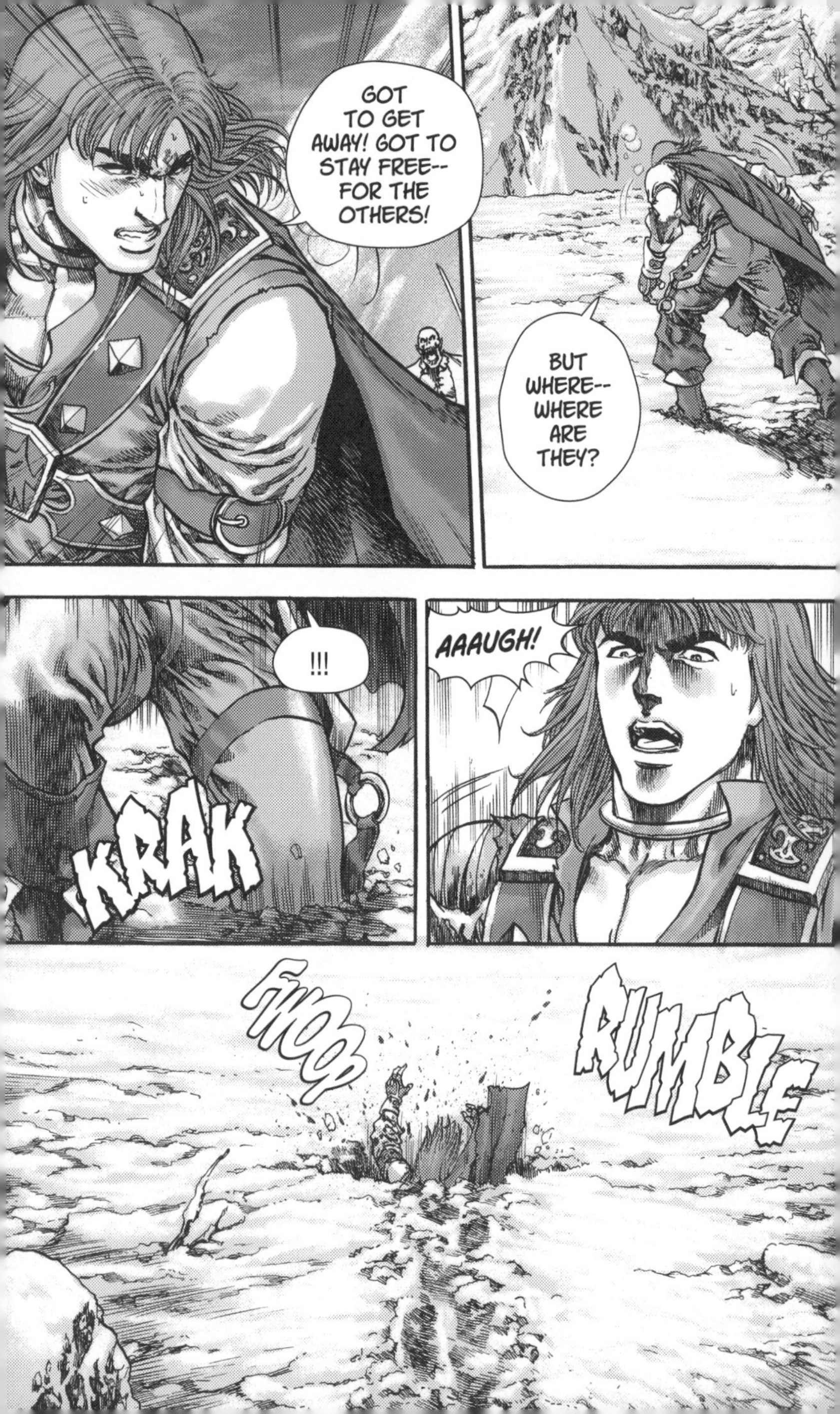
GOT TO GET AWAY! GOT TO STAY FREE-- FOR THE OTHERS!
BUT WHERE-- WHERE ARE THEY?
!!!
KRAK
AAAUGH!
FWOOM
RUMBLE

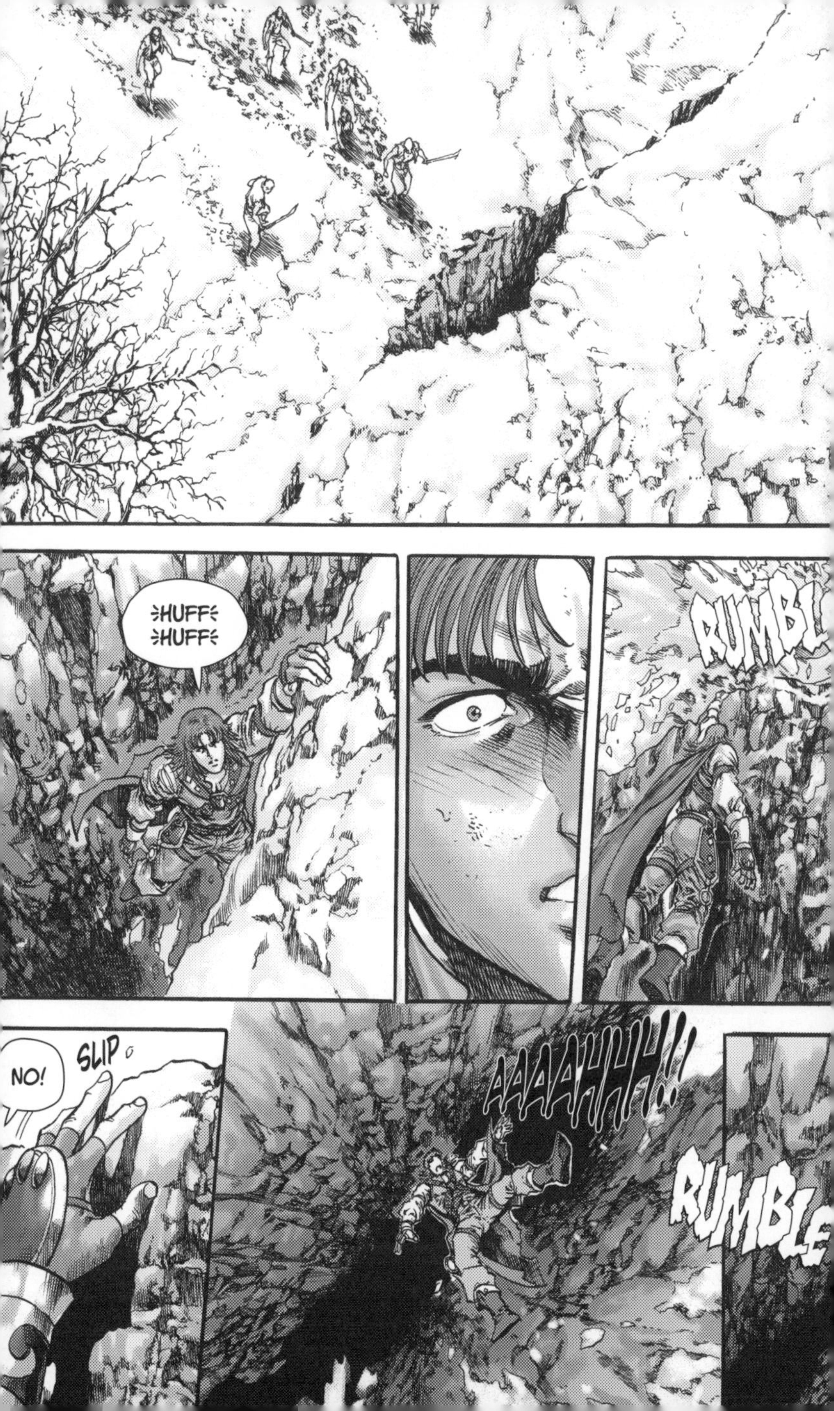

HUFF
HUFF
RUMBL
NO!
SLIP
AAAAHHH!!
RUMBLE

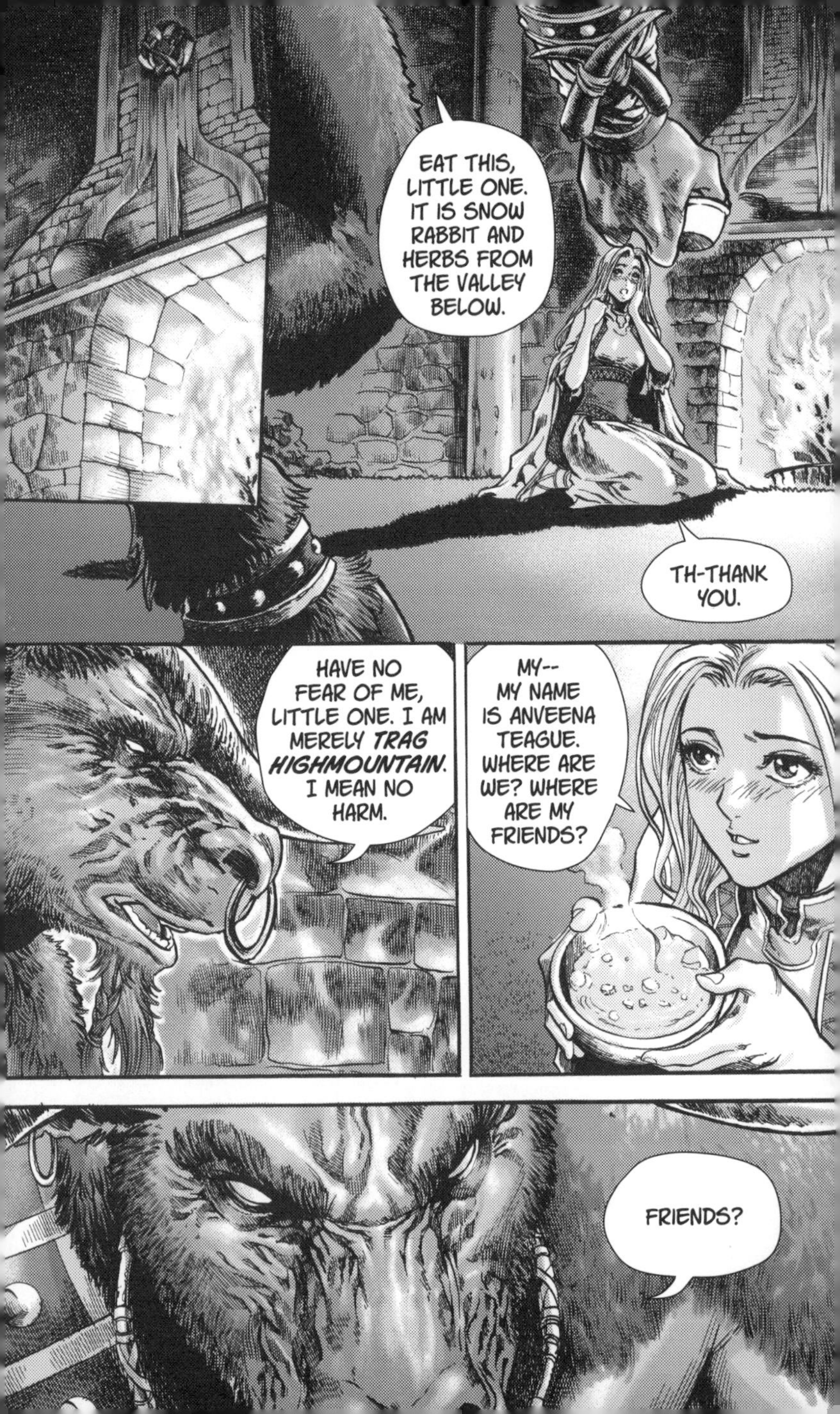
EAT THIS, LITTLE ONE. IT IS SNOW RABBIT AND HERBS FROM THE VALLEY BELOW.
TH-THANK YOU.
HAVE NO FEAR OF ME, LITTLE ONE. I AM MERELY *TRAG HIGHMOUNTAIN*. I MEAN NO HARM.
MY-- MY NAME IS ANVEENA TEAGUE. WHERE ARE WE? WHERE ARE MY FRIENDS?
FRIENDS?

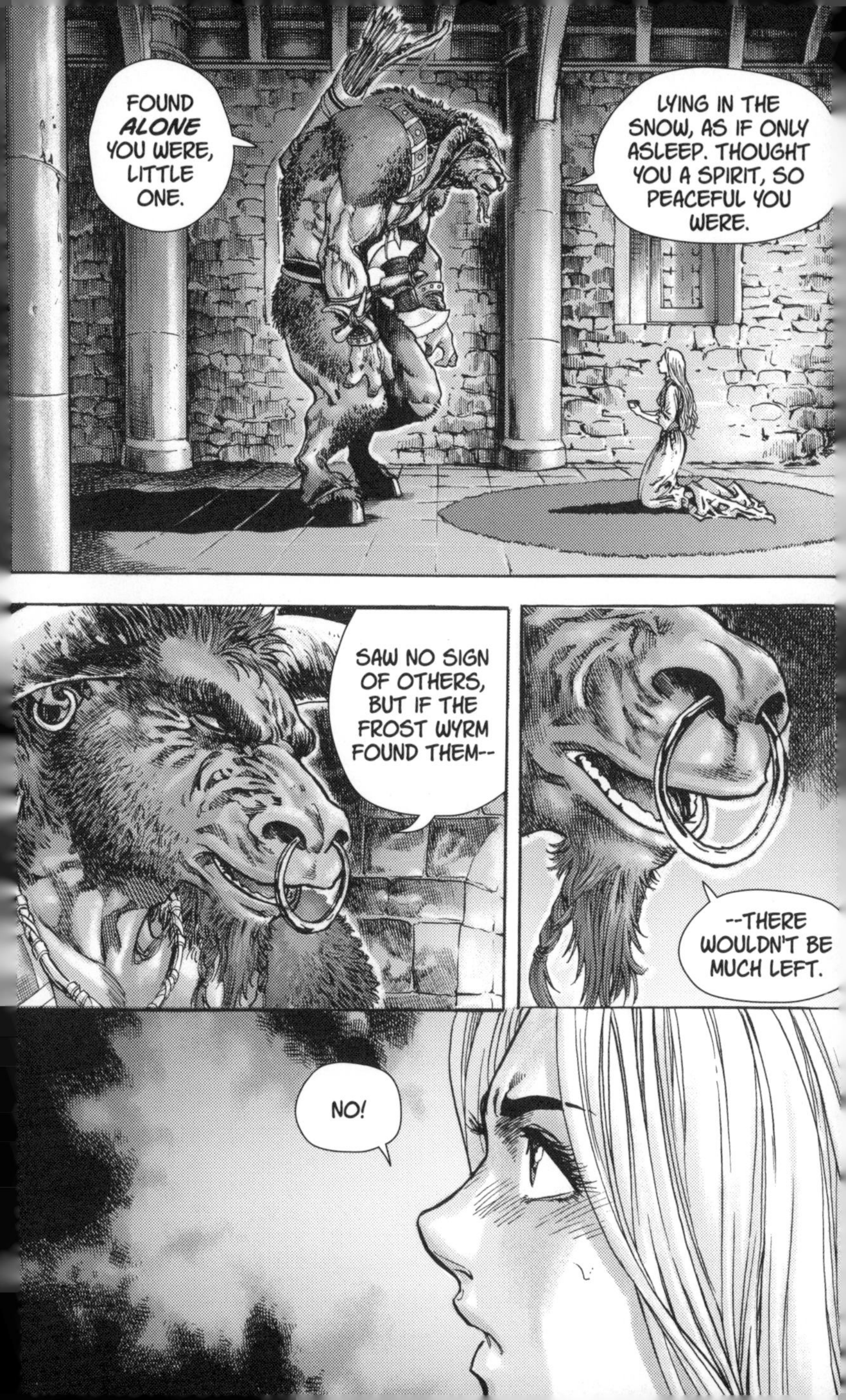
FOUND *ALONE* YOU WERE, LITTLE ONE.
LYING IN THE SNOW, AS IF ONLY ASLEEP. THOUGHT YOU A SPIRIT, SO PEACEFUL YOU WERE.
SAW NO SIGN OF OTHERS, BUT IF THE FROST WYRM FOUND THEM--
--THERE WOULDN'T BE MUCH LEFT.
NO!

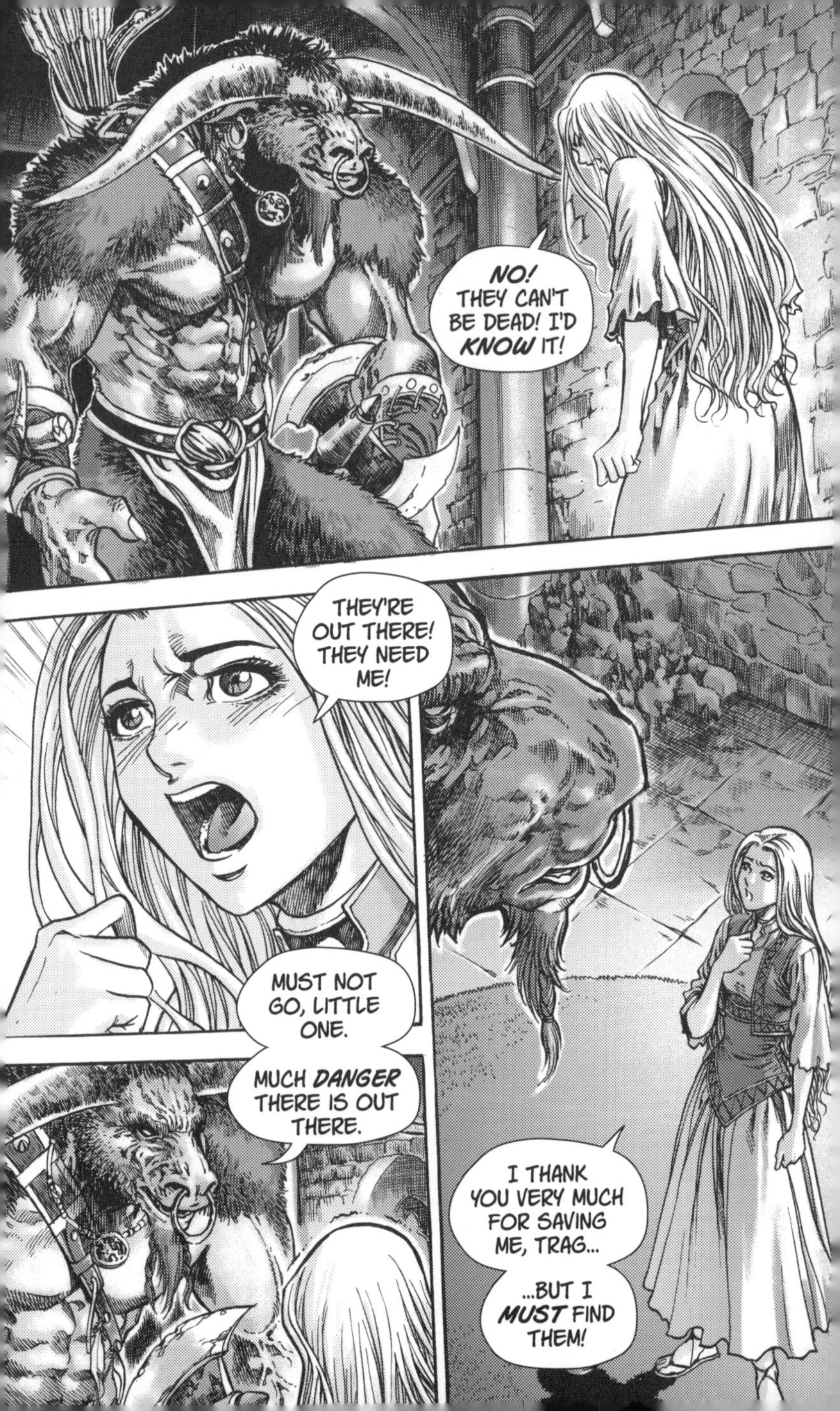

NO! THEY CAN'T BE DEAD! I'D KNOW IT!
THEY'RE OUT THERE! THEY NEED ME!
MUST NOT GO, LITTLE ONE.
MUCH DANGER THERE IS OUT THERE.
I THANK YOU VERY MUCH FOR SAVING ME, TRAG...
...BUT I MUST FIND THEM!

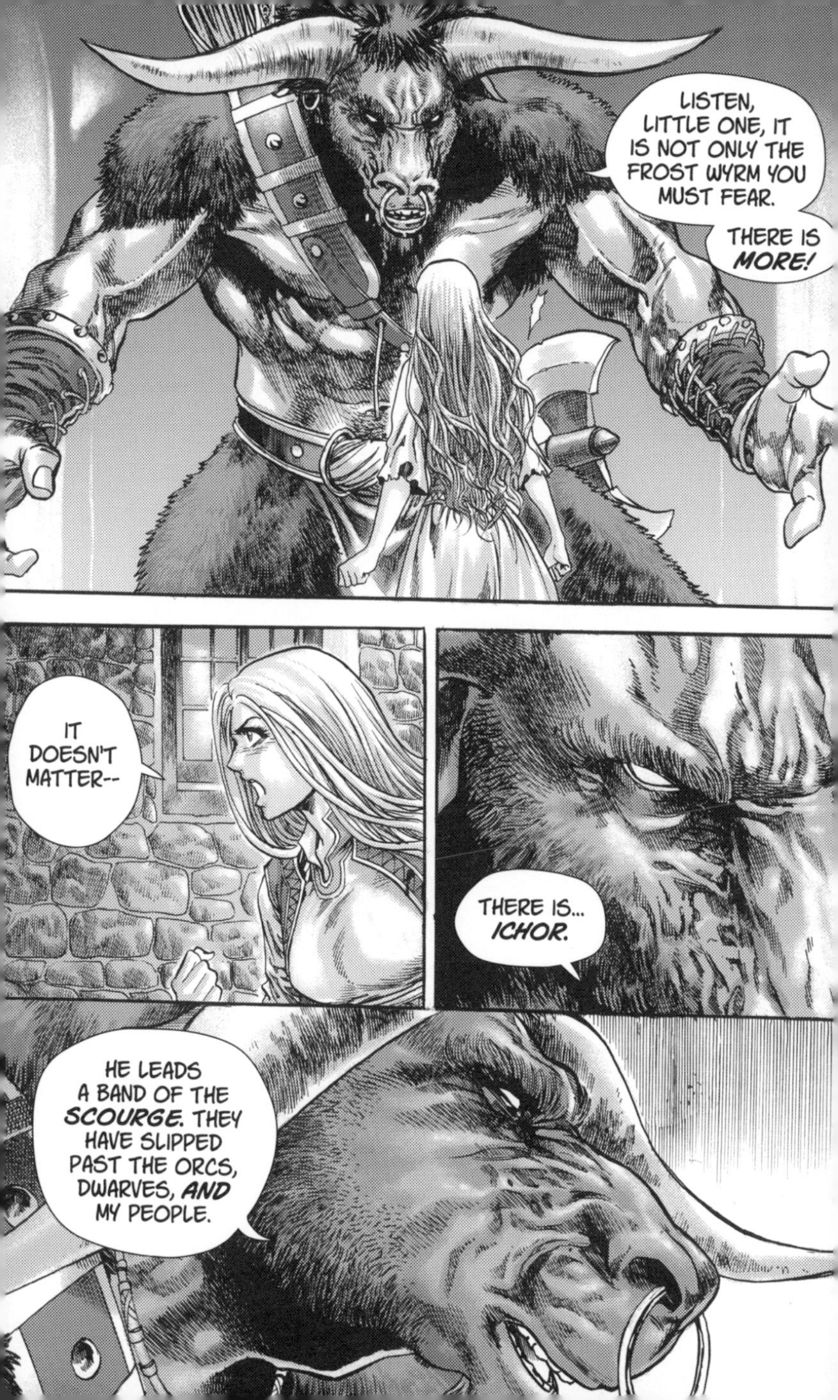
LISTEN, LITTLE ONE, IT IS NOT ONLY THE FROST WYRM YOU MUST FEAR.
THERE IS *MORE!*
IT DOESN'T MATTER--
THERE IS... *ICHOR.*
HE LEADS A BAND OF THE *SCOURGE.* THEY HAVE SLIPPED PAST THE ORCS, DWARVES, *AND* MY PEOPLE.

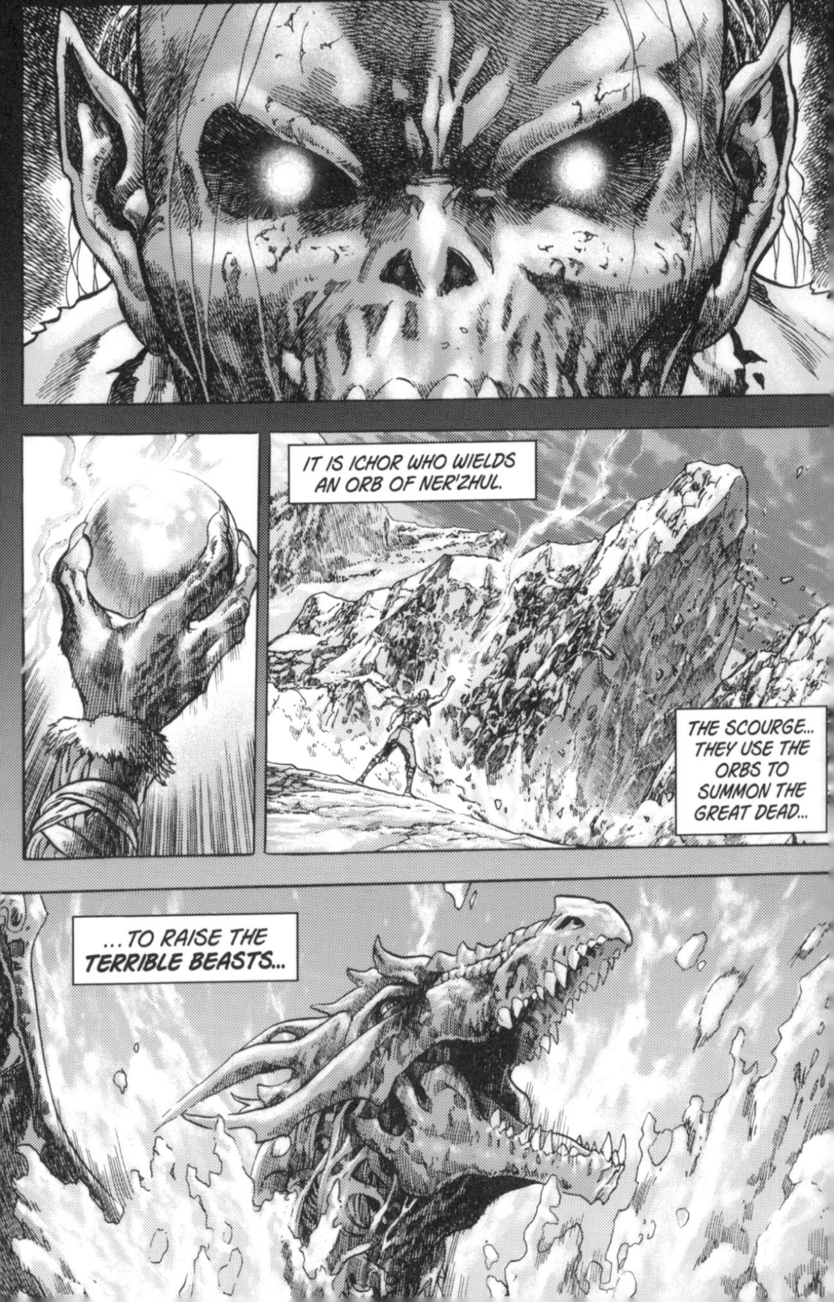
IT IS ICHOR WHO WIELDS AN ORB OF NER'ZHUL.
THE SCOURGE... THEY USE THE ORBS TO SUMMON THE GREAT DEAD...
...TO RAISE THE TERRIBLE BEASTS...

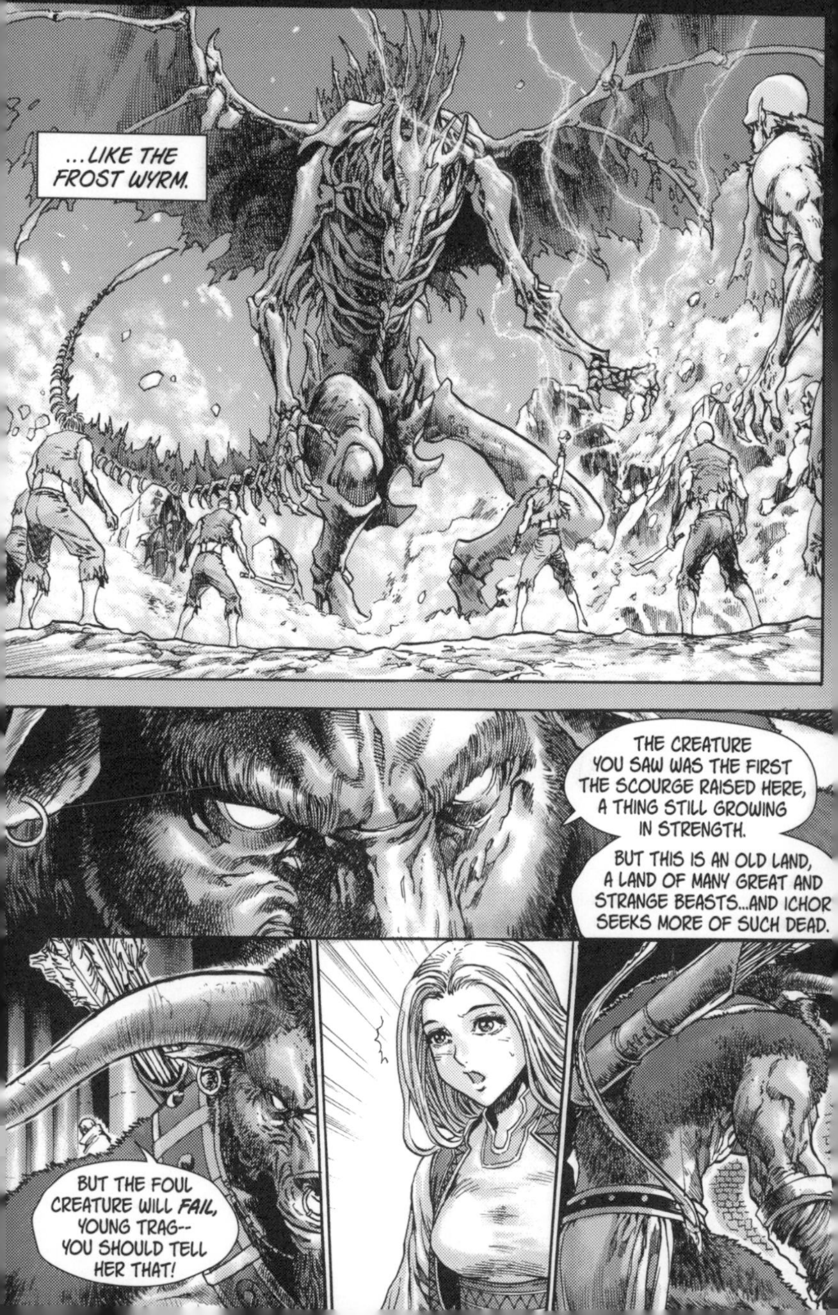
...LIKE THE FROST WYRM.
THE CREATURE YOU SAW WAS THE FIRST THE SCOURGE RAISED HERE, A THING STILL GROWING IN STRENGTH.
BUT THIS IS AN OLD LAND, A LAND OF MANY GREAT AND STRANGE BEASTS...AND ICHOR SEEKS MORE OF SUCH DEAD.
BUT THE FOUL CREATURE WILL *FAIL*, YOUNG TRAG-- YOU SHOULD TELL HER THAT!

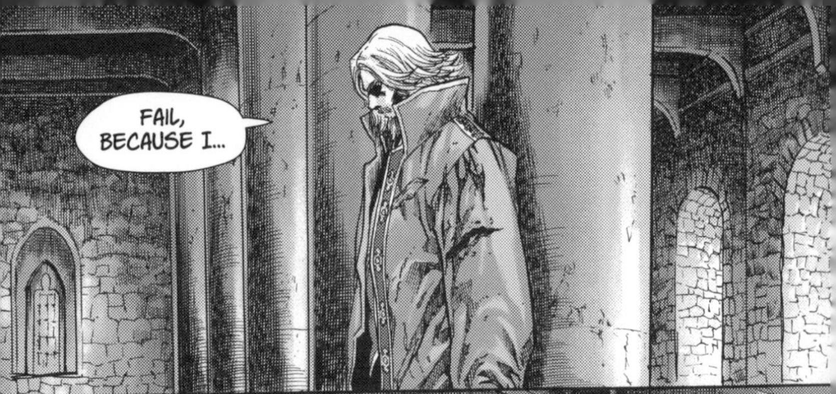
FAIL, BECAUSE I...
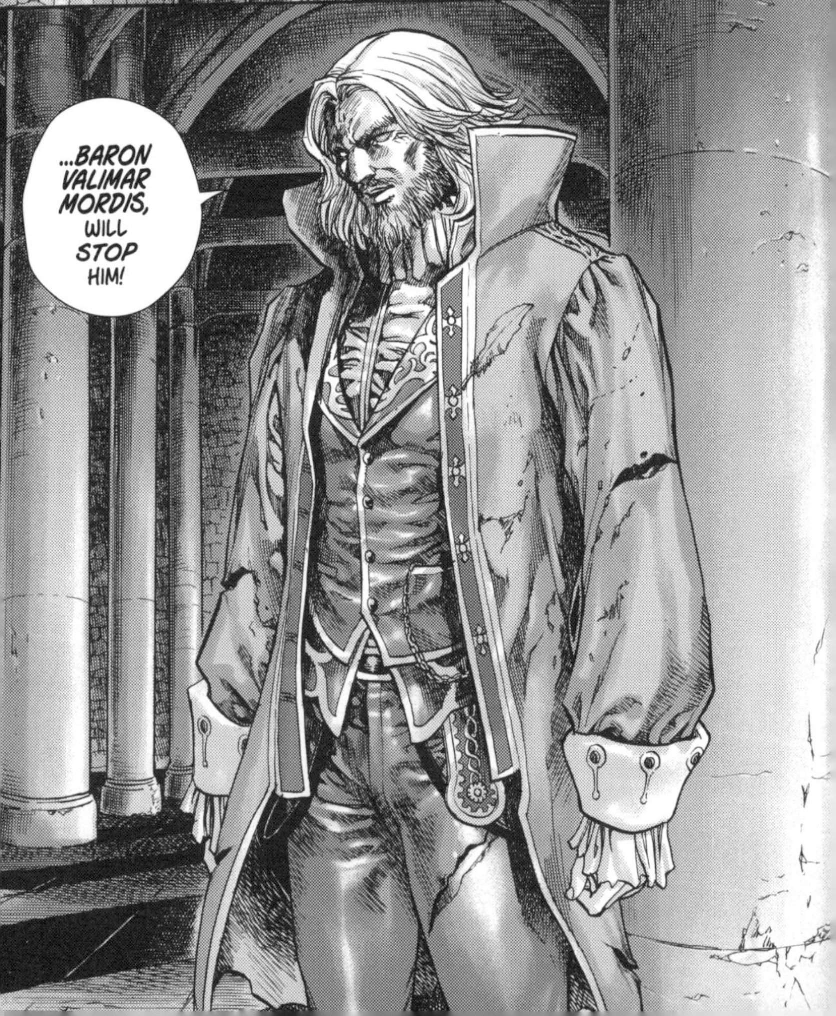
...BARON VALIMAR MORDIS, WILL STOP HIM!

CHAPTER TWO
BARON MORDIS

B-BOREL...

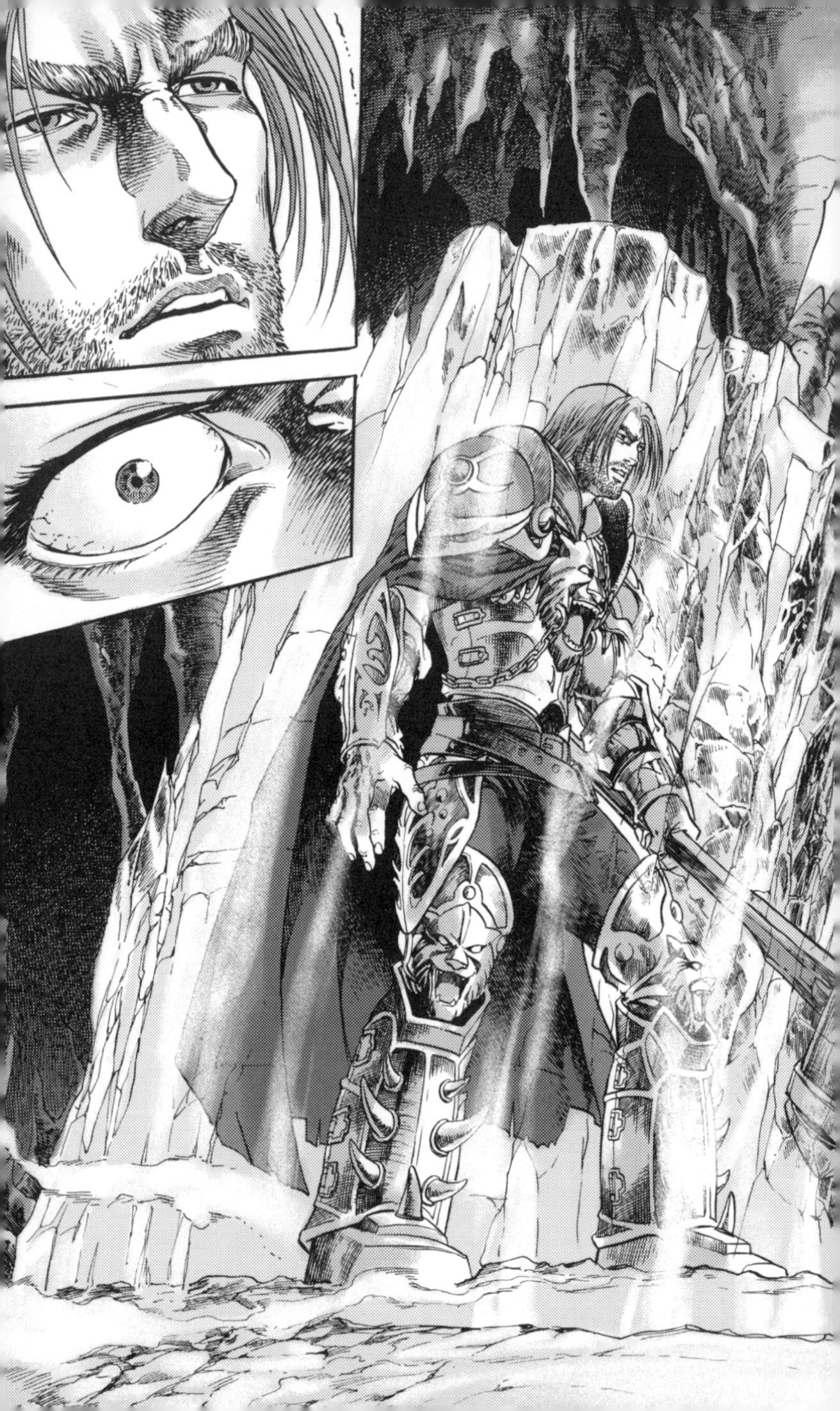

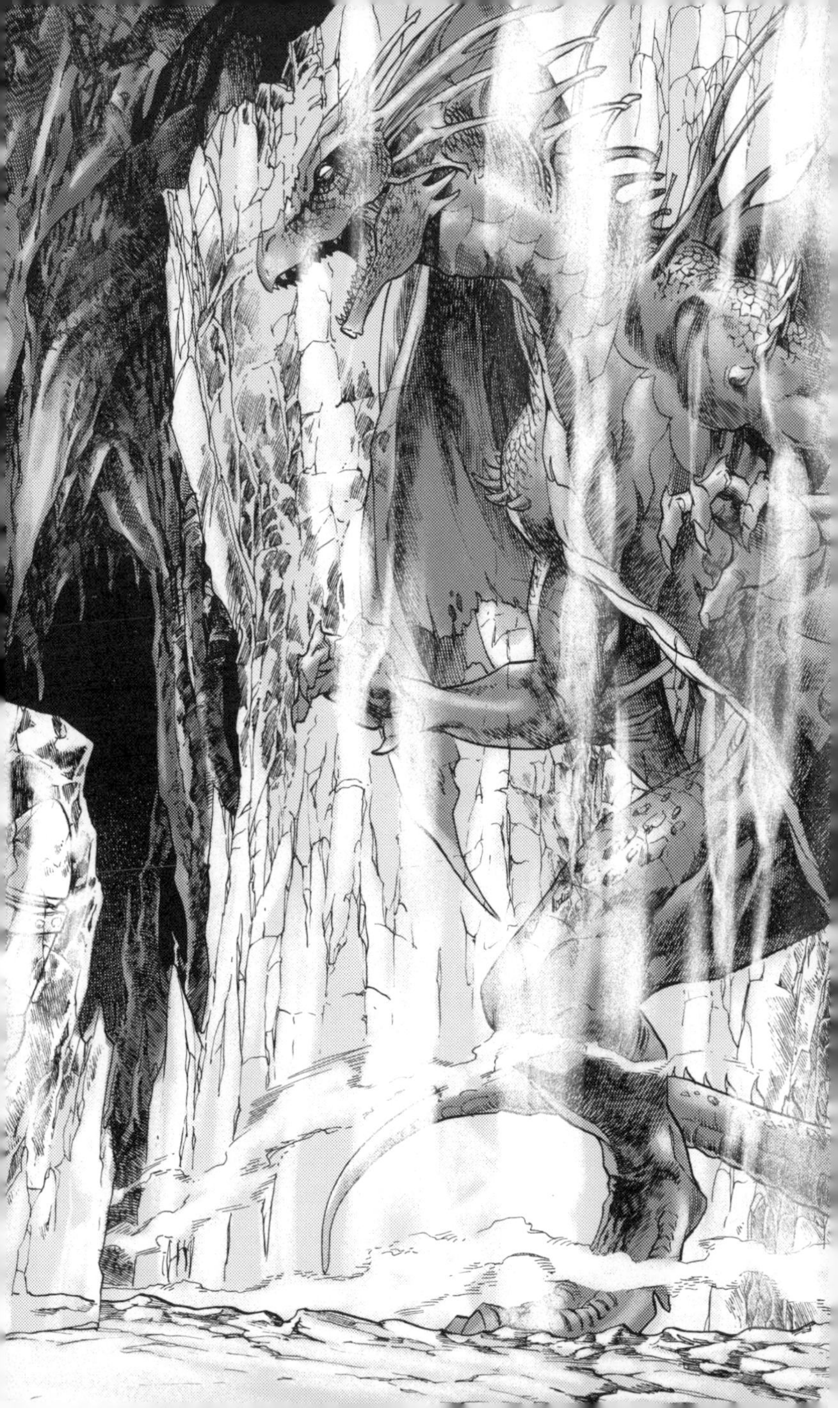

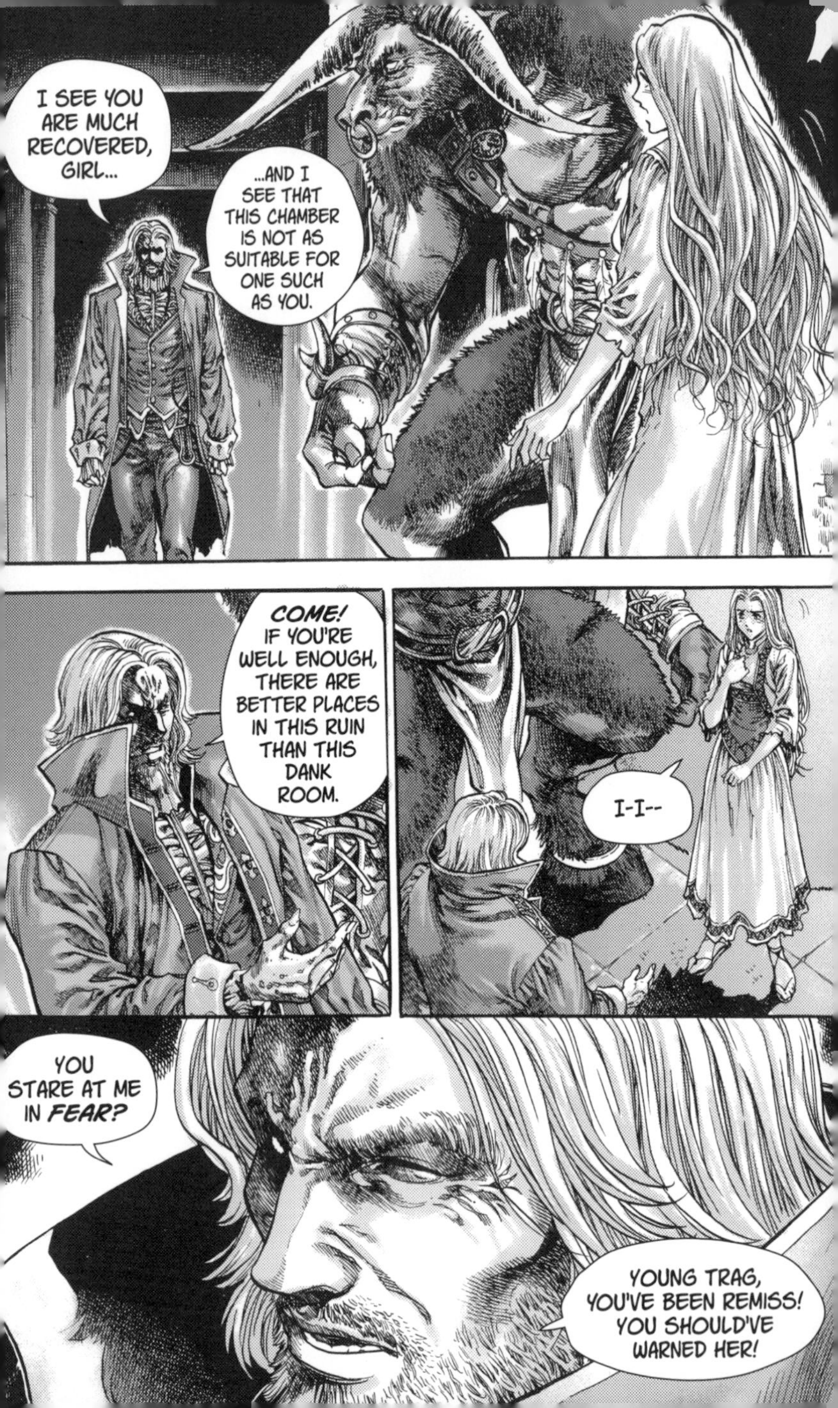
I SEE YOU ARE MUCH RECOVERED, GIRL...
...AND I SEE THAT THIS CHAMBER IS NOT AS SUITABLE FOR ONE SUCH AS YOU.
COME! IF YOU'RE WELL ENOUGH, THERE ARE BETTER PLACES IN THIS RUIN THAN THIS DANK ROOM.
I-I--
YOU STARE AT ME IN FEAR?
YOUNG TRAG, YOU'VE BEEN REMISS! YOU SHOULD'VE WARNED HER!

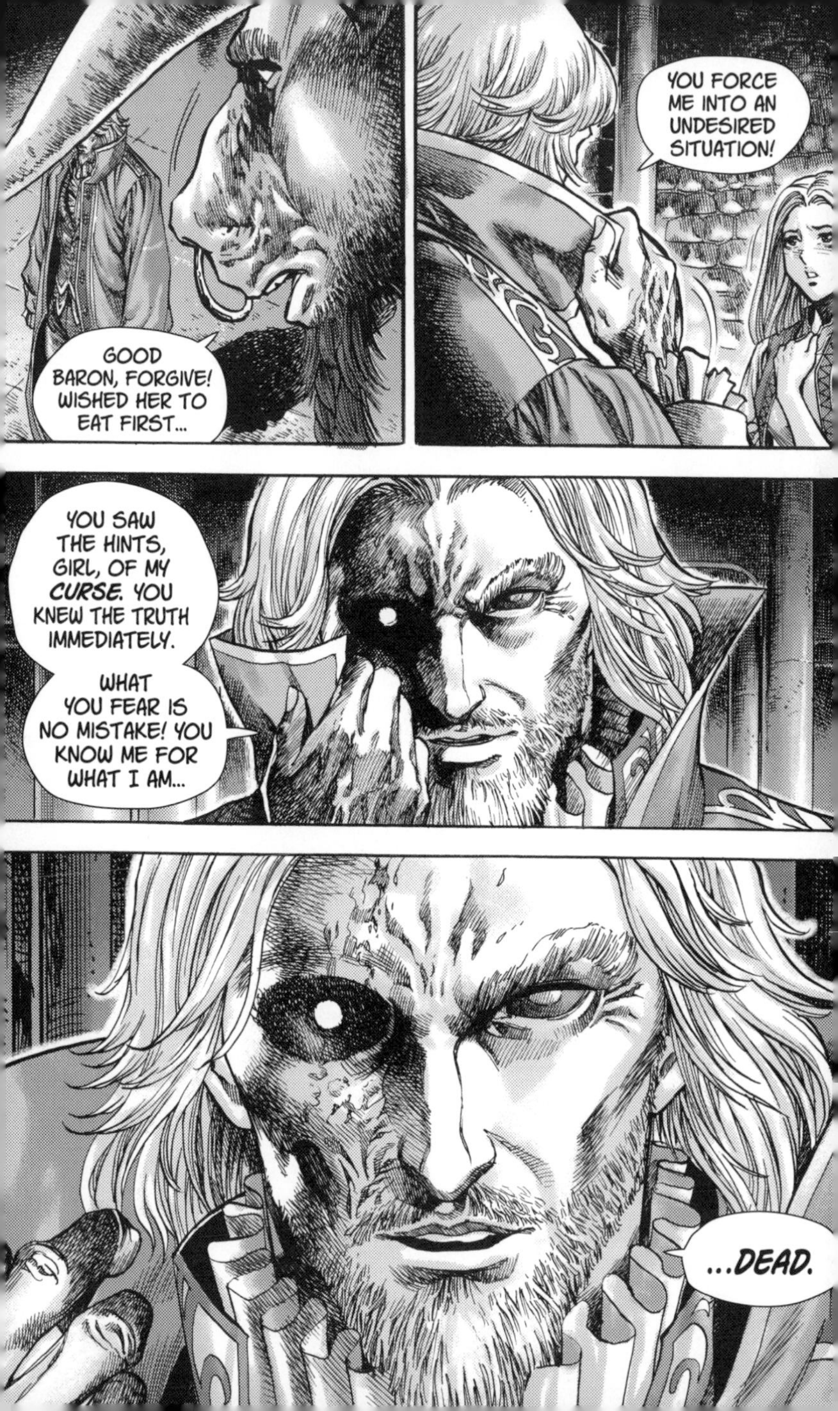
GOOD BARON, FORGIVE! WISHED HER TO EAT FIRST...
YOU FORCE ME INTO AN UNDESIRED SITUATION!
YOU SAW THE HINTS, GIRL, OF MY *CURSE*. YOU KNEW THE TRUTH IMMEDIATELY.
WHAT YOU FEAR IS NO MISTAKE! YOU KNOW ME FOR WHAT I AM...
...*DEAD.*

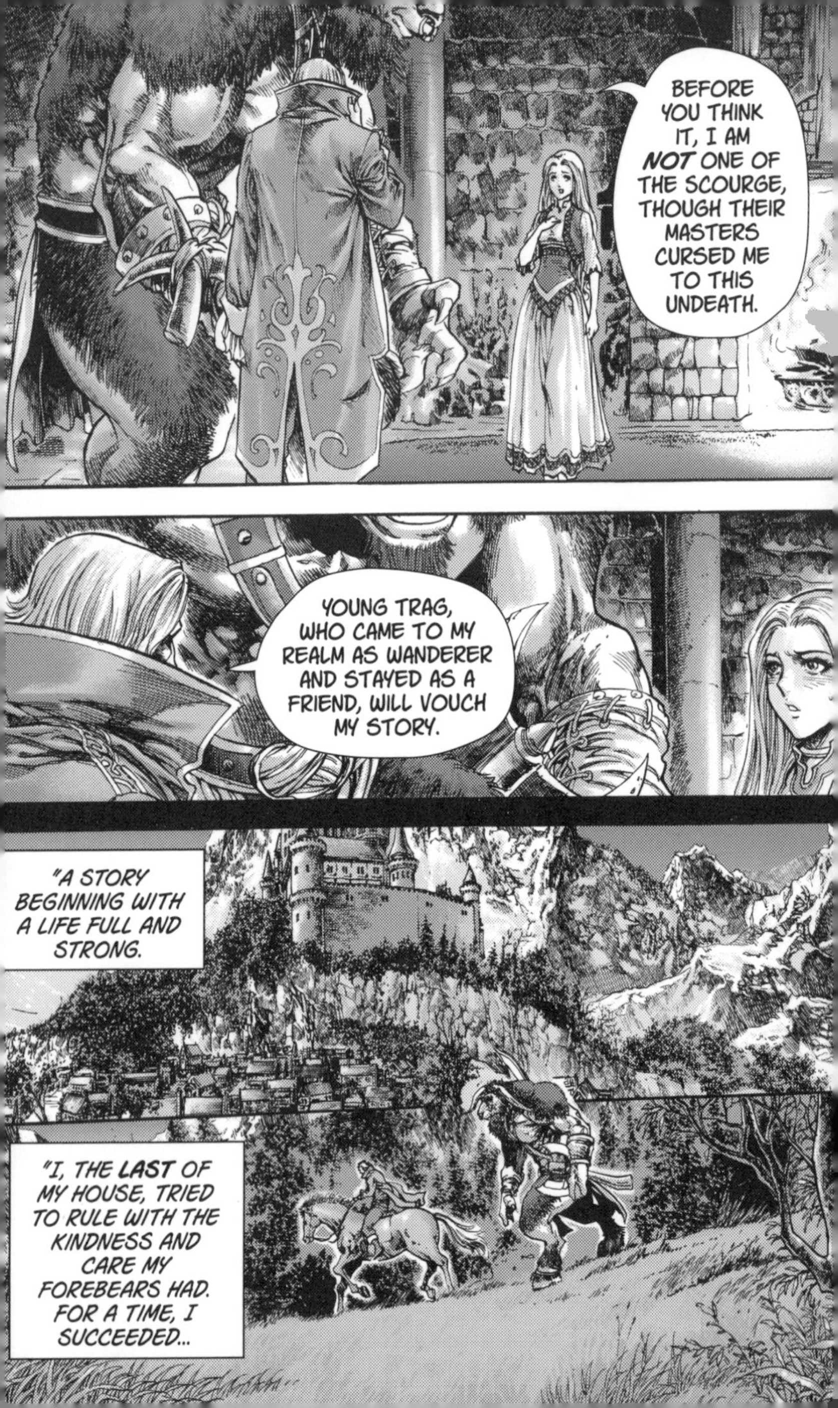
BEFORE YOU THINK IT, I AM *NOT* ONE OF THE SCOURGE, THOUGH THEIR MASTERS CURSED ME TO THIS UNDEATH.
YOUNG TRAG, WHO CAME TO MY REALM AS WANDERER AND STAYED AS A FRIEND, WILL VOUCH MY STORY.
"A STORY BEGINNING WITH A LIFE FULL AND STRONG.
"I, THE **LAST** OF MY HOUSE, TRIED TO RULE WITH THE KINDNESS AND CARE MY FOREBEARS HAD. FOR A TIME, I SUCCEEDED...

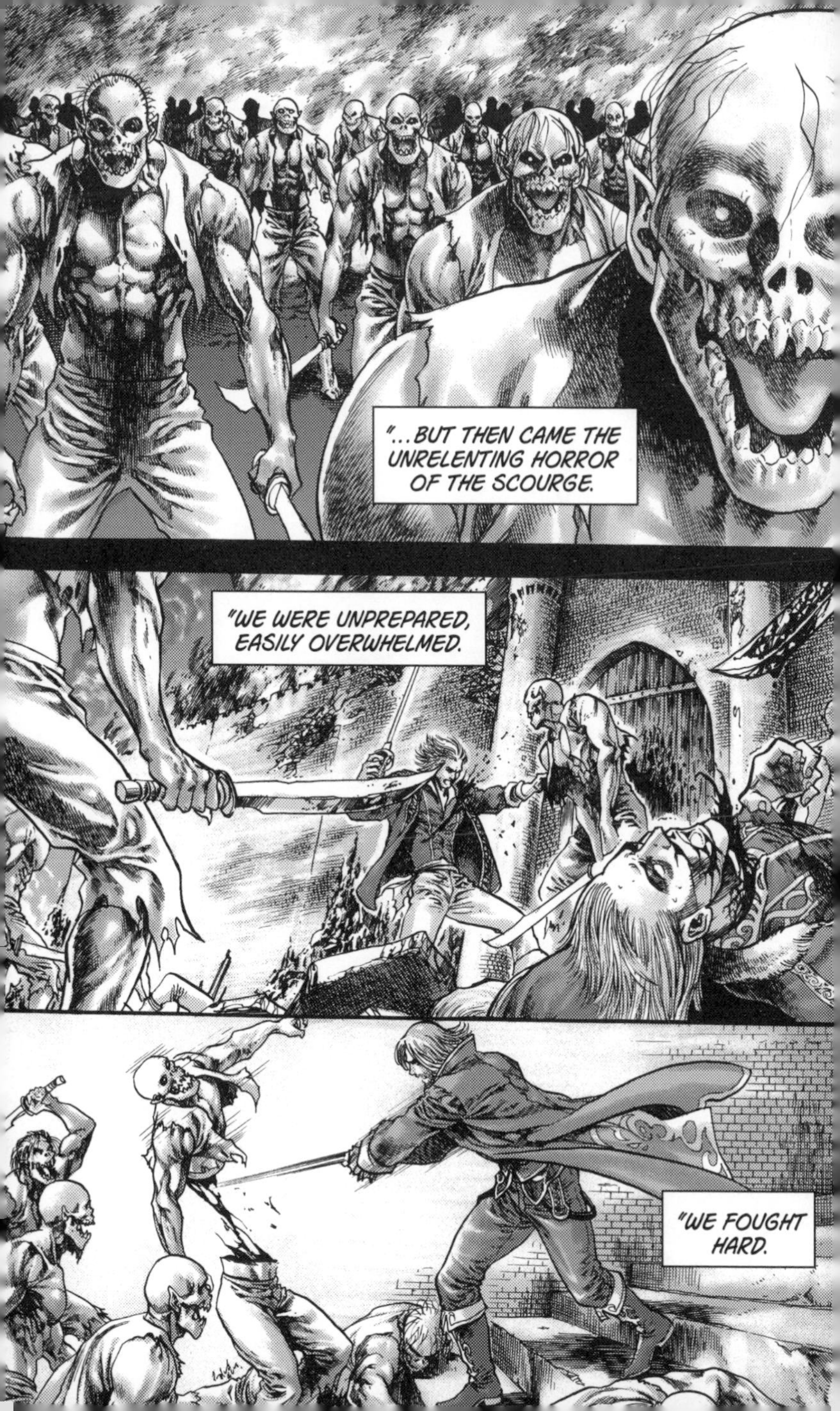
"...BUT THEN CAME THE UNRELENTING HORROR OF THE SCOURGE.
"WE WERE UNPREPARED, EASILY OVERWHELMED.
"WE FOUGHT HARD.

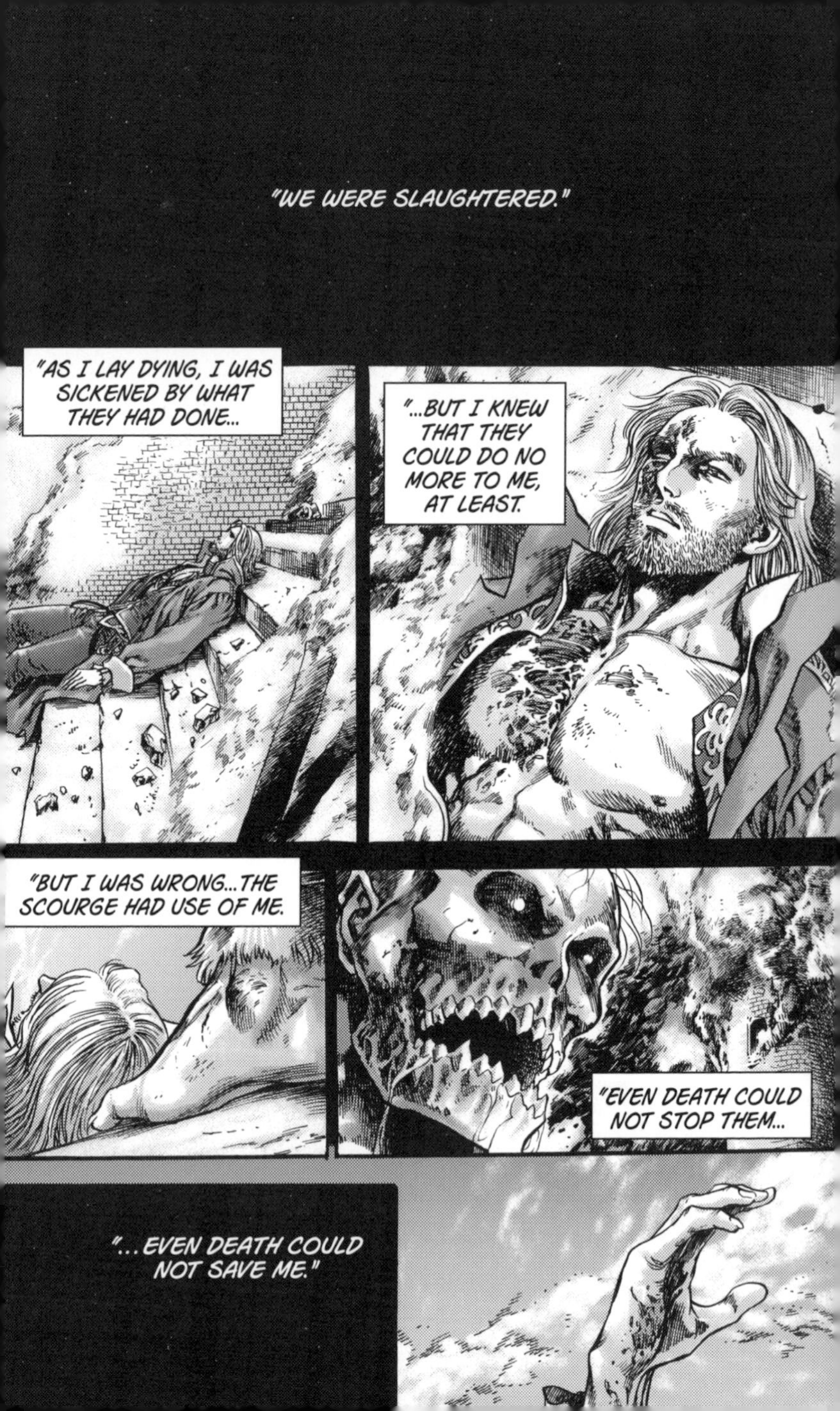
"WE WERE SLAUGHTERED."
"AS I LAY DYING, I WAS SICKENED BY WHAT THEY HAD DONE...
"...BUT I KNEW THAT THEY COULD DO NO MORE TO ME, AT LEAST.
"BUT I WAS WRONG...THE SCOURGE HAD USE OF ME.
"EVEN DEATH COULD NOT STOP THEM...
"...EVEN DEATH COULD NOT SAVE ME."

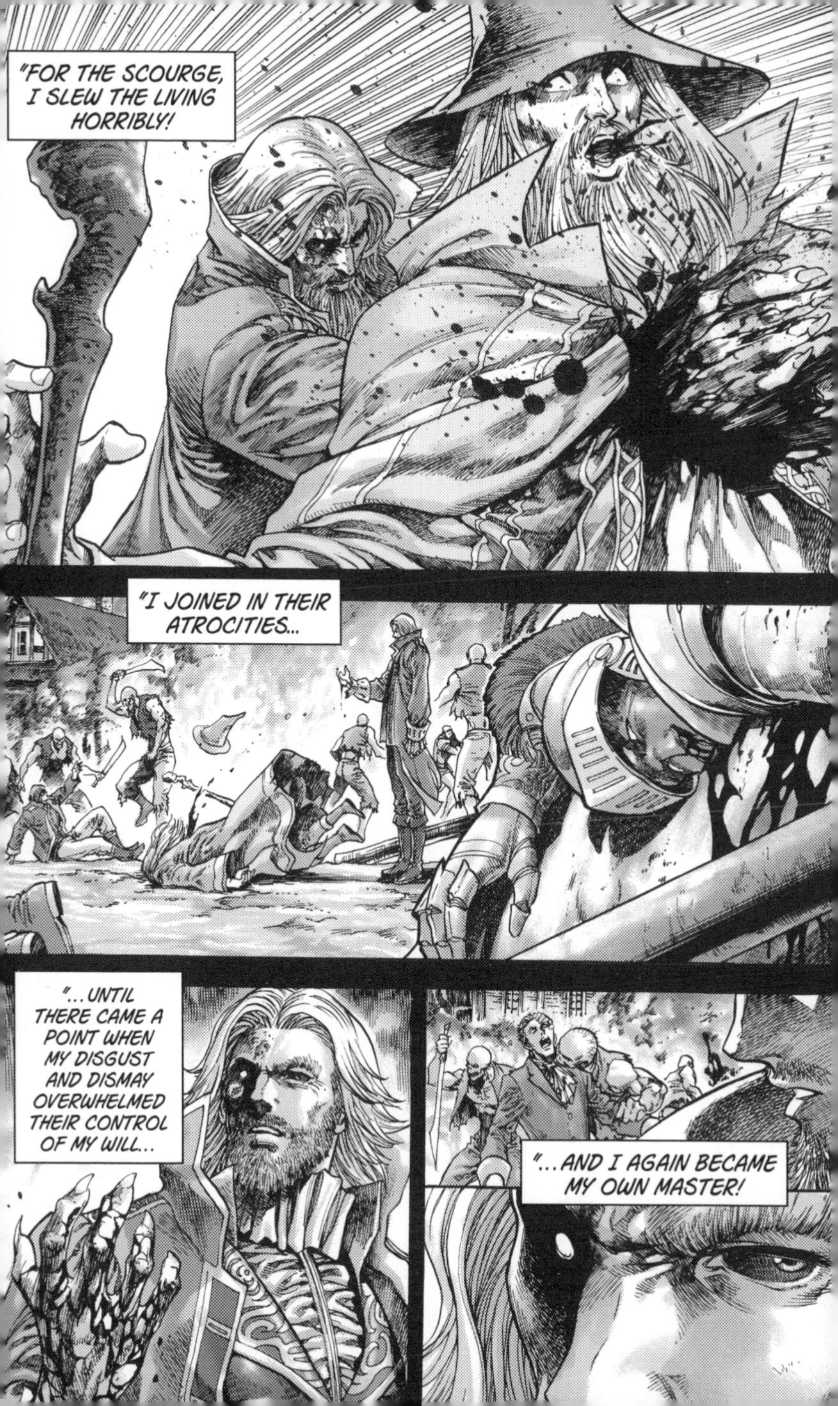
"FOR THE SCOURGE, I SLEW THE LIVING HORRIBLY!
"I JOINED IN THEIR ATROCITIES...
"...UNTIL THERE CAME A POINT WHEN MY DISGUST AND DISMAY OVERWHELMED THEIR CONTROL OF MY WILL...
"...AND I AGAIN BECAME MY OWN MASTER!

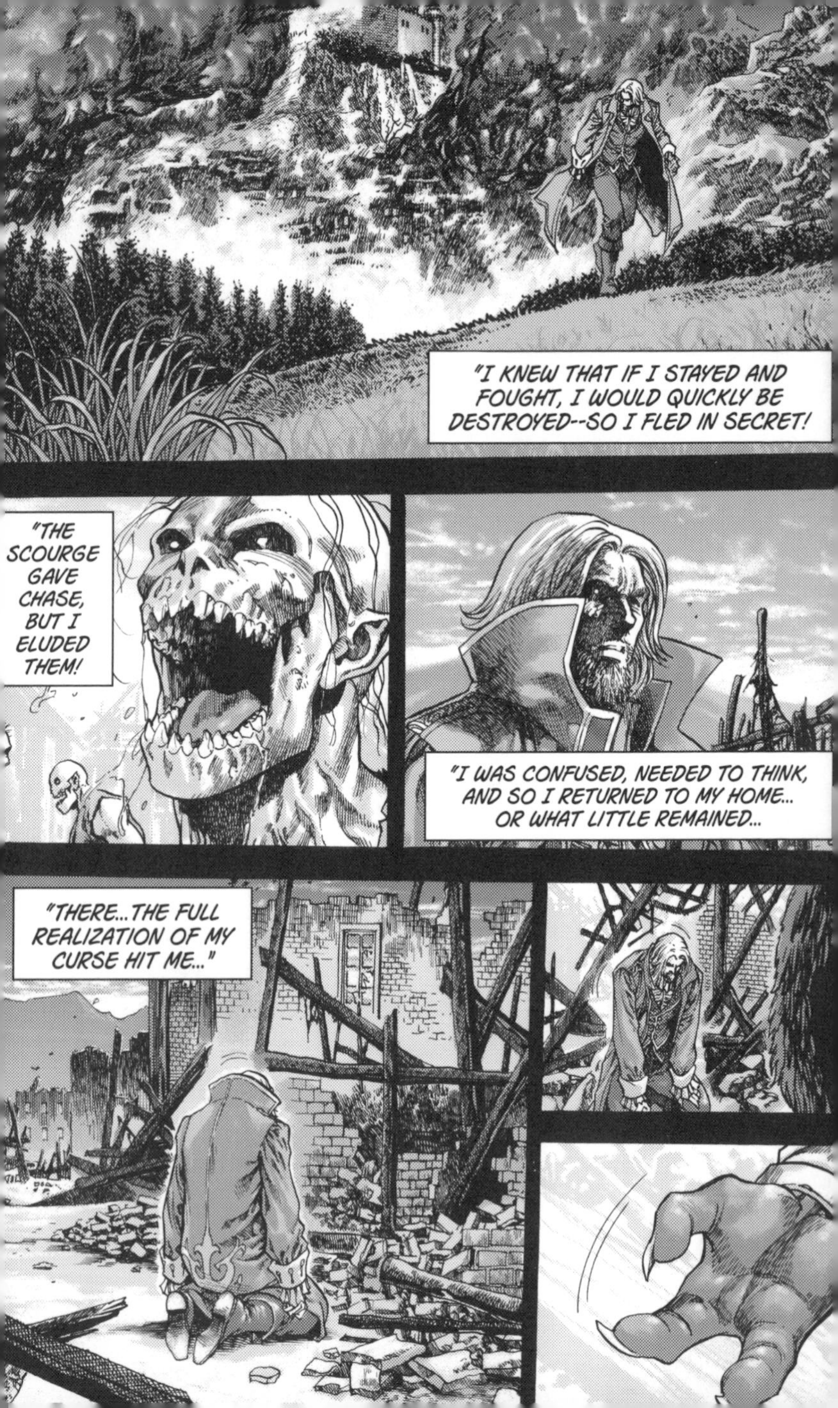
"I KNEW THAT IF I STAYED AND FOUGHT, I WOULD QUICKLY BE DESTROYED--SO I FLED IN SECRET!
"THE SCOURGE GAVE CHASE, BUT I ELUDED THEM!
"I WAS CONFUSED, NEEDED TO THINK, AND SO I RETURNED TO MY HOME... OR WHAT LITTLE REMAINED...
"THERE...THE FULL REALIZATION OF MY CURSE HIT ME..."

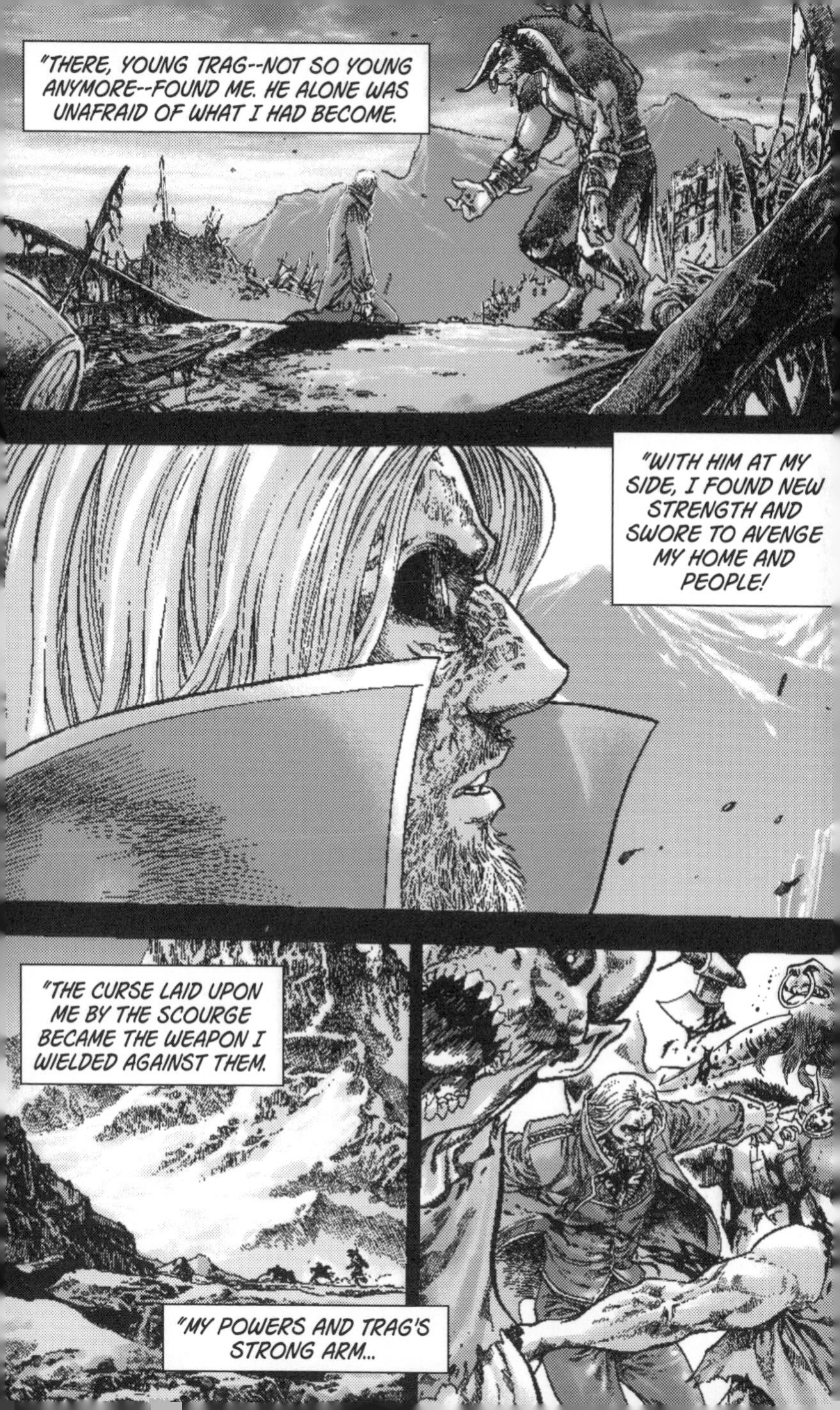
"THERE, YOUNG TRAG--NOT SO YOUNG ANYMORE--FOUND ME. HE ALONE WAS UNAFRAID OF WHAT I HAD BECOME.
"WITH HIM AT MY SIDE, I FOUND NEW STRENGTH AND SWORE TO AVENGE MY HOME AND PEOPLE!
"THE CURSE LAID UPON ME BY THE SCOURGE BECAME THE WEAPON I WIELDED AGAINST THEM.
"MY POWERS AND TRAG'S STRONG ARM...

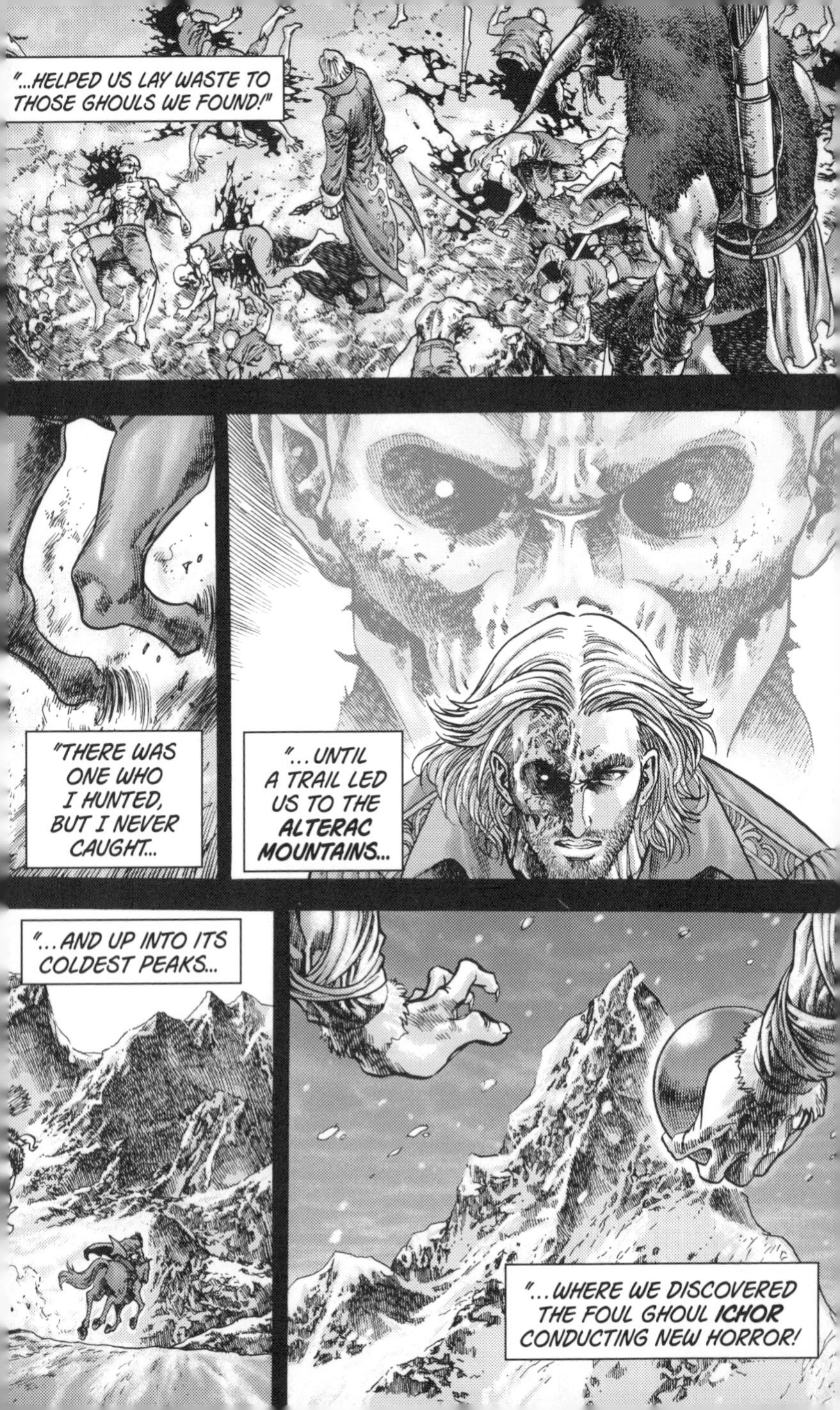
"...HELPED US LAY WASTE TO THOSE GHOULS WE FOUND!"
"THERE WAS ONE WHO I HUNTED, BUT I NEVER CAUGHT...
"...UNTIL A TRAIL LED US TO THE **ALTERAC MOUNTAINS**...
"...AND UP INTO ITS COLDEST PEAKS...
"...WHERE WE DISCOVERED THE FOUL GHOUL **ICHOR** CONDUCTING NEW HORROR!

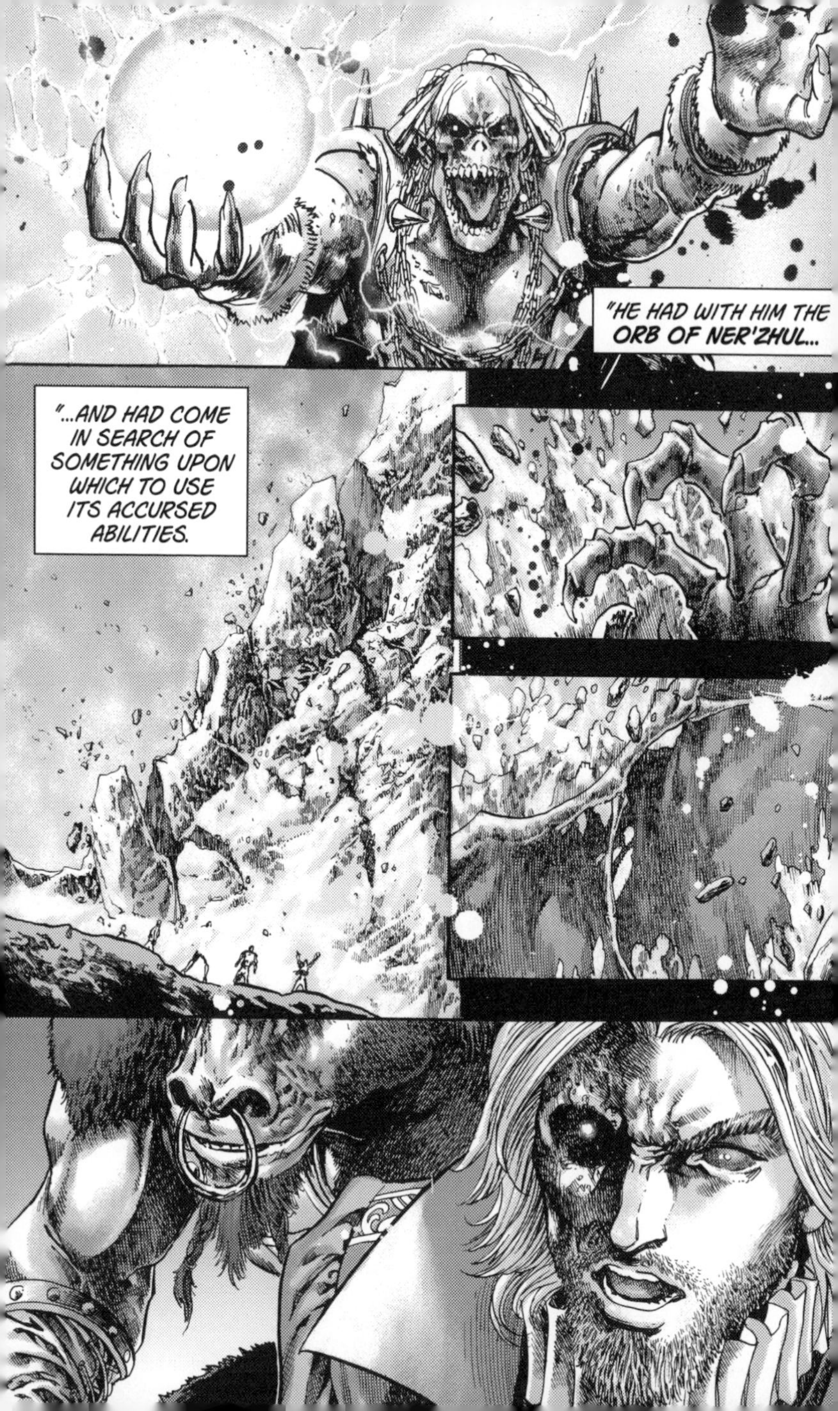
"HE HAD WITH HIM THE ORB OF NER'ZHUL...
"...AND HAD COME IN SEARCH OF SOMETHING UPON WHICH TO USE ITS ACCURSED ABILITIES.

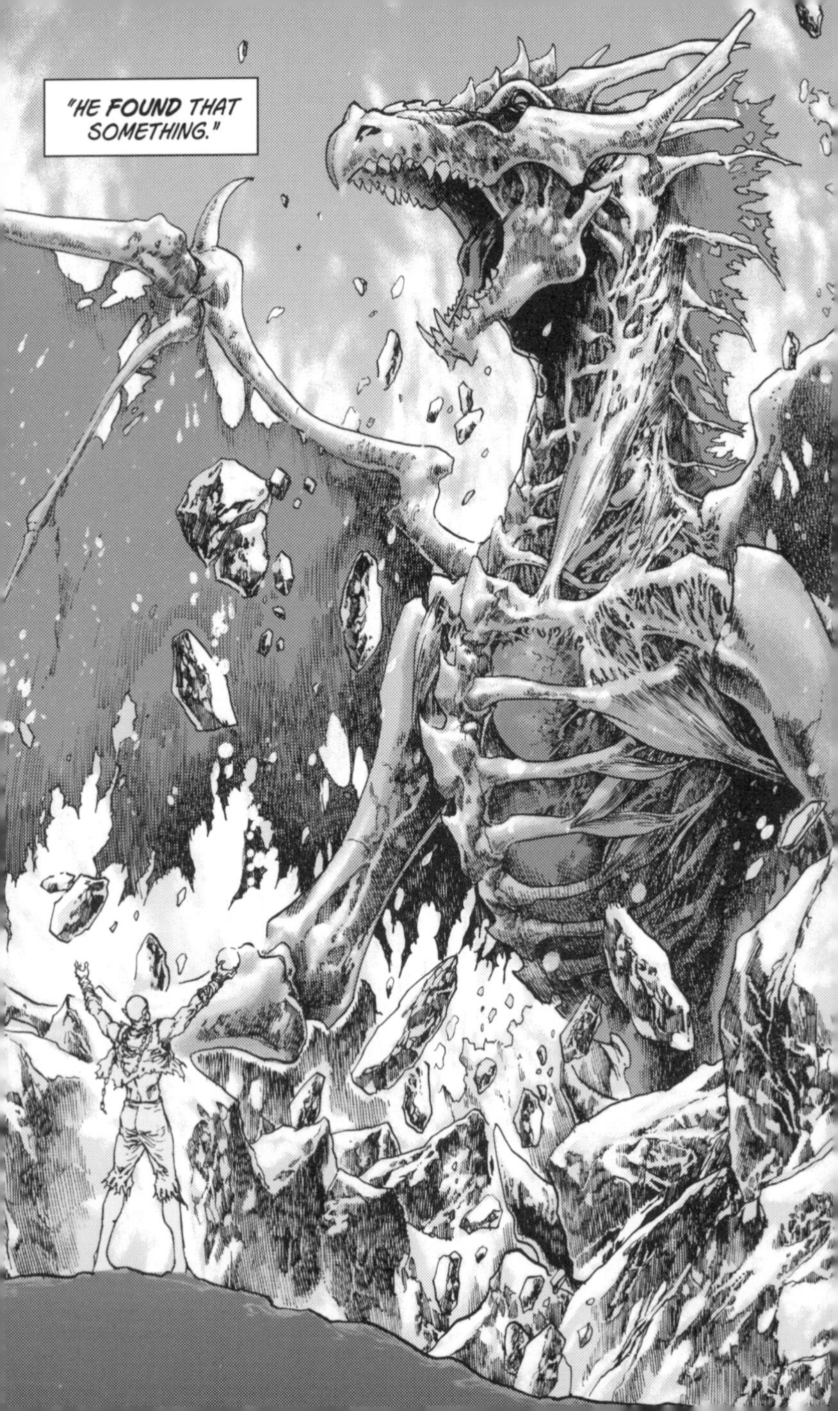
"HE FOUND THAT SOMETHING."

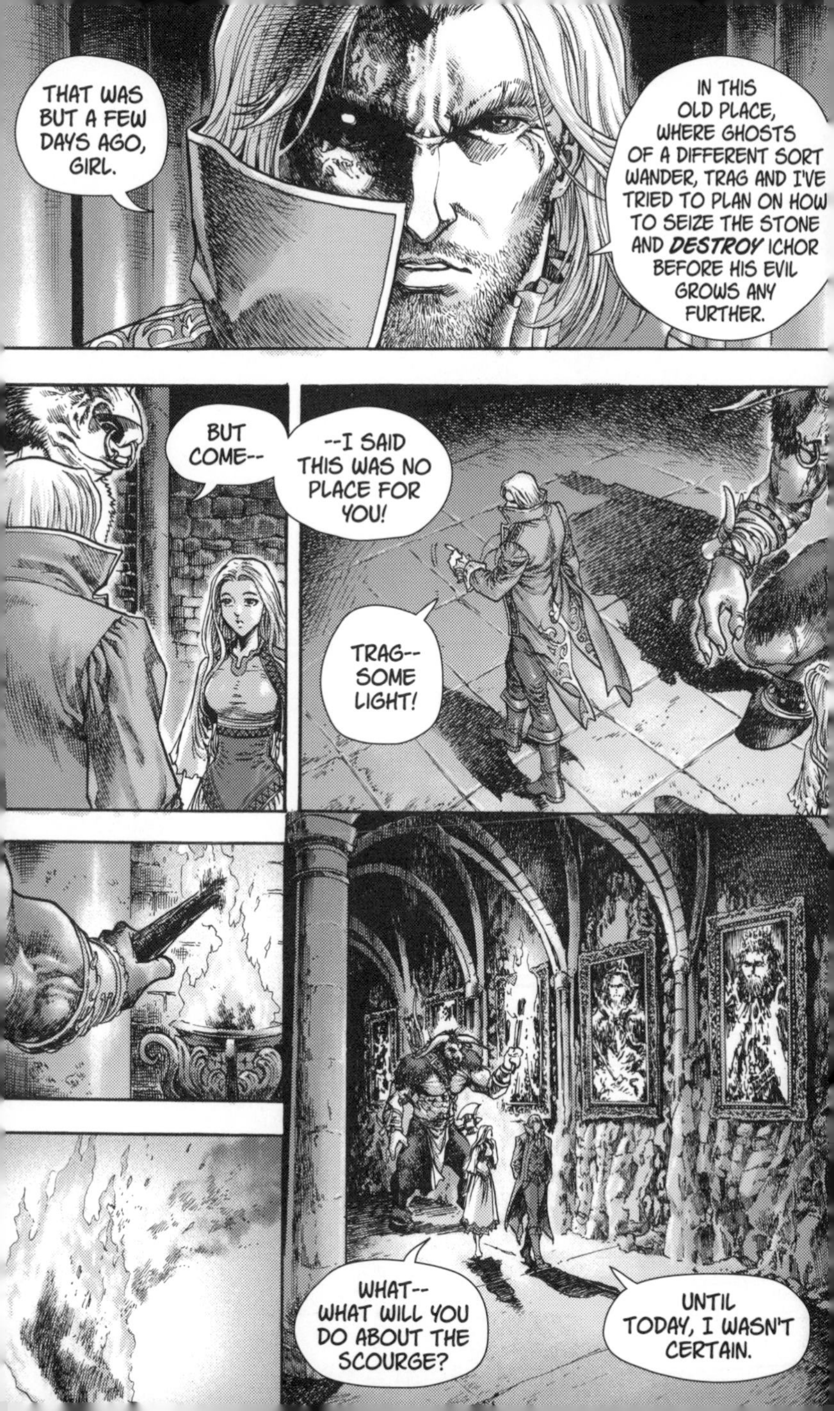
THAT WAS BUT A FEW DAYS AGO, GIRL.
IN THIS OLD PLACE, WHERE GHOSTS OF A DIFFERENT SORT WANDER, TRAG AND I'VE TRIED TO PLAN ON HOW TO SEIZE THE STONE AND ***DESTROY*** ICHOR BEFORE HIS EVIL GROWS ANY FURTHER.
BUT COME--
--I SAID THIS WAS NO PLACE FOR YOU!
TRAG-- SOME LIGHT!
WHAT-- WHAT WILL YOU DO ABOUT THE SCOURGE?
UNTIL TODAY, I WASN'T CERTAIN.

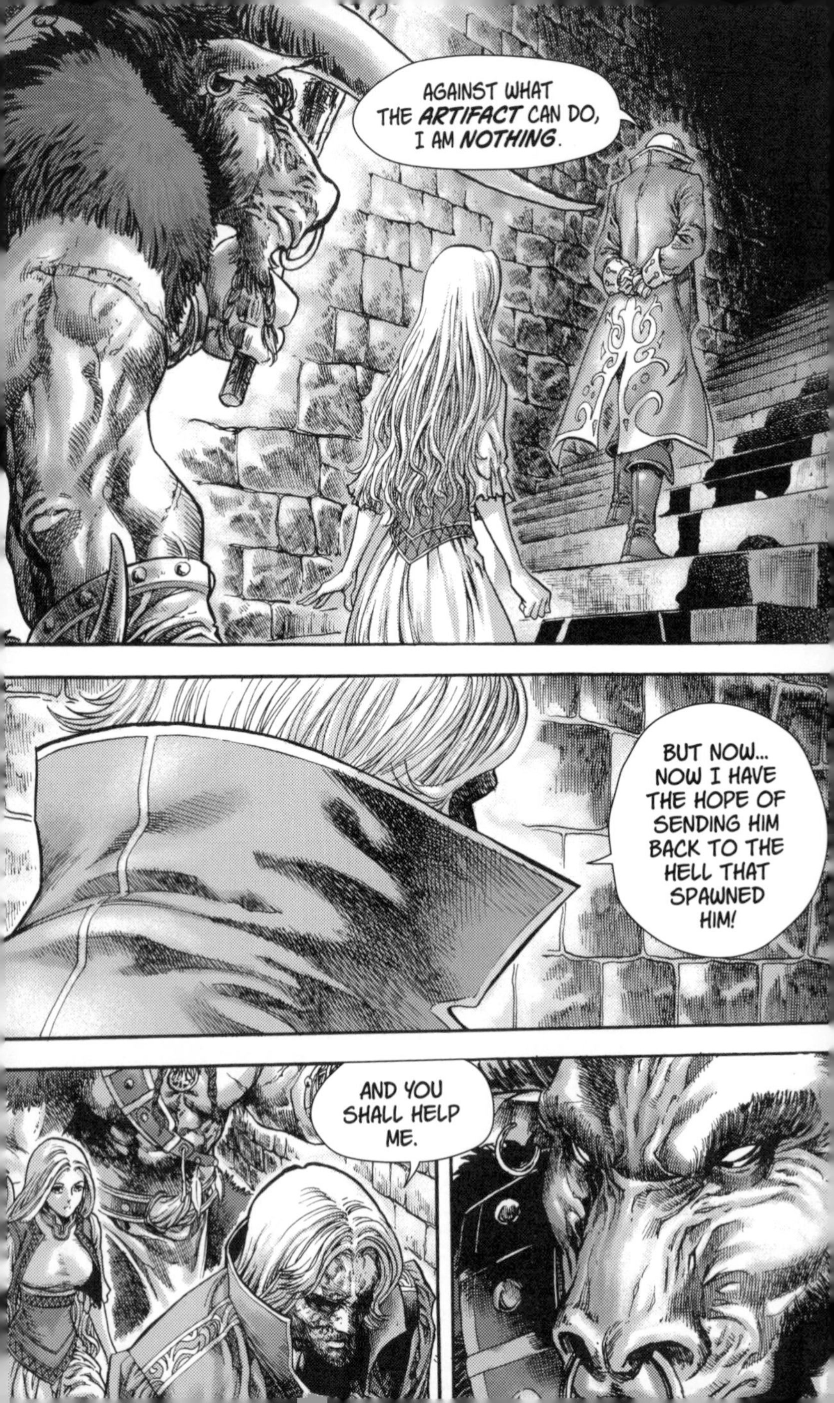
AGAINST WHAT THE **ARTIFACT** CAN DO, I AM **NOTHING**.
BUT NOW... NOW I HAVE THE HOPE OF SENDING HIM BACK TO THE HELL THAT SPAWNED HIM!
AND YOU SHALL HELP ME.

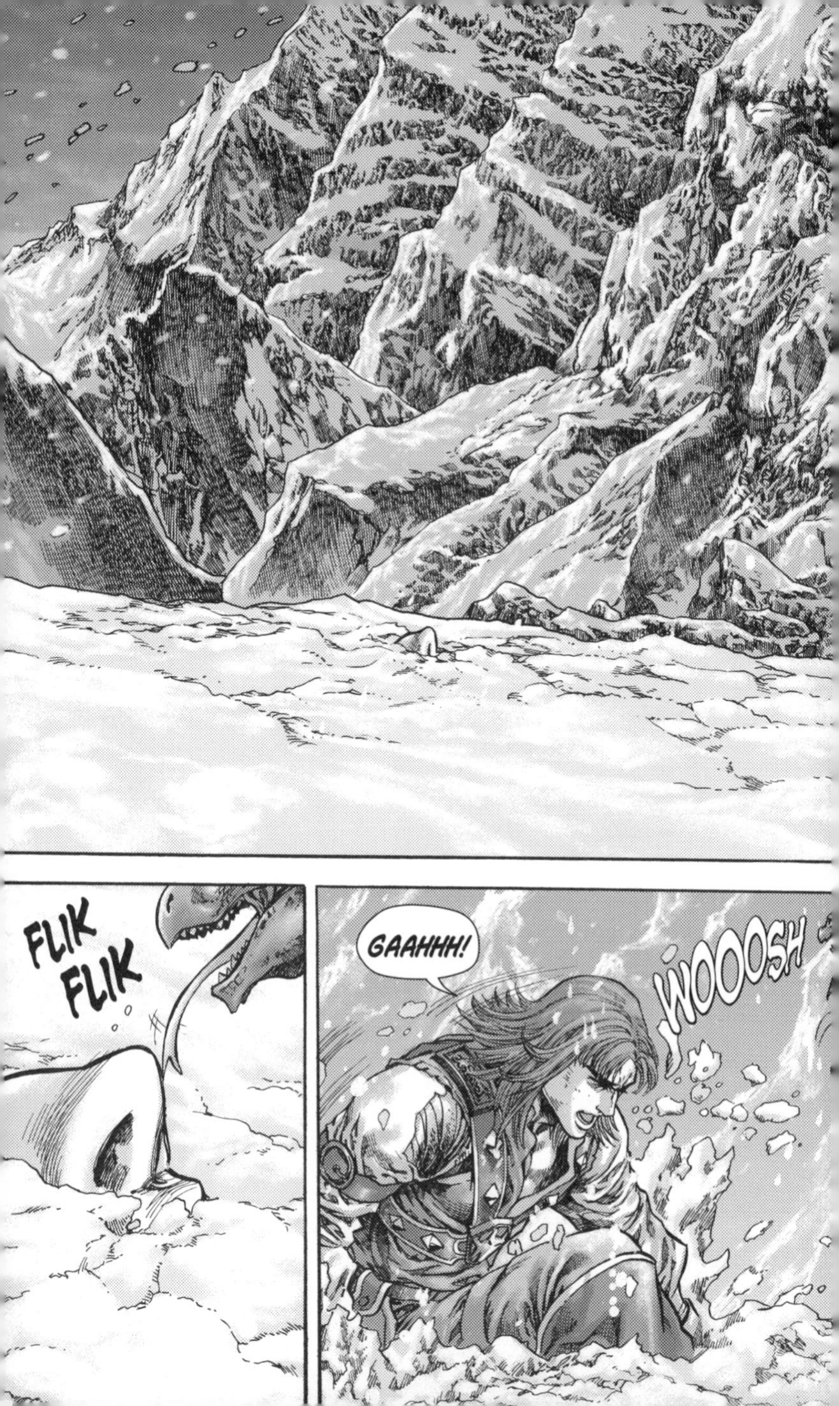
FLIK
FLIK
GAAHHH!
WOOOSH

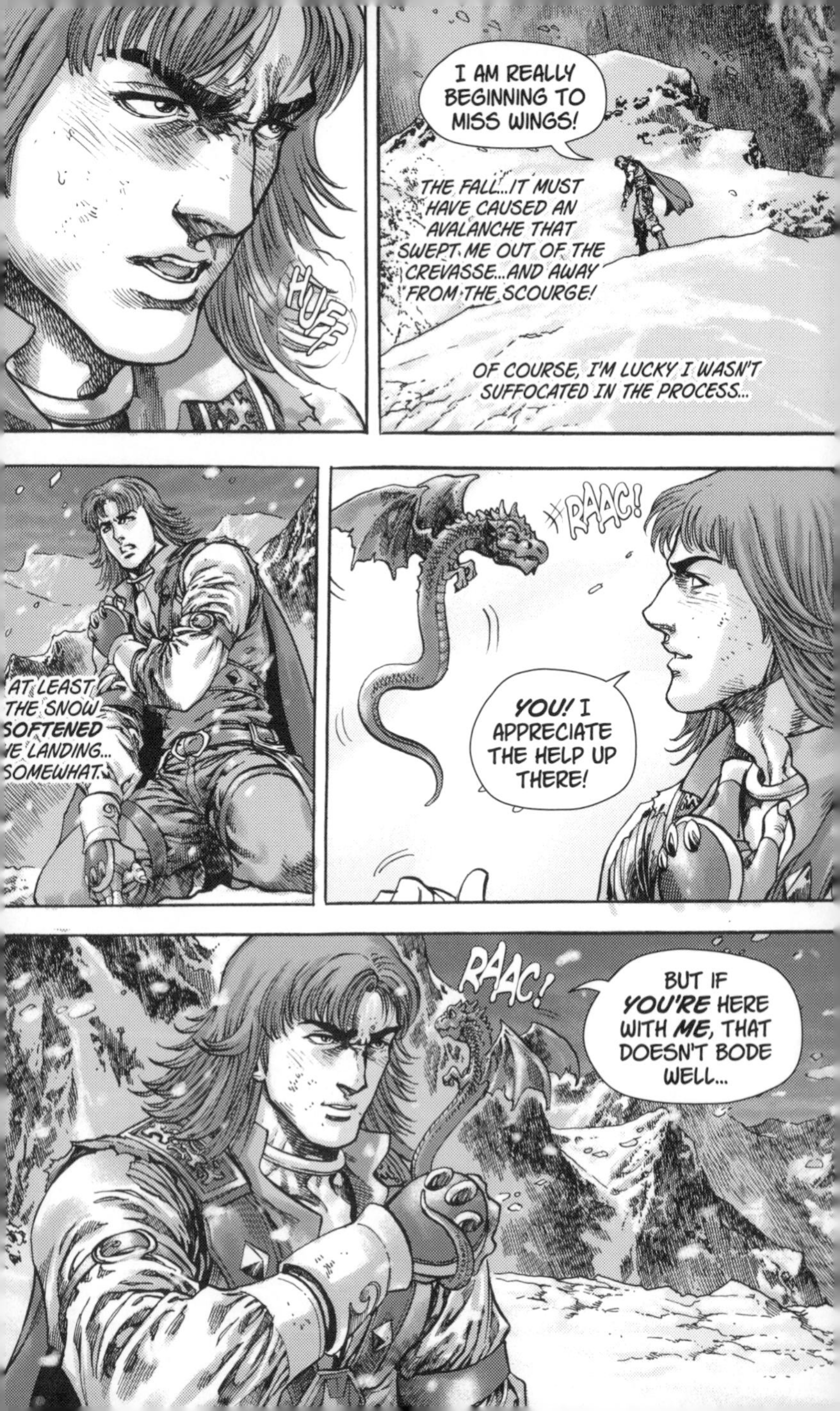
HUFF
I AM REALLY BEGINNING TO MISS WINGS!
THE FALL...IT MUST HAVE CAUSED AN AVALANCHE THAT SWEPT ME OUT OF THE CREVASSE...AND AWAY FROM THE SCOURGE!
OF COURSE, I'M LUCKY I WASN'T SUFFOCATED IN THE PROCESS...
AT LEAST THE SNOW SOFTENED HE LANDING... SOMEWHAT.
RAAC!
YOU! I APPRECIATE THE HELP UP THERE!
RAAC!
BUT IF YOU'RE HERE WITH ME, THAT DOESN'T BODE WELL...

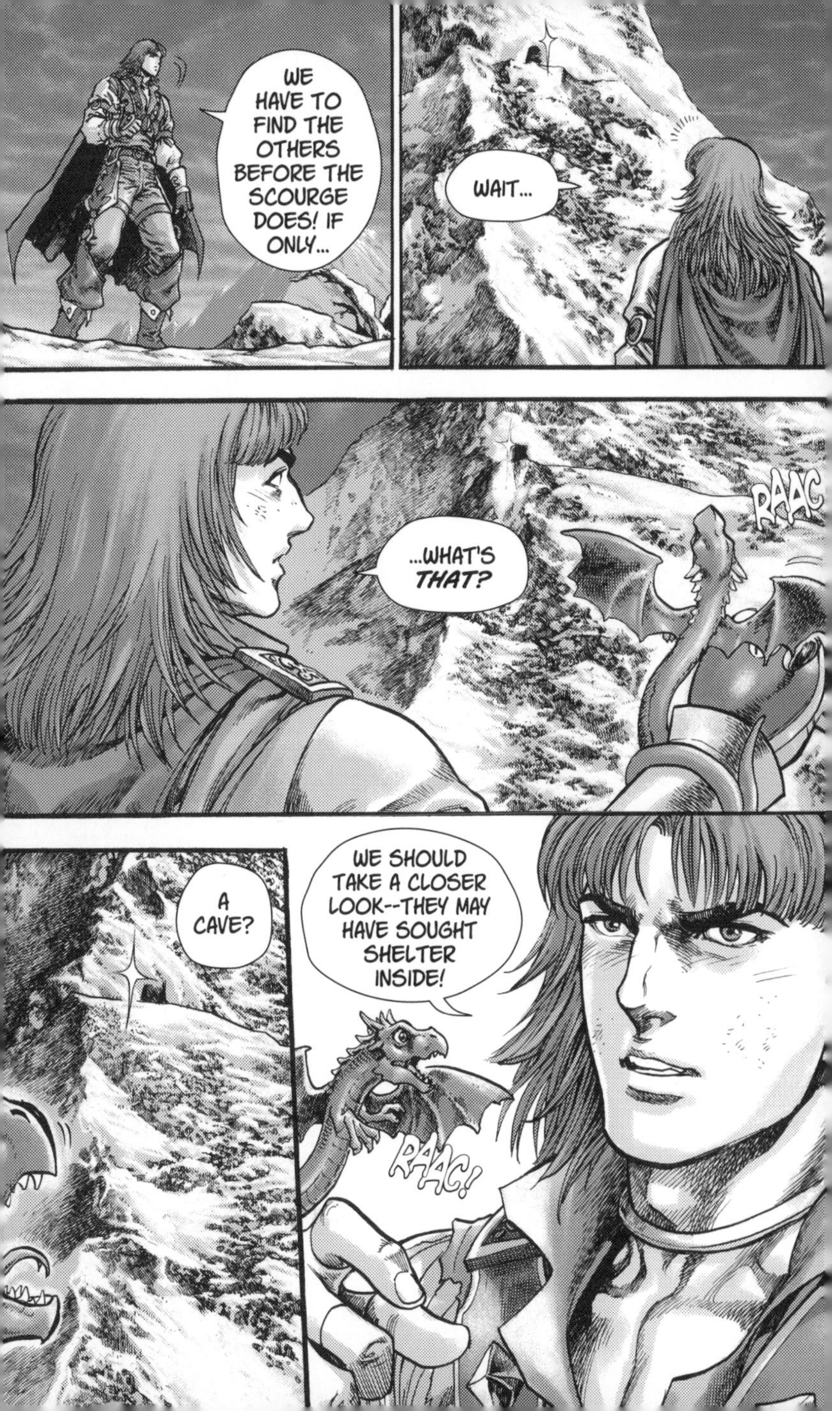
WE HAVE TO FIND THE OTHERS BEFORE THE SCOURGE DOES! IF ONLY...
WAIT...
RAAC
...WHAT'S *THAT?*
A CAVE?
WE SHOULD TAKE A CLOSER LOOK--THEY MAY HAVE SOUGHT SHELTER INSIDE!
RAAC!

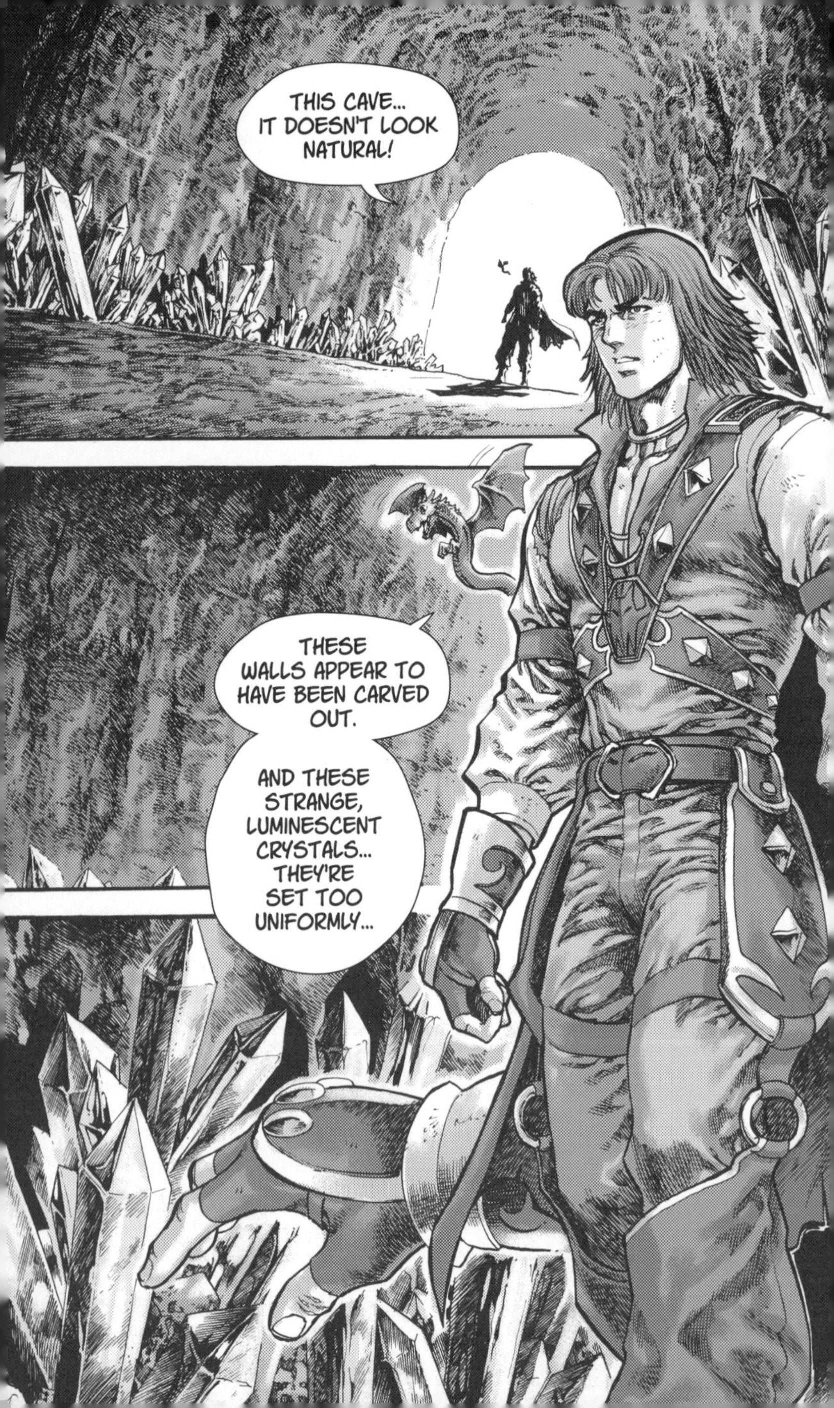
THIS CAVE... IT DOESN'T LOOK NATURAL!
THESE WALLS APPEAR TO HAVE BEEN CARVED OUT.
AND THESE STRANGE, LUMINESCENT CRYSTALS... THEY'RE SET TOO UNIFORMLY...

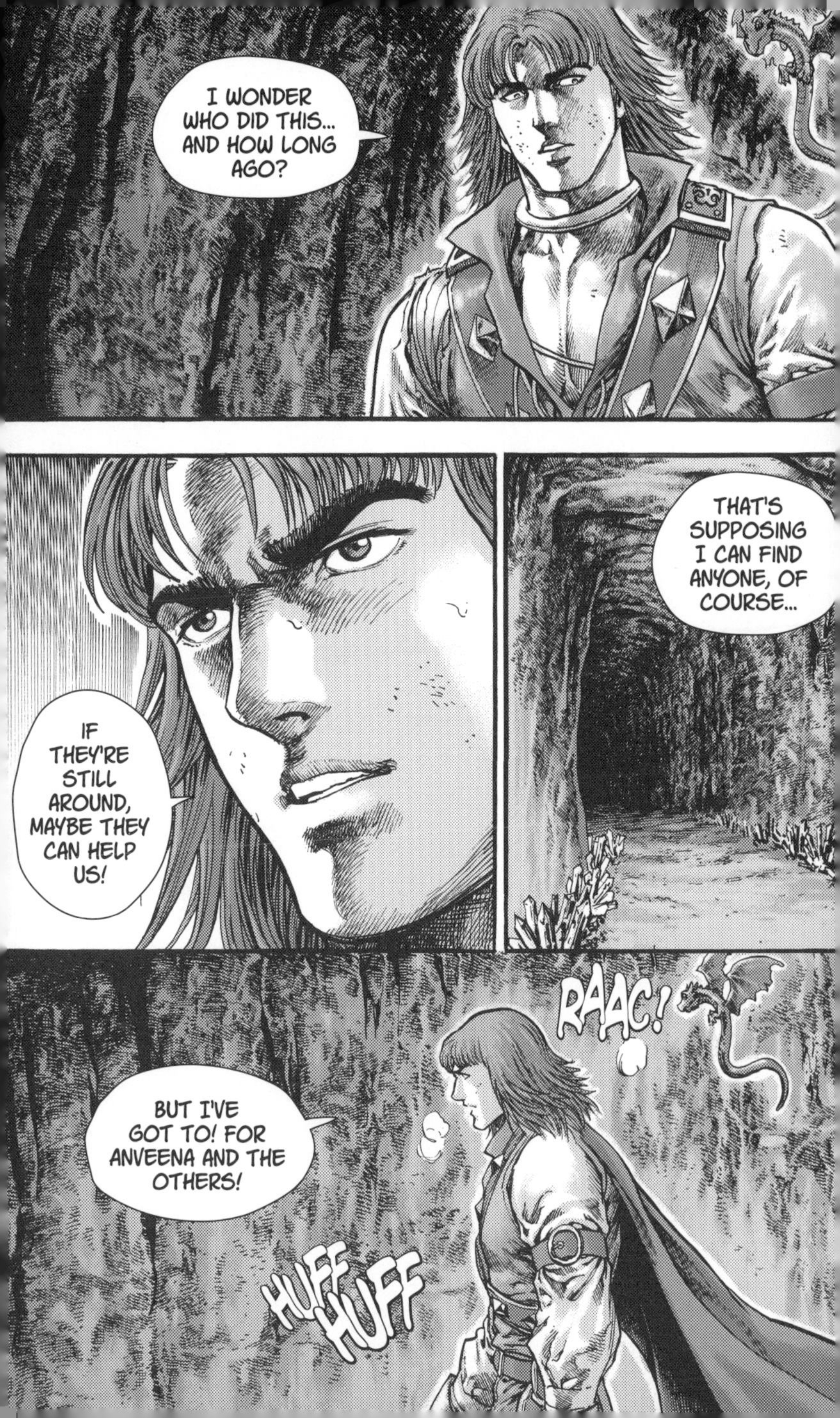
I WONDER WHO DID THIS... AND HOW LONG AGO?
IF THEY'RE STILL AROUND, MAYBE THEY CAN HELP US!
THAT'S SUPPOSING I CAN FIND ANYONE, OF COURSE...
RAAC!
BUT I'VE GOT TO! FOR ANVEENA AND THE OTHERS!
HUFF HUFF

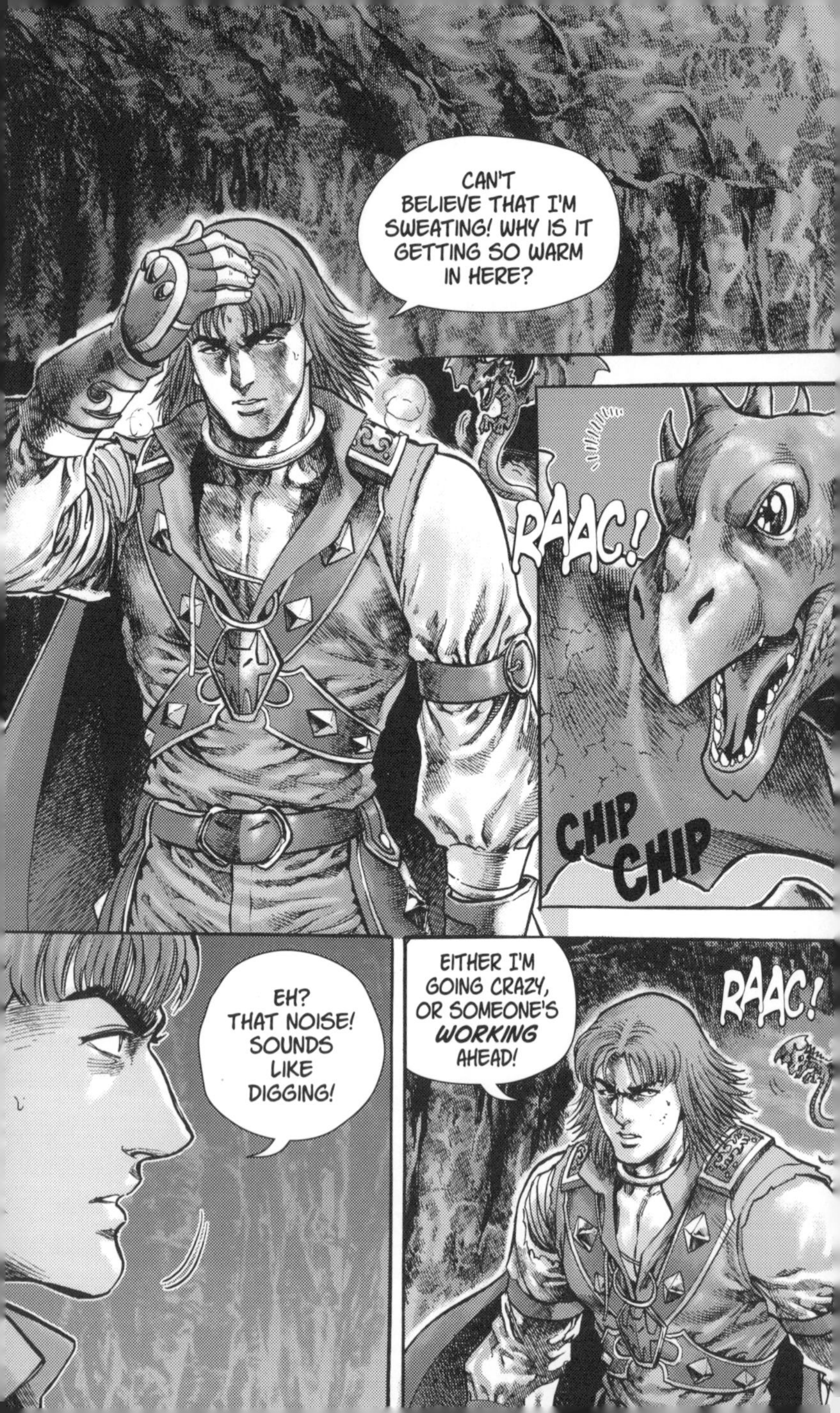
CAN'T BELIEVE THAT I'M SWEATING! WHY IS IT GETTING SO WARM IN HERE?
RAAC!
CHIP CHIP
EH? THAT NOISE! SOUNDS LIKE DIGGING!
EITHER I'M GOING CRAZY, OR SOMEONE'S ***WORKING*** AHEAD!
RAAC!

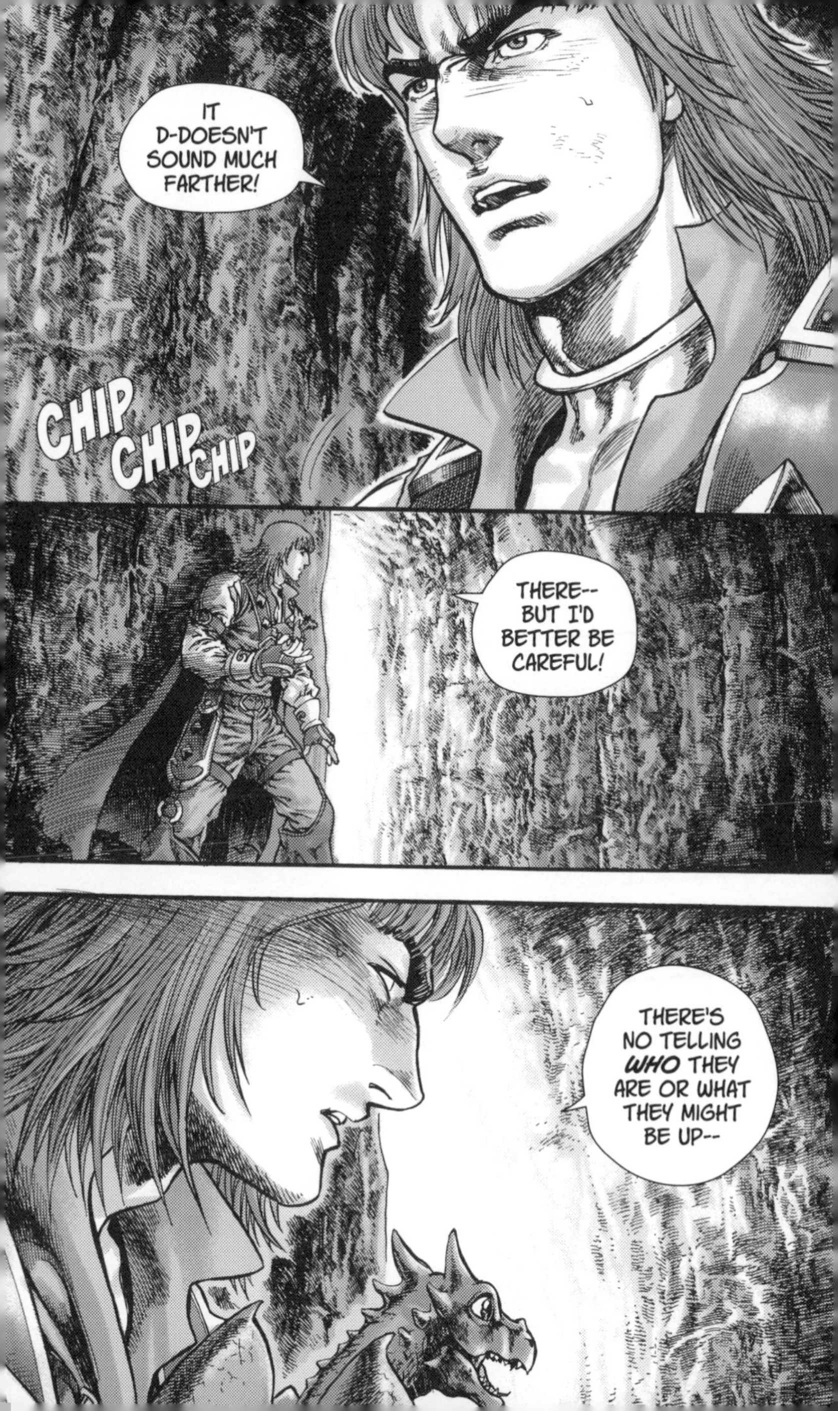
IT D-DOESN'T SOUND MUCH FARTHER!
CHIP CHIP CHIP
THERE-- BUT I'D BETTER BE CAREFUL!
THERE'S NO TELLING ***WHO*** THEY ARE OR WHAT THEY MIGHT BE UP--

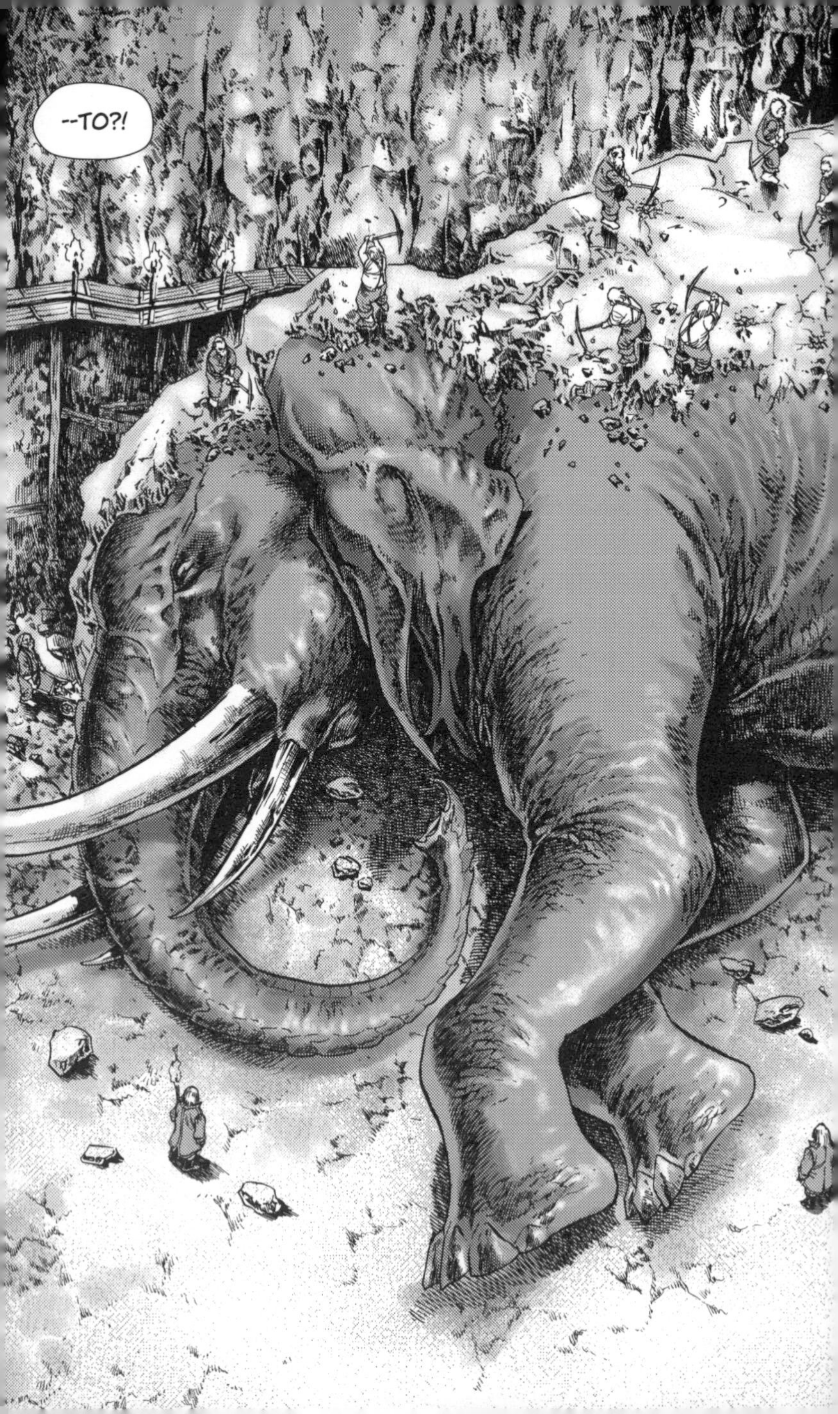
--TO?!

CHAPTER THREE

CAVERNS OF THE DEAD

KRAK

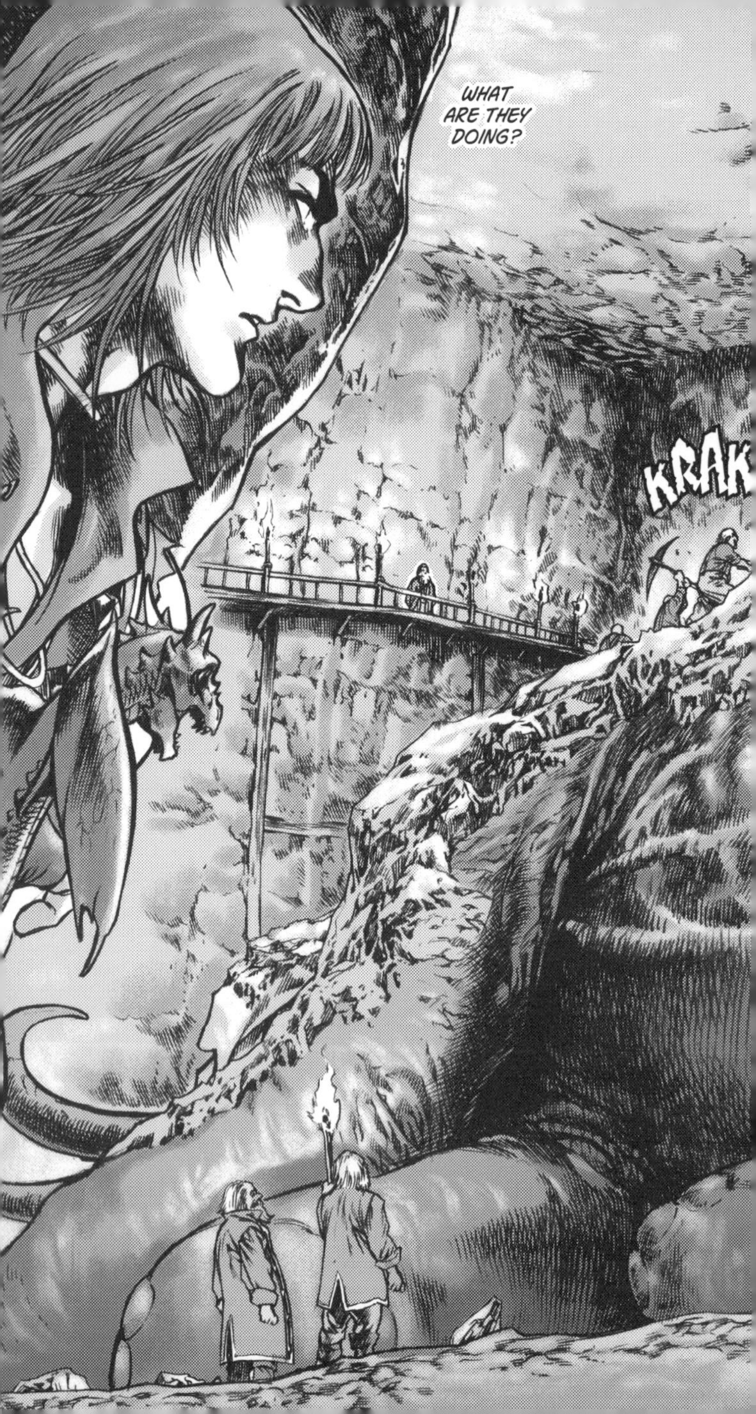
WHAT ARE THEY DOING?
KRAK

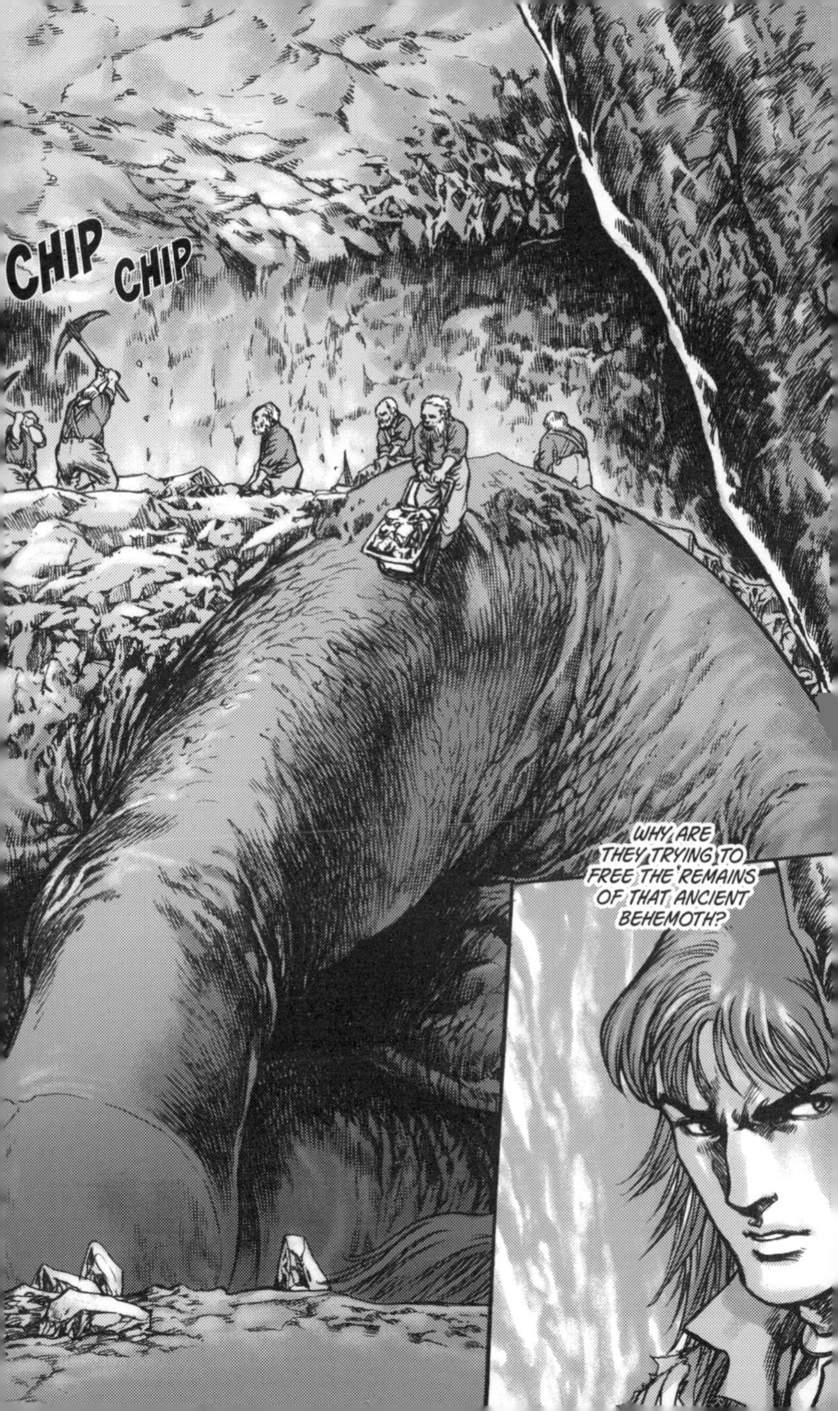
CHIP CHIP
WHY ARE THEY TRYING TO FREE THE REMAINS OF THAT ANCIENT BEHEMOTH?

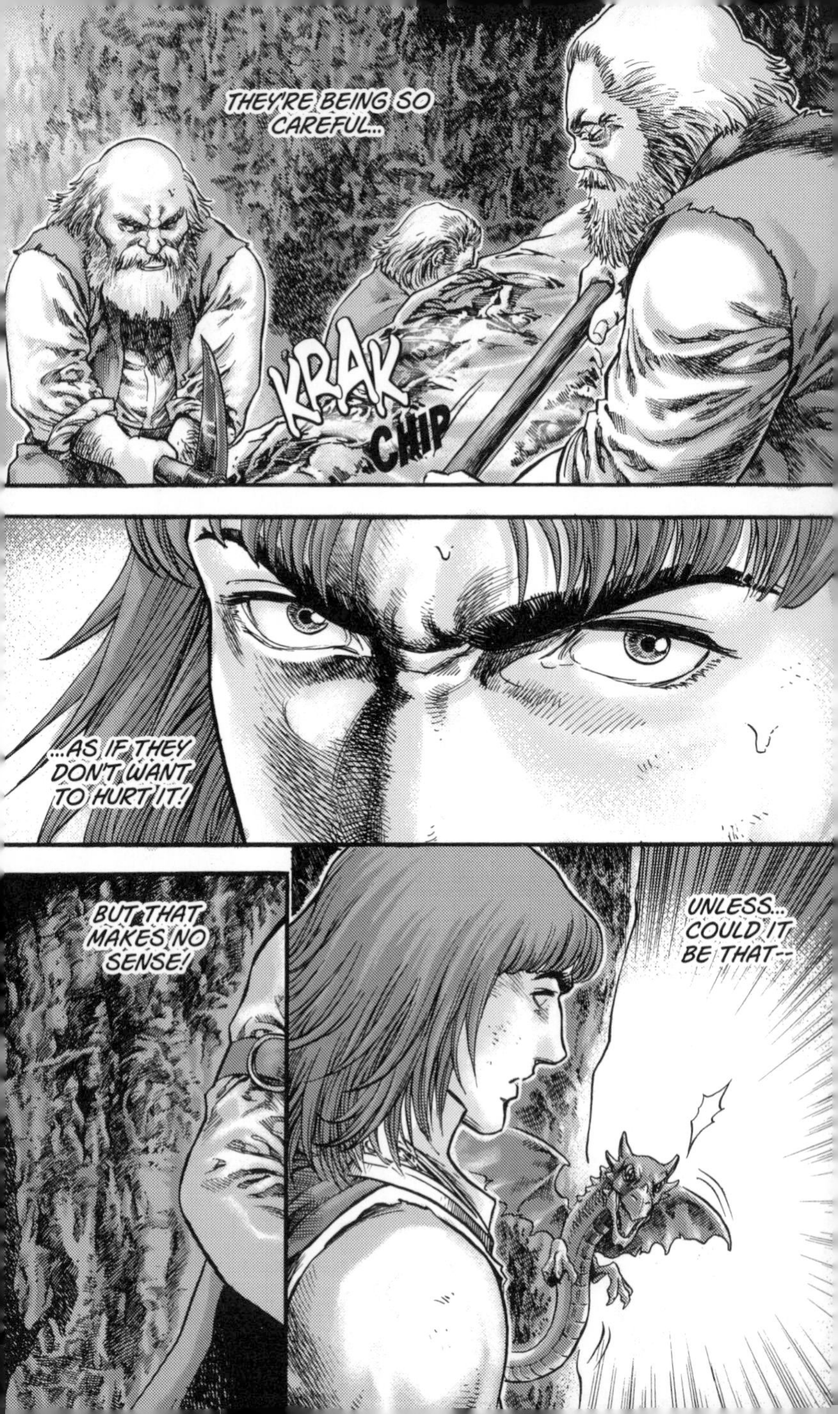
THEY'RE BEING SO CAREFUL...
KRAK
CHIP
...AS IF THEY DON'T WANT TO HURT IT!
BUT THAT MAKES NO SENSE!
UNLESS... COULD IT BE THAT--

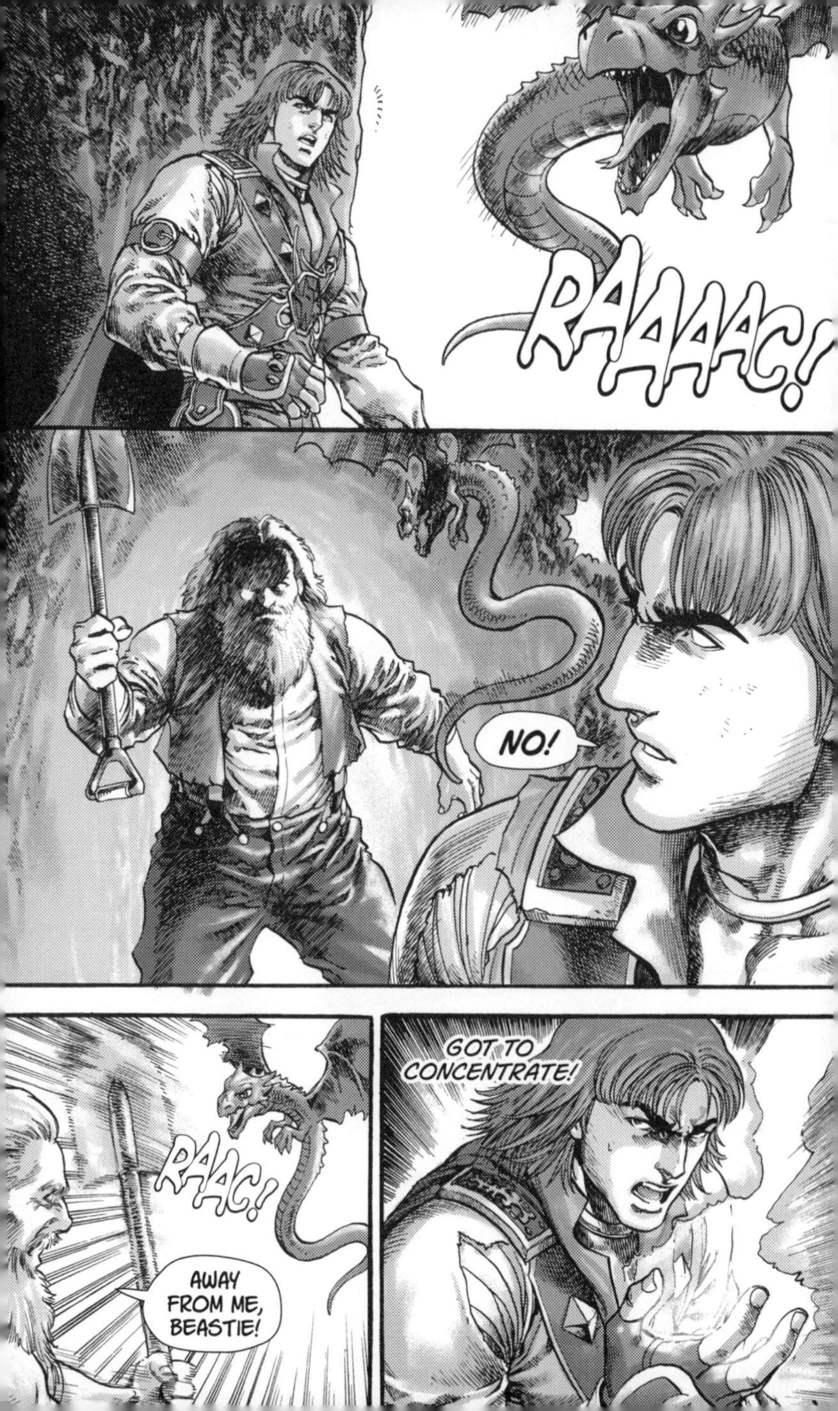
RAAAAAC!
NO!
RAAC!
AWAY FROM ME, BEASTIE!
GOT TO CONCENTRATE!

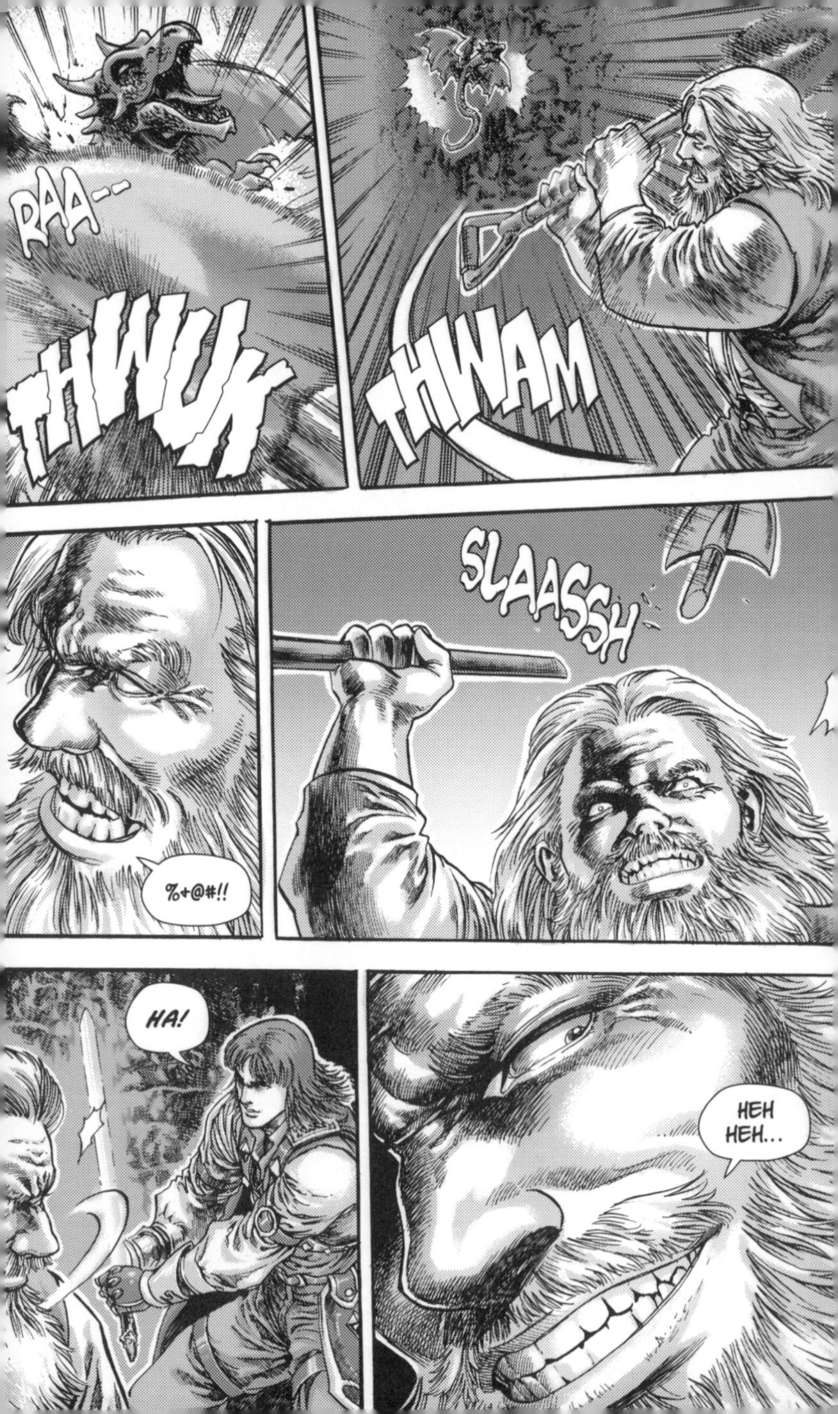
RAA--
THWUK
THWAM
%+@#!!
SLAASSH
HA!
HEH HEH...

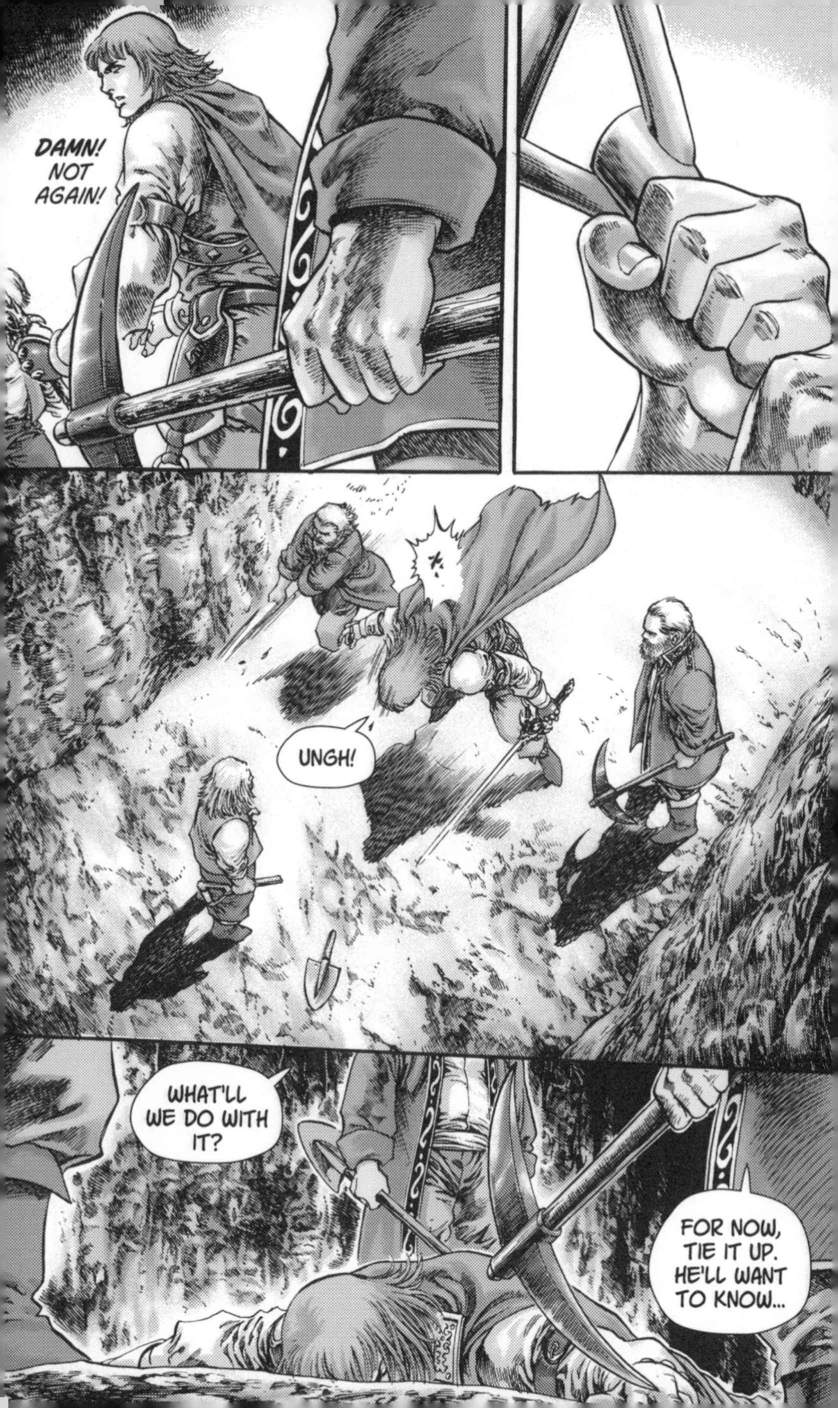
DAMN! NOT AGAIN!
UNGH!
WHAT'LL WE DO WITH IT?
FOR NOW, TIE IT UP. HE'LL WANT TO KNOW...

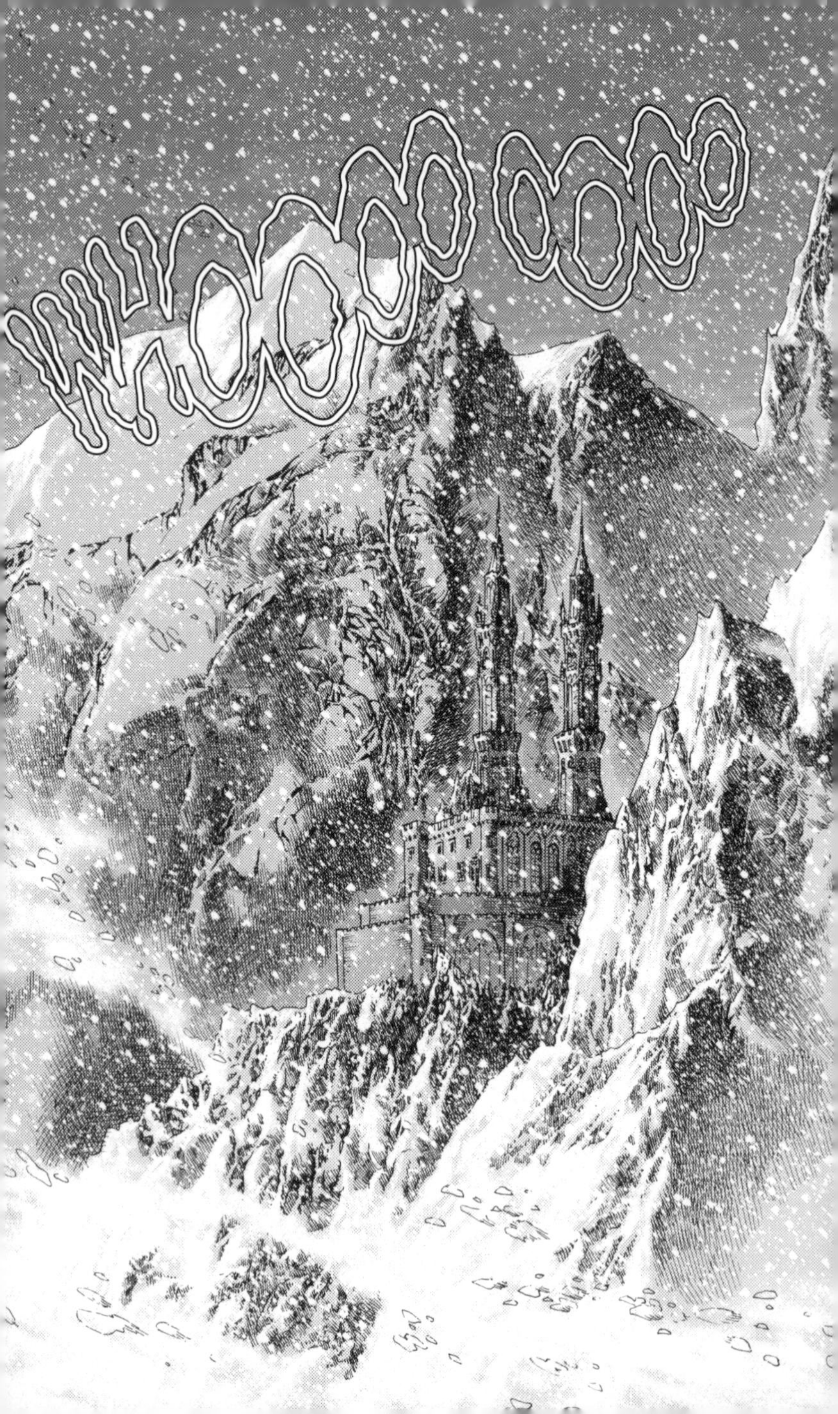
WHOOOOOOOO

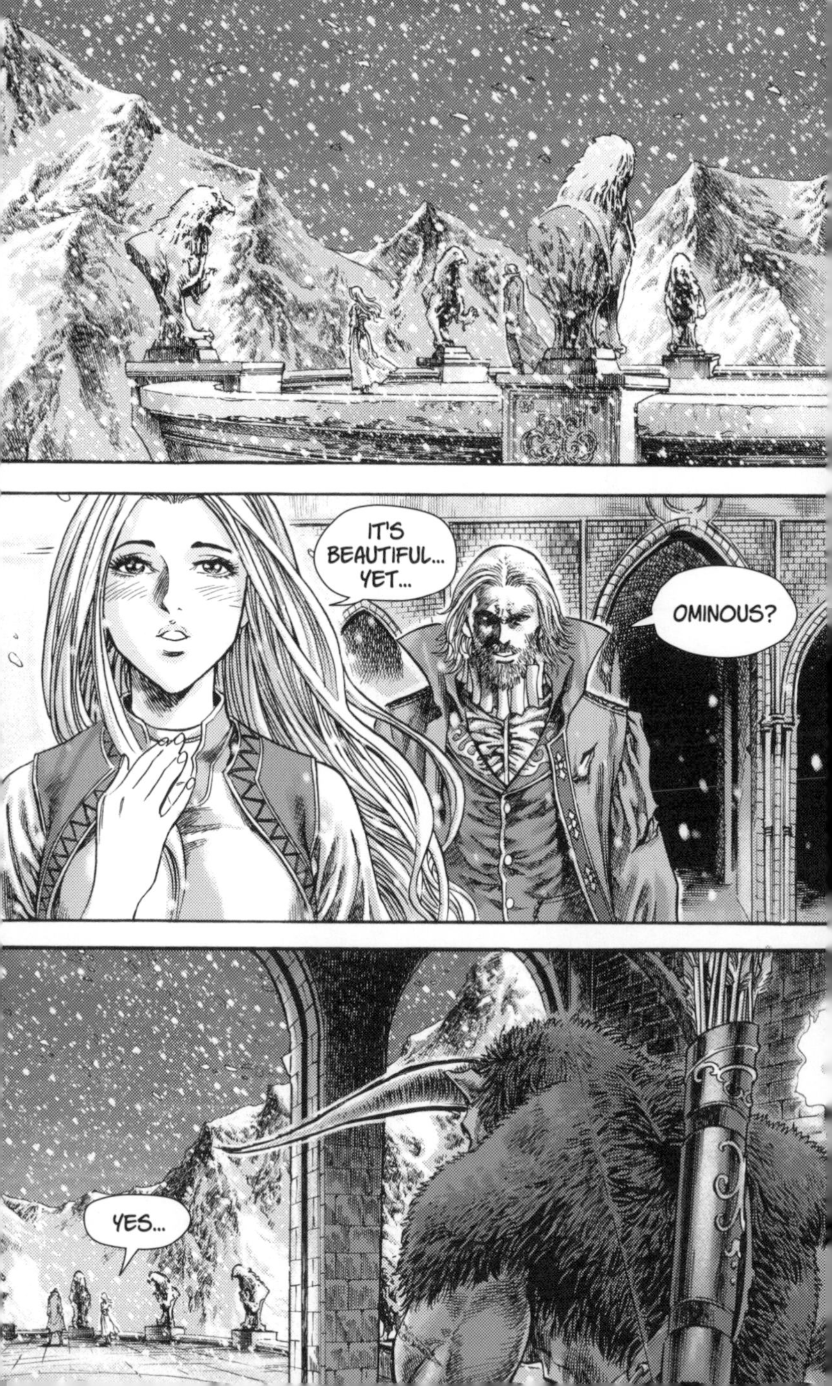
IT'S BEAUTIFUL... YET...
OMINOUS?
YES...

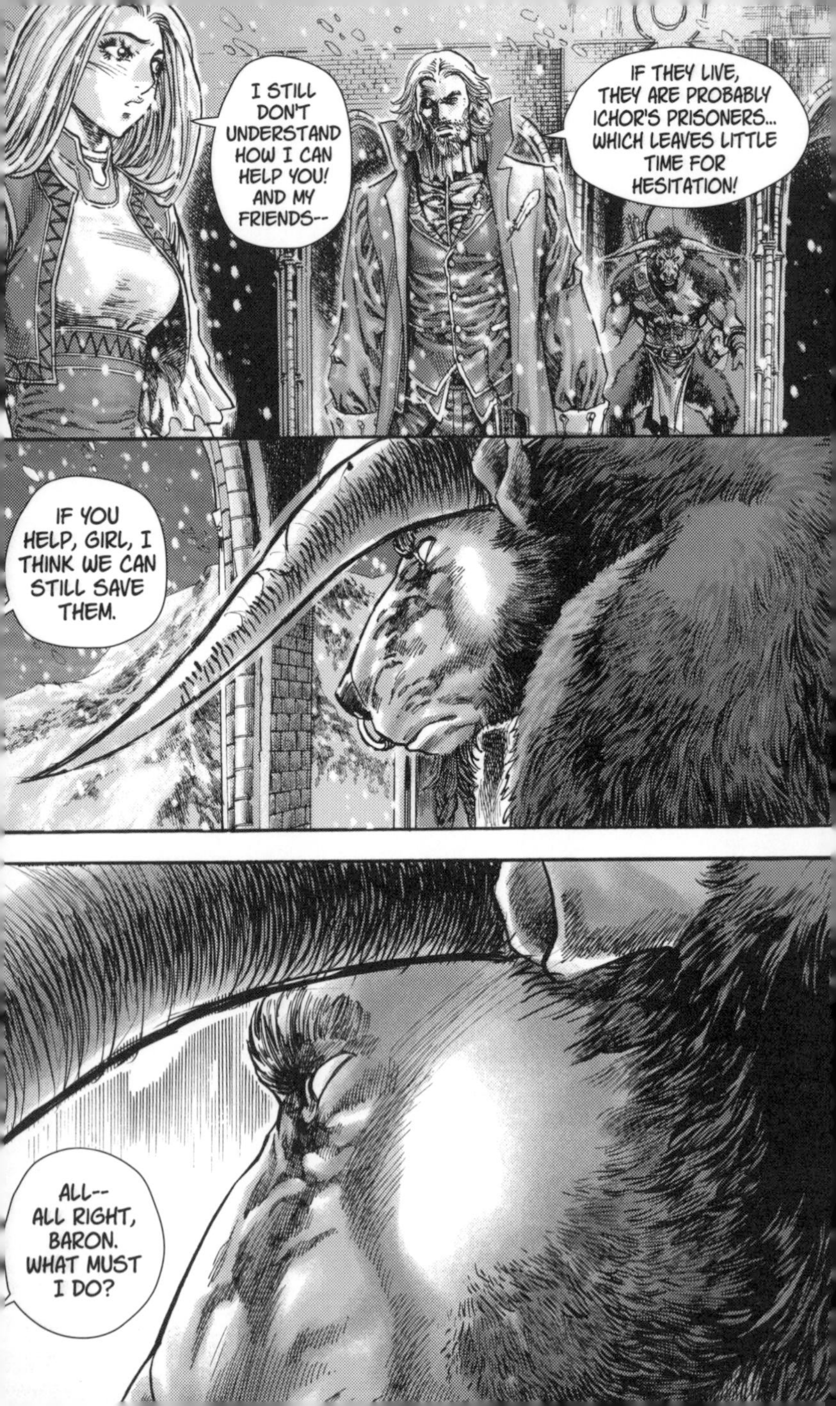
I STILL DON'T UNDERSTAND HOW I CAN HELP YOU! AND MY FRIENDS--
IF THEY LIVE, THEY ARE PROBABLY ICHOR'S PRISONERS... WHICH LEAVES LITTLE TIME FOR HESITATION!
IF YOU HELP, GIRL, I THINK WE CAN STILL SAVE THEM.
ALL-- ALL RIGHT, BARON. WHAT MUST I DO?

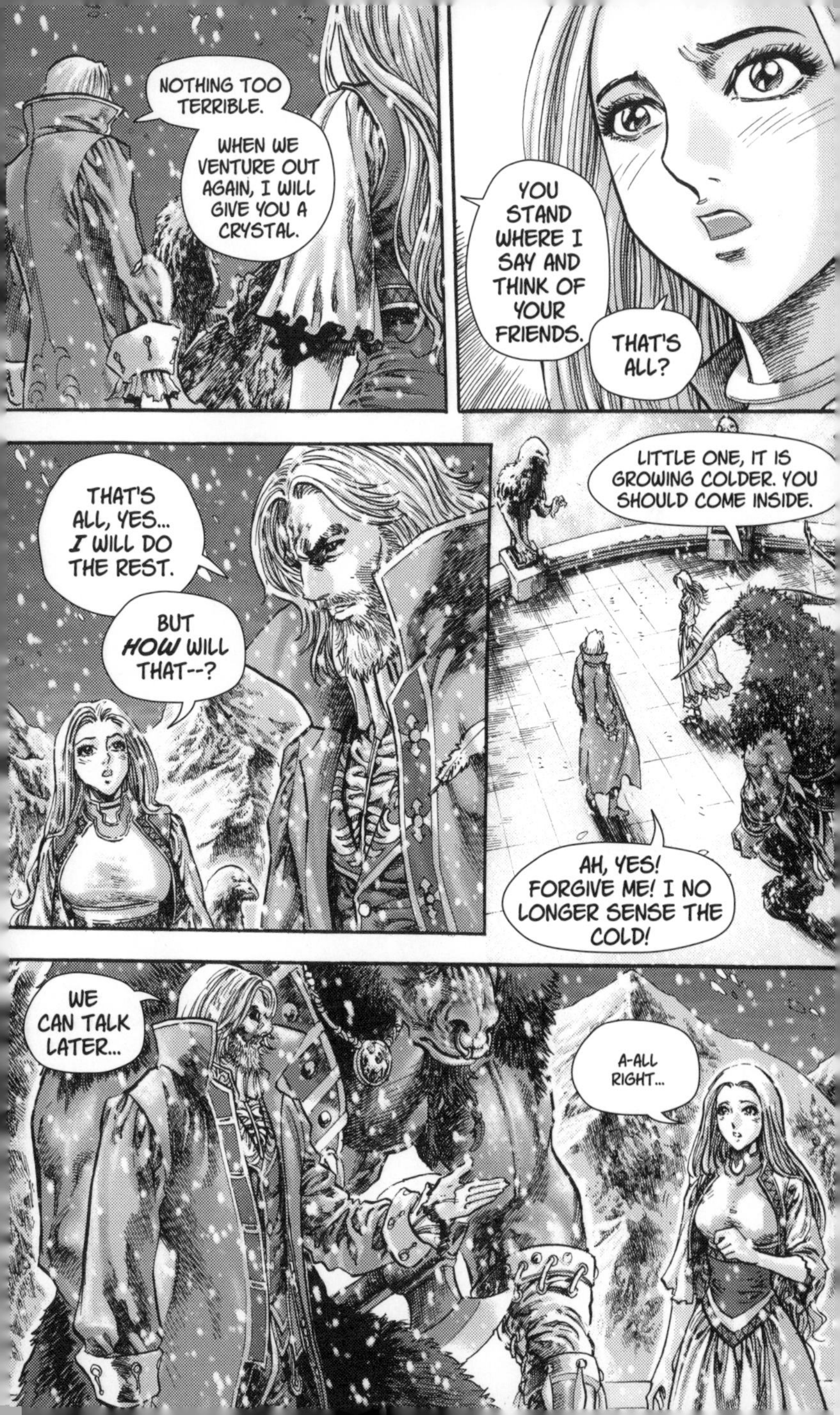
NOTHING TOO TERRIBLE.
WHEN WE VENTURE OUT AGAIN, I WILL GIVE YOU A CRYSTAL.
YOU STAND WHERE I SAY AND THINK OF YOUR FRIENDS.
THAT'S ALL?
THAT'S ALL, YES... *I* WILL DO THE REST.
BUT ***HOW*** WILL THAT--?
LITTLE ONE, IT IS GROWING COLDER. YOU SHOULD COME INSIDE.
AH, YES! FORGIVE ME! I NO LONGER SENSE THE COLD!
WE CAN TALK LATER...
A-ALL RIGHT...

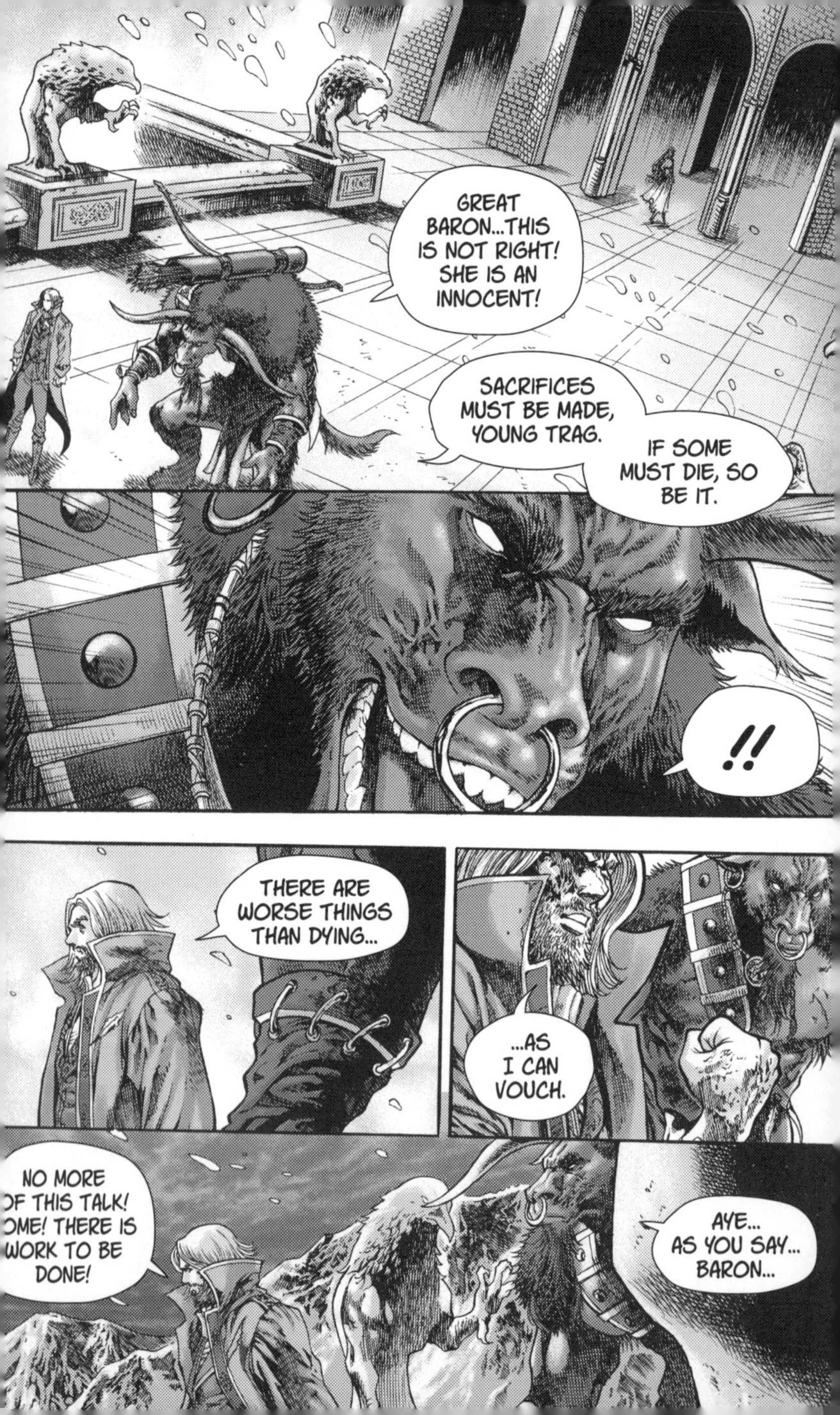
GREAT BARON...THIS IS NOT RIGHT! SHE IS AN INNOCENT!
SACRIFICES MUST BE MADE, YOUNG TRAG.
IF SOME MUST DIE, SO BE IT.
!!
THERE ARE WORSE THINGS THAN DYING...
...AS I CAN VOUCH.
NO MORE OF THIS TALK! COME! THERE IS WORK TO BE DONE!
AYE... AS YOU SAY... BARON...

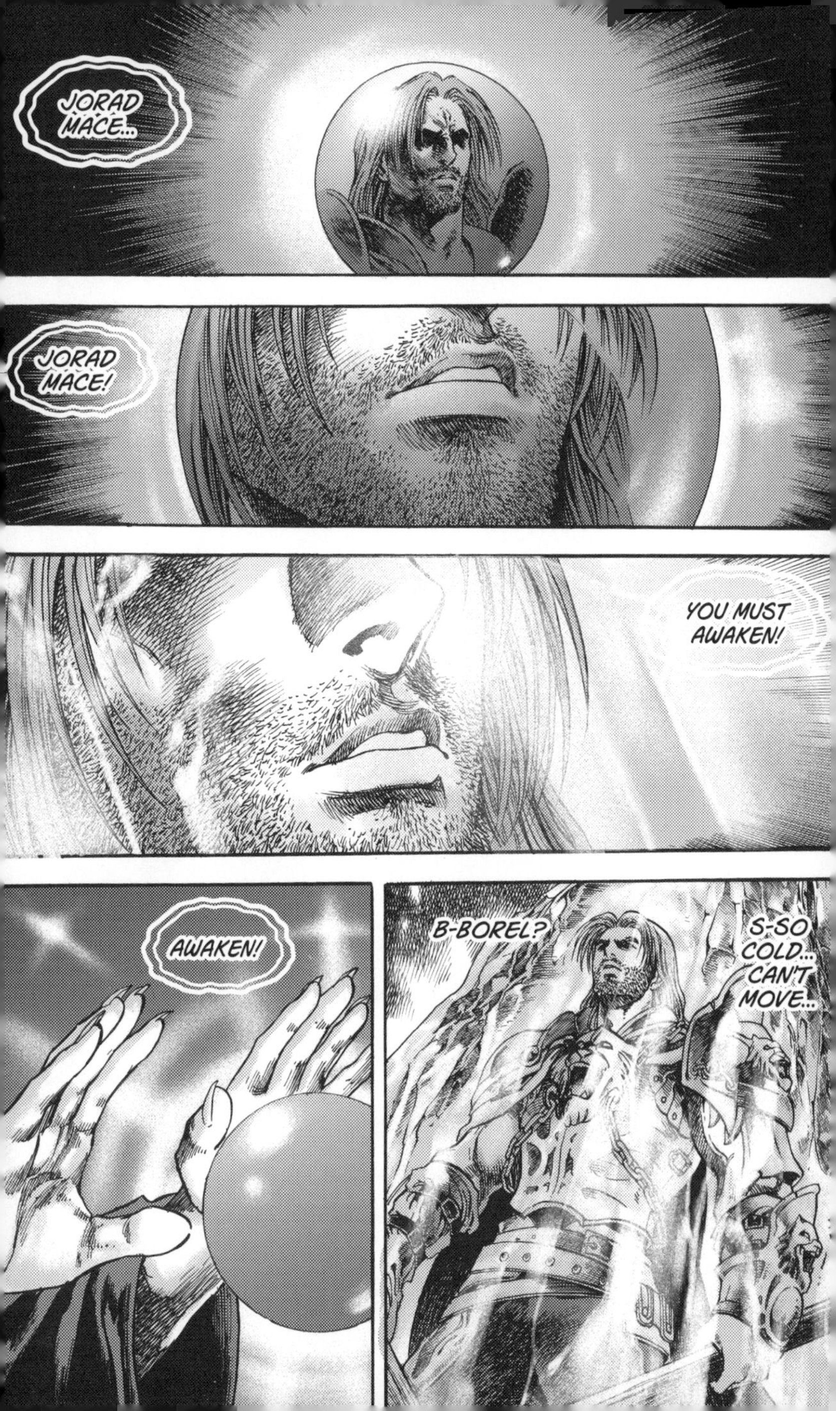
JORAD MACE...
JORAD MACE!
YOU MUST AWAKEN!
AWAKEN!
B-BOREL?
S-SO COLD... CAN'T MOVE...

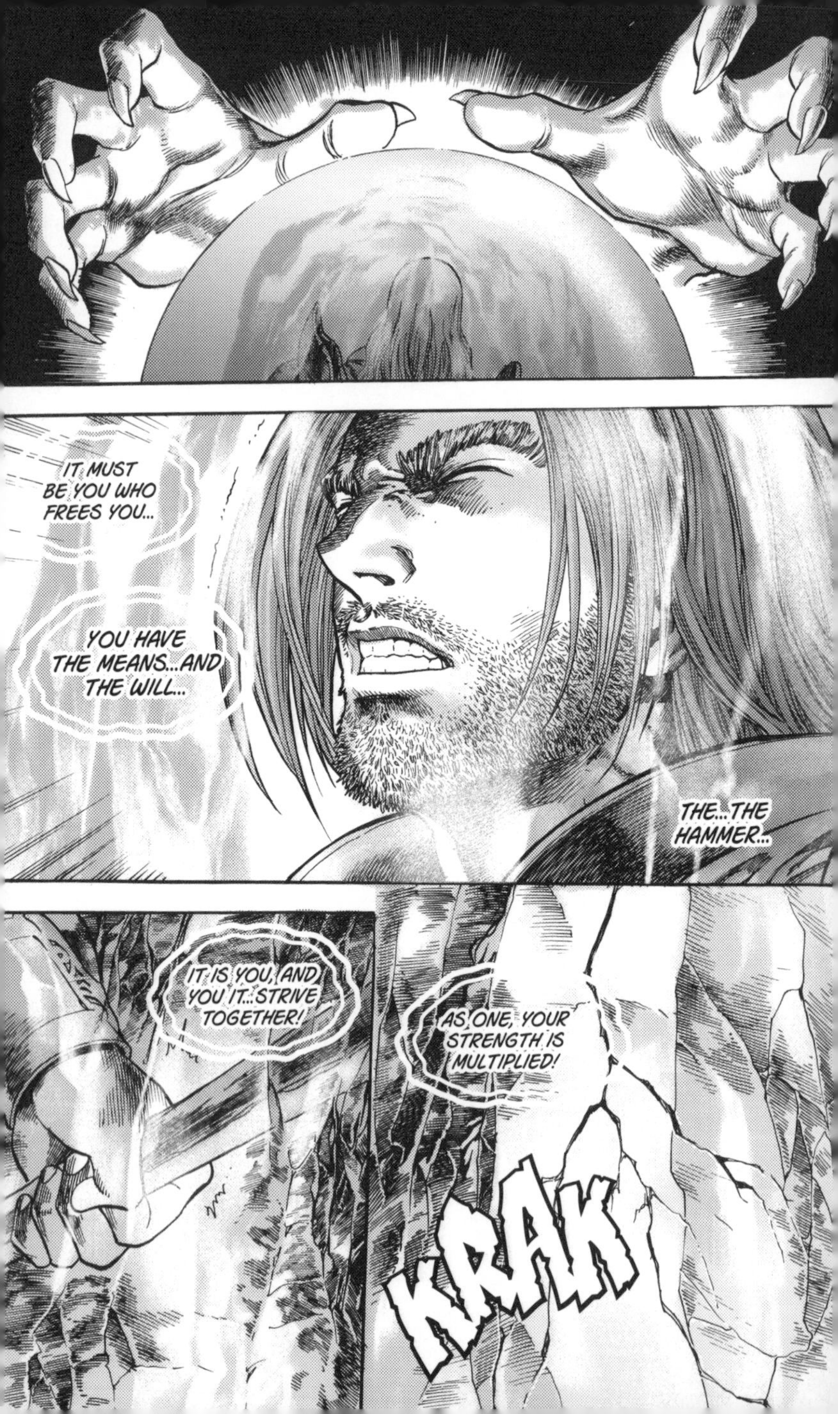
IT MUST BE YOU WHO FREES YOU...
YOU HAVE THE MEANS...AND THE WILL...
THE...THE HAMMER...
IT IS YOU, AND YOU IT...STRIVE TOGETHER!
AS ONE, YOUR STRENGTH IS MULTIPLIED!
KRAK

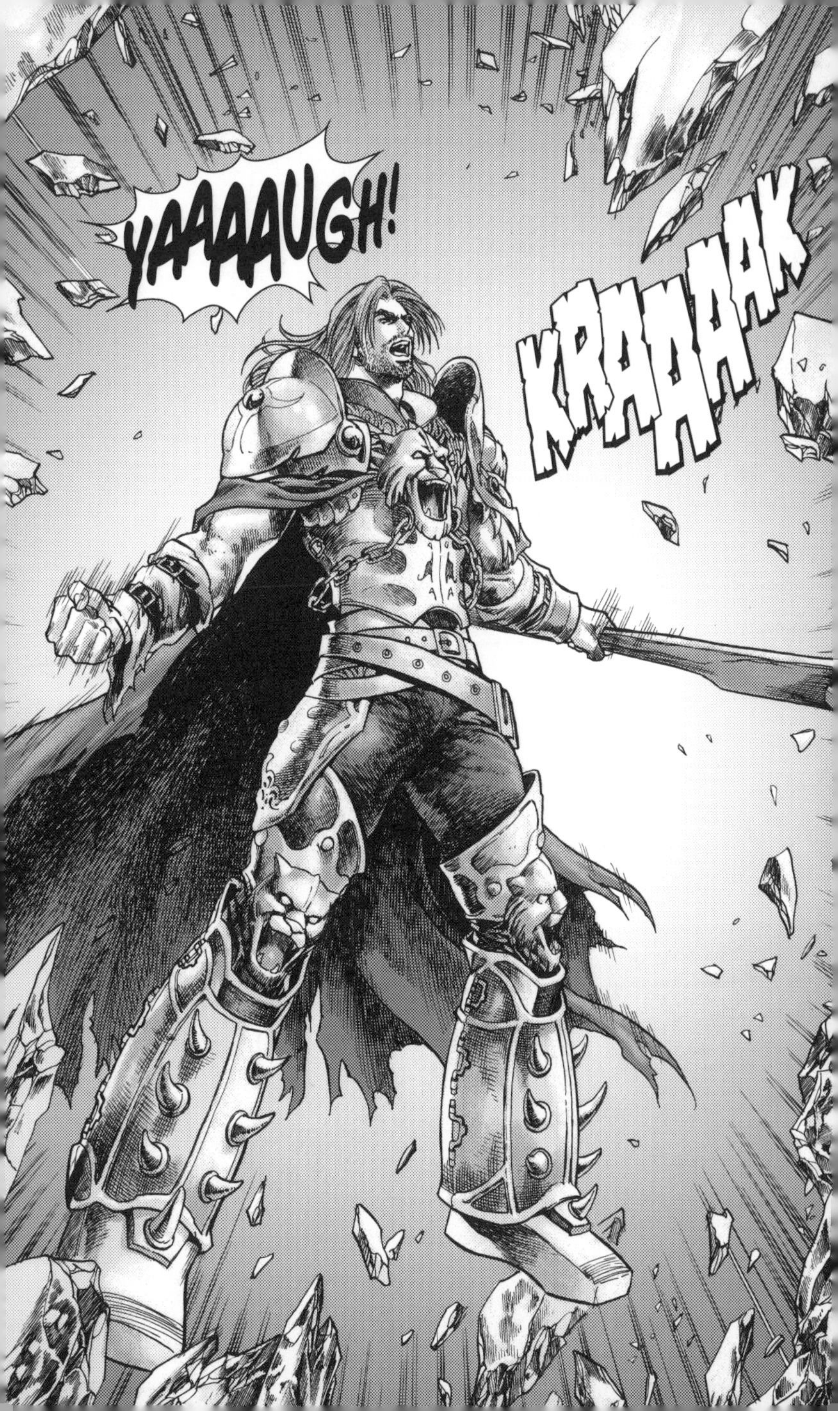

YAAAAUGH!
KRAAAAK

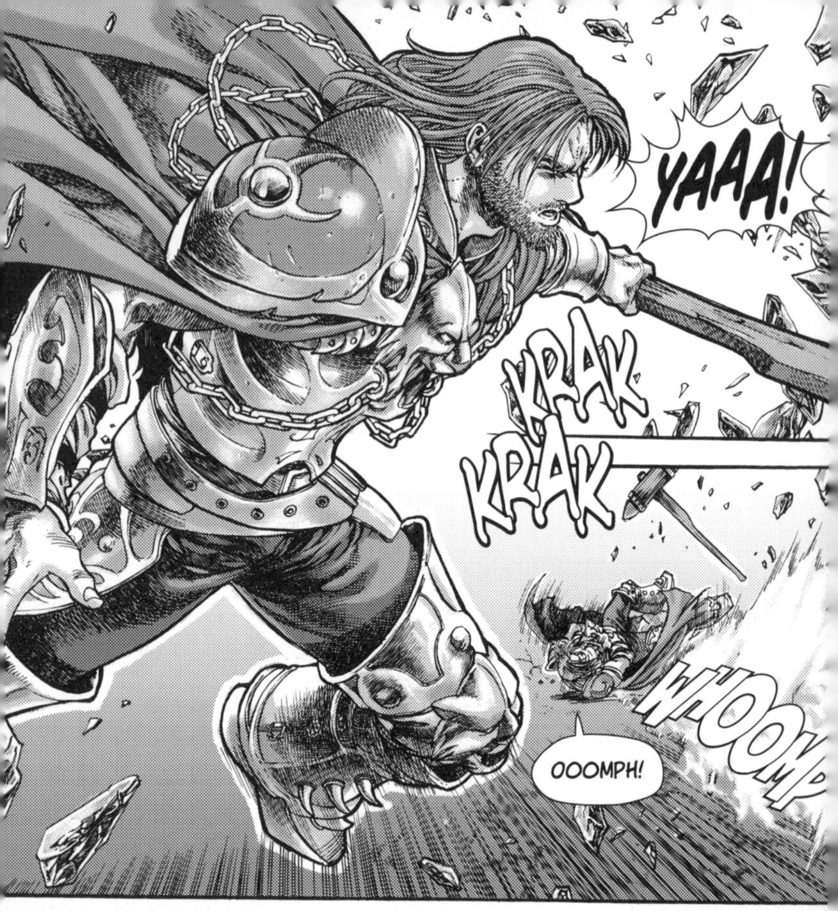
YAAAA!
KRAK
KRAK
WHOOMP
OOOMPH!
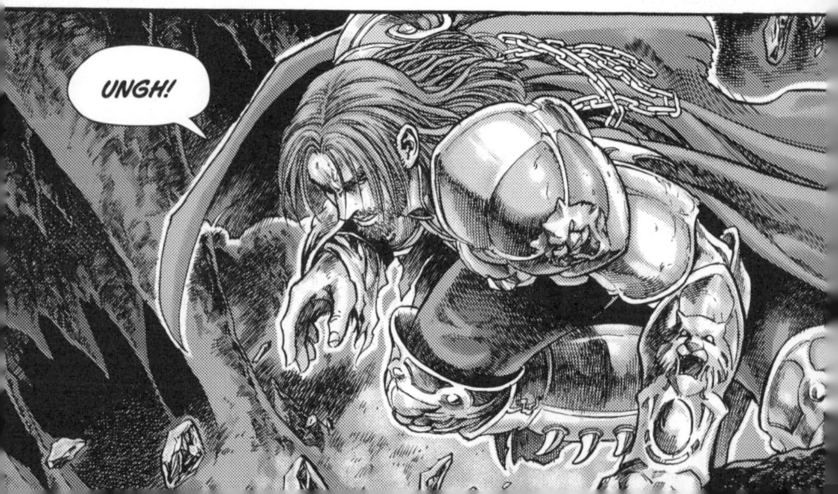
UNGH!

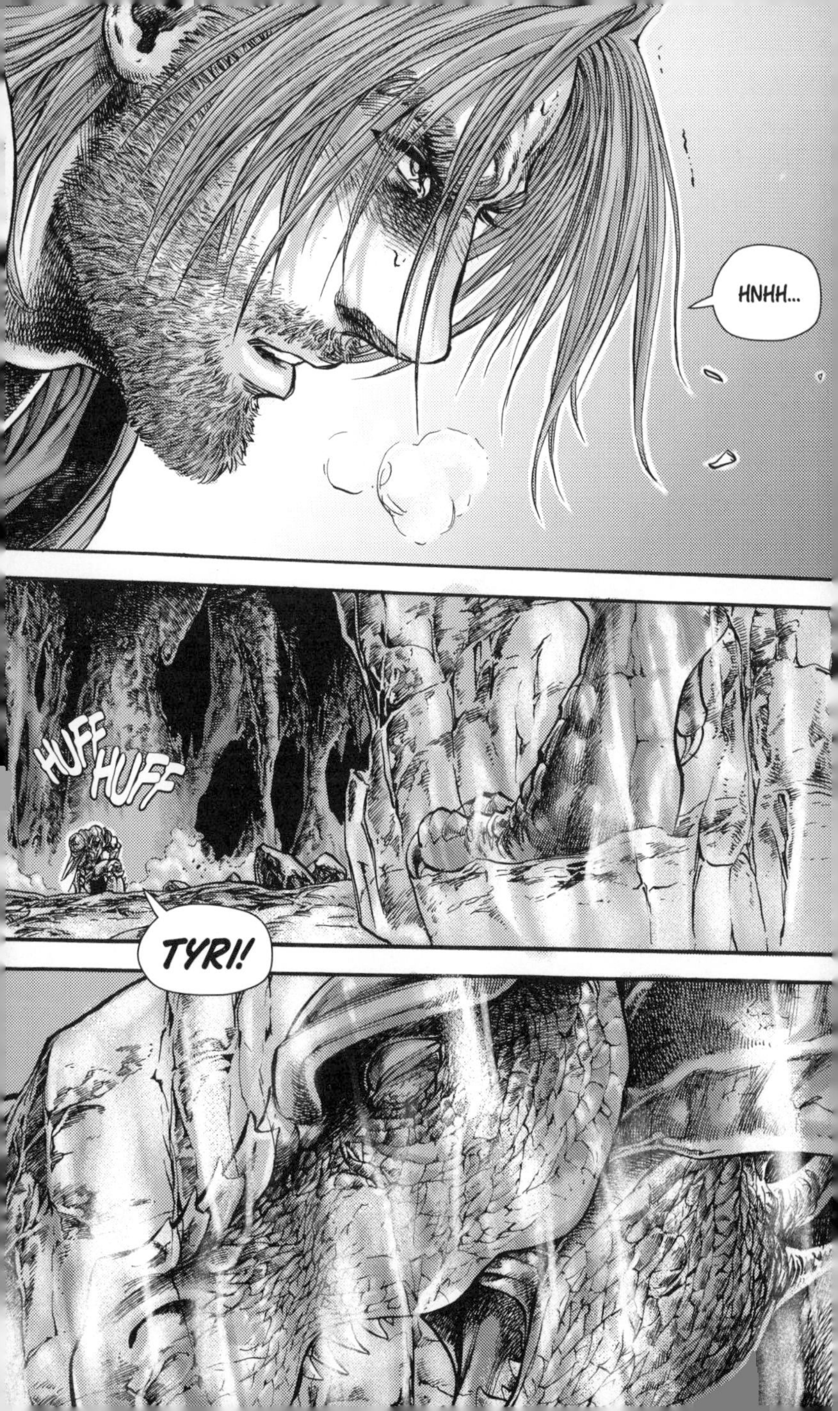
HNHH...
HUFF HUFF
TYRI!

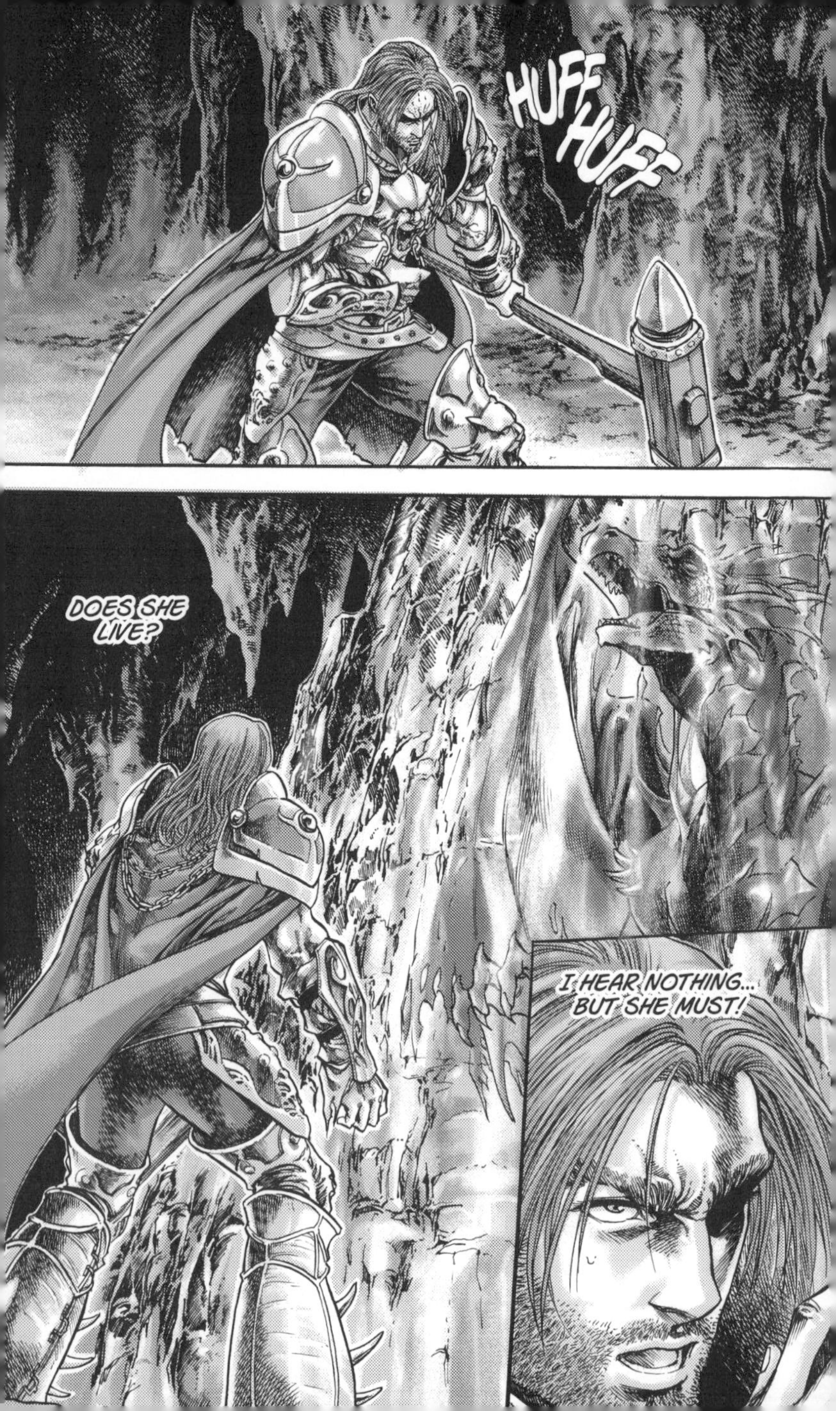
HUFF HUFF
DOES SHE LIVE?
I HEAR NOTHING... BUT SHE MUST!

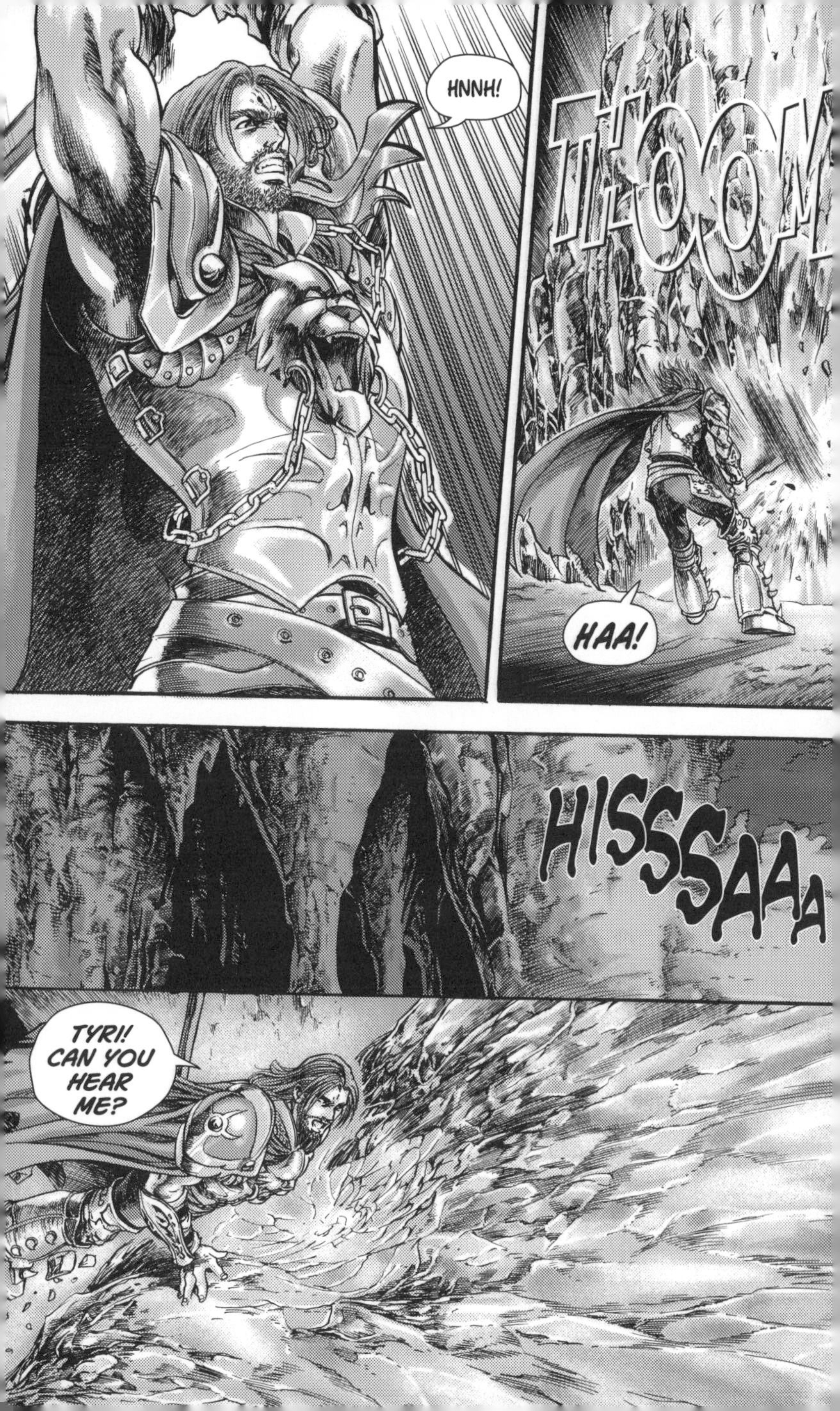
HNNH!
THOOM
HAA!
HISSSAAAA
TYRI! CAN YOU HEAR ME?

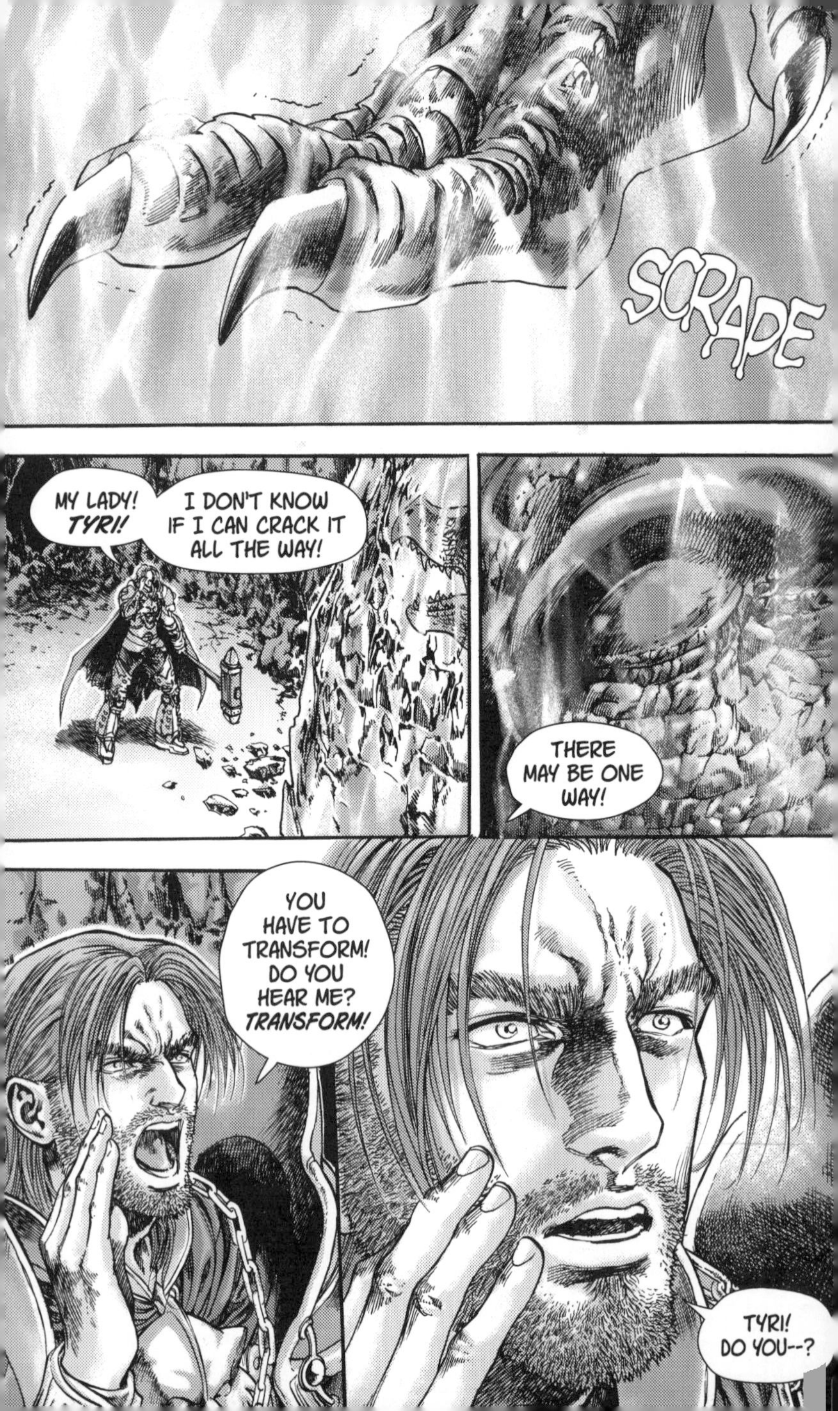
SCRAPE
MY LADY! TYRI!
I DON'T KNOW IF I CAN CRACK IT ALL THE WAY!
THERE MAY BE ONE WAY!
YOU HAVE TO TRANSFORM! DO YOU HEAR ME? TRANSFORM!
TYRI! DO YOU--?

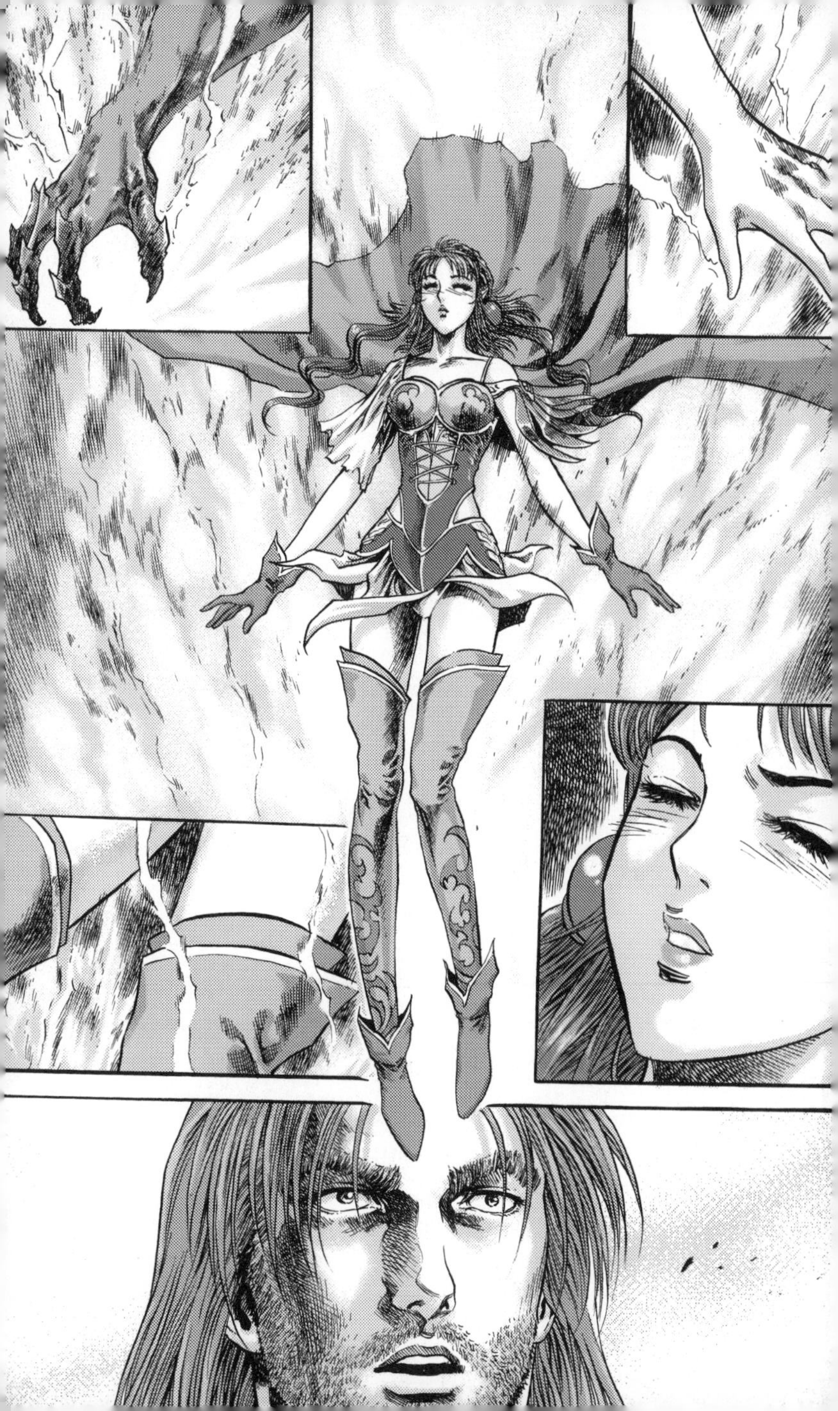

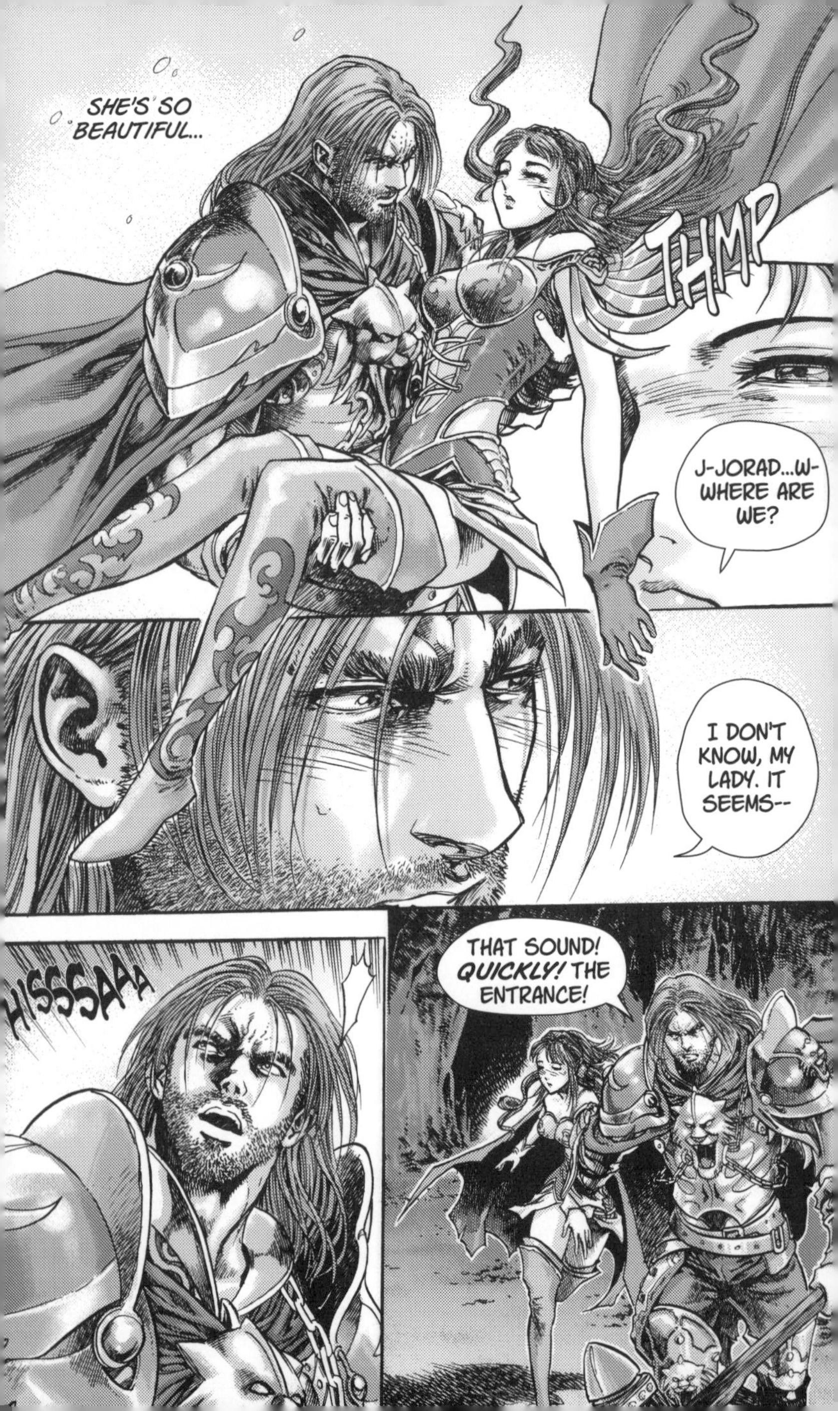

SHE'S SO BEAUTIFUL...
THMP
J-JORAD...W-WHERE ARE WE?
I DON'T KNOW, MY LADY. IT SEEMS--
HISSSAAA
THAT SOUND! *QUICKLY!* THE ENTRANCE!

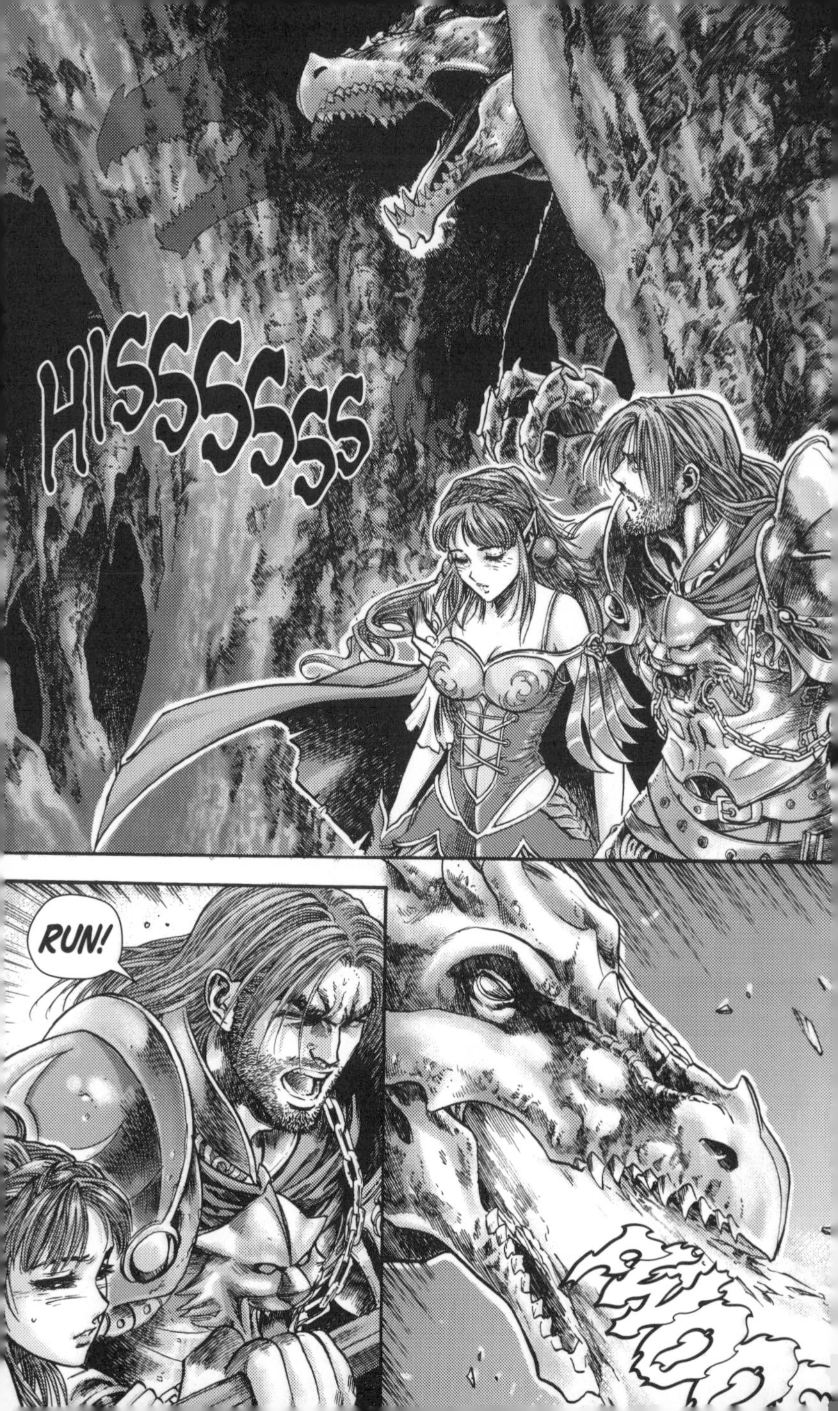
HISSSSSSS
RUN!

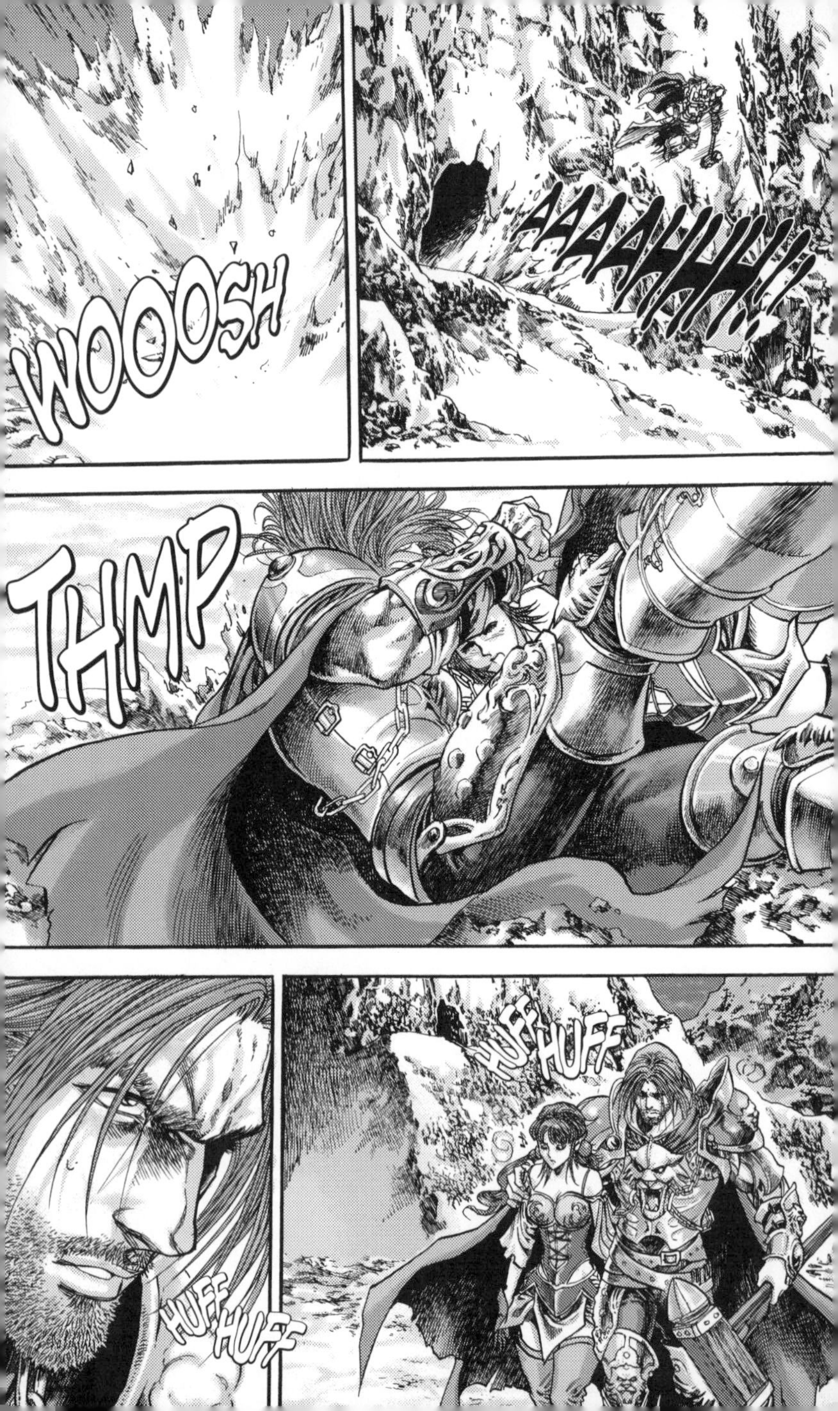
WOOOSH
AAAAHHH!!!
THMP
HUFF HUFF
HUFF HUFF

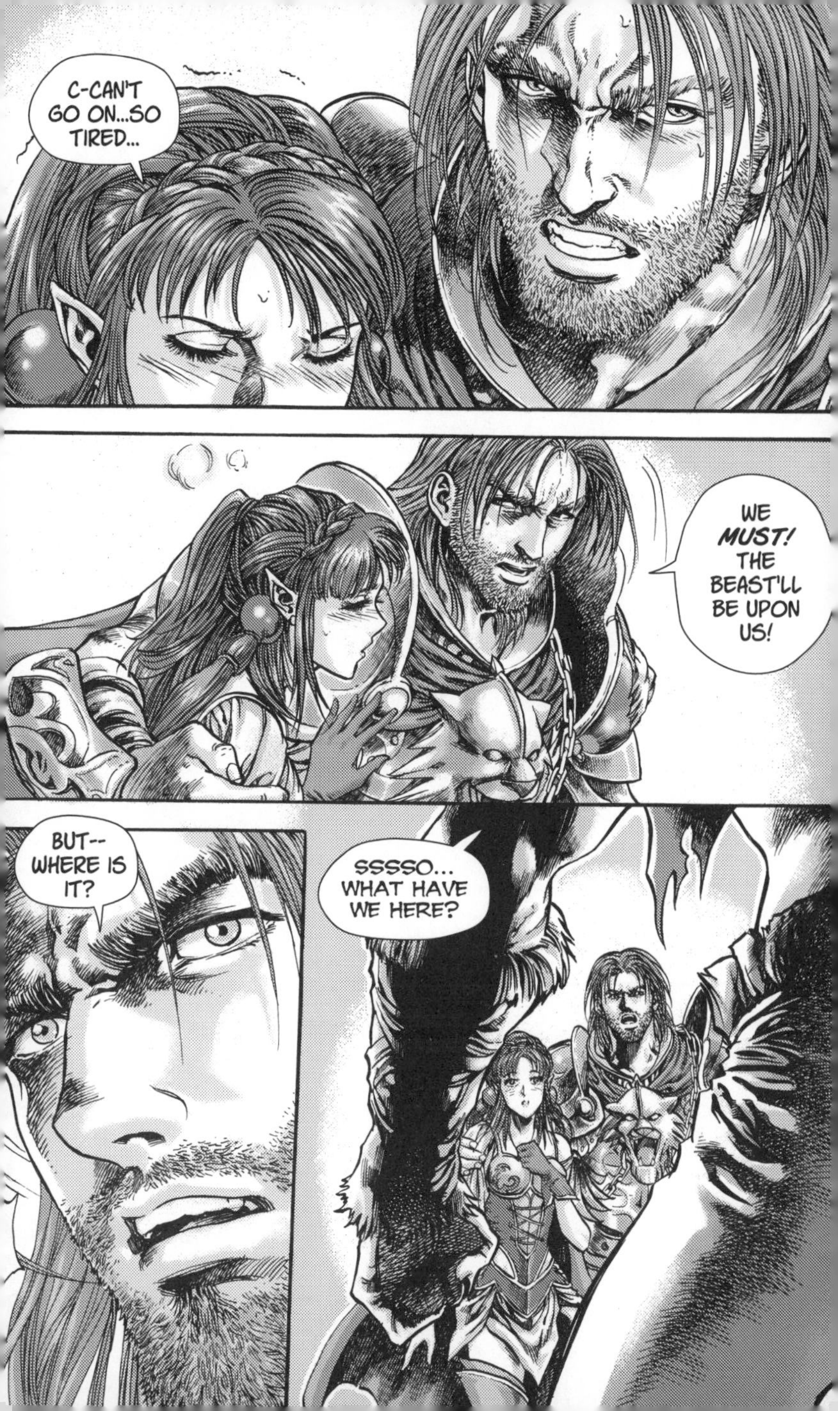
C-CAN'T GO ON...SO TIRED...
WE *MUST!* THE BEAST'LL BE UPON US!
BUT-- WHERE IS IT?
SSSSO... WHAT HAVE WE HERE?

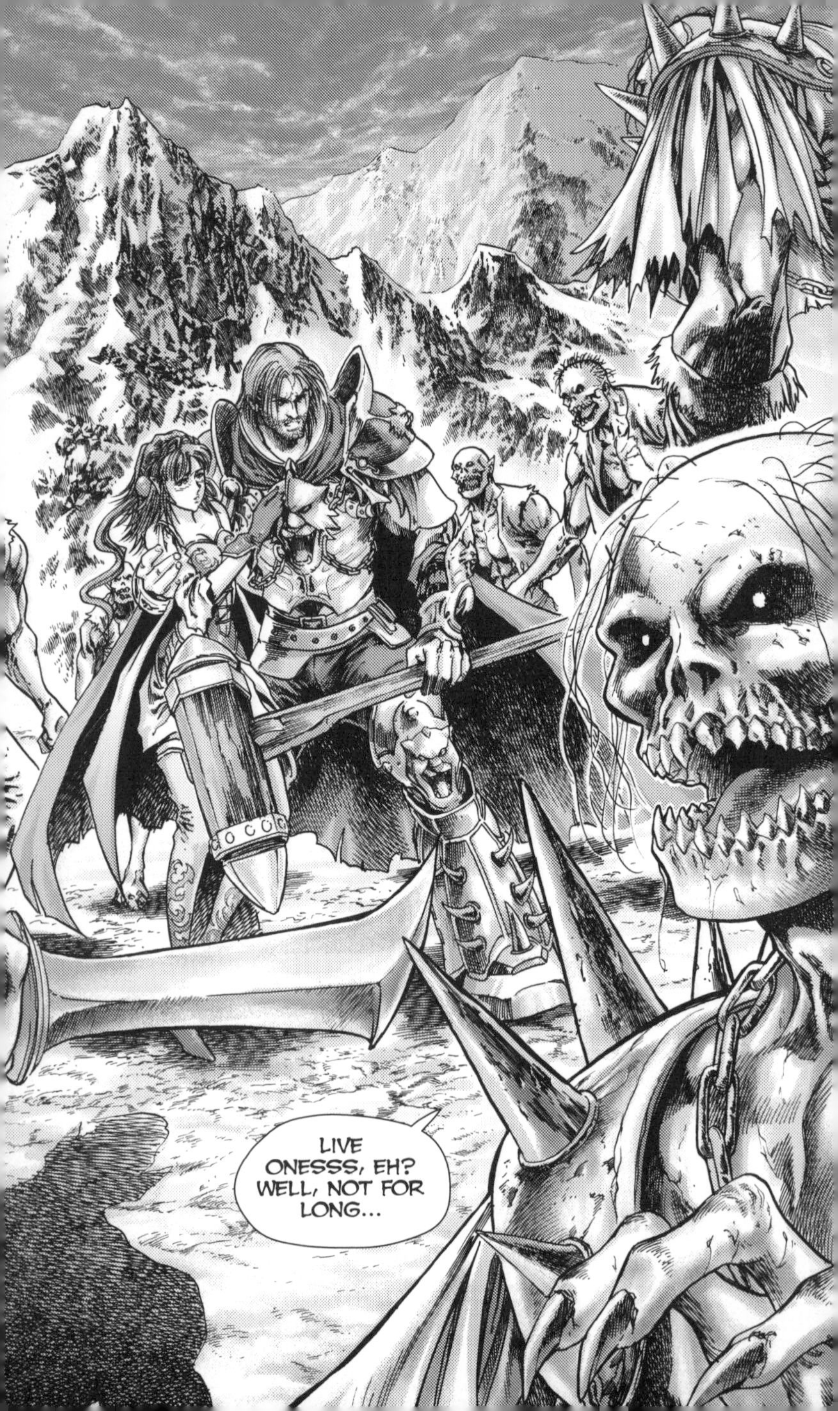
LIVE ONESSS, EH? WELL, NOT FOR LONG...

CHAPTER FOUR
THE DWELLERS BENEATH

UNNGH...
WHERE--?

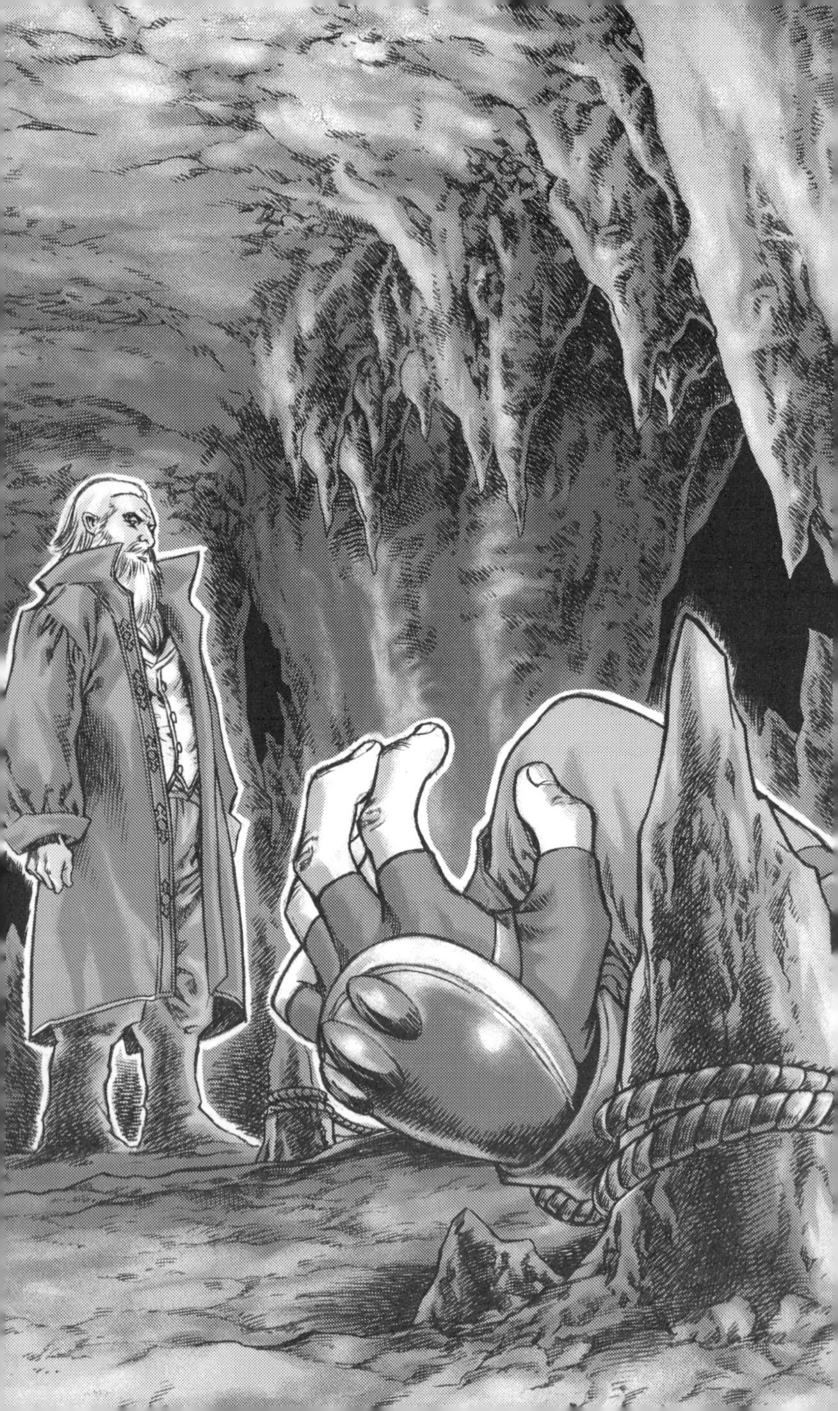

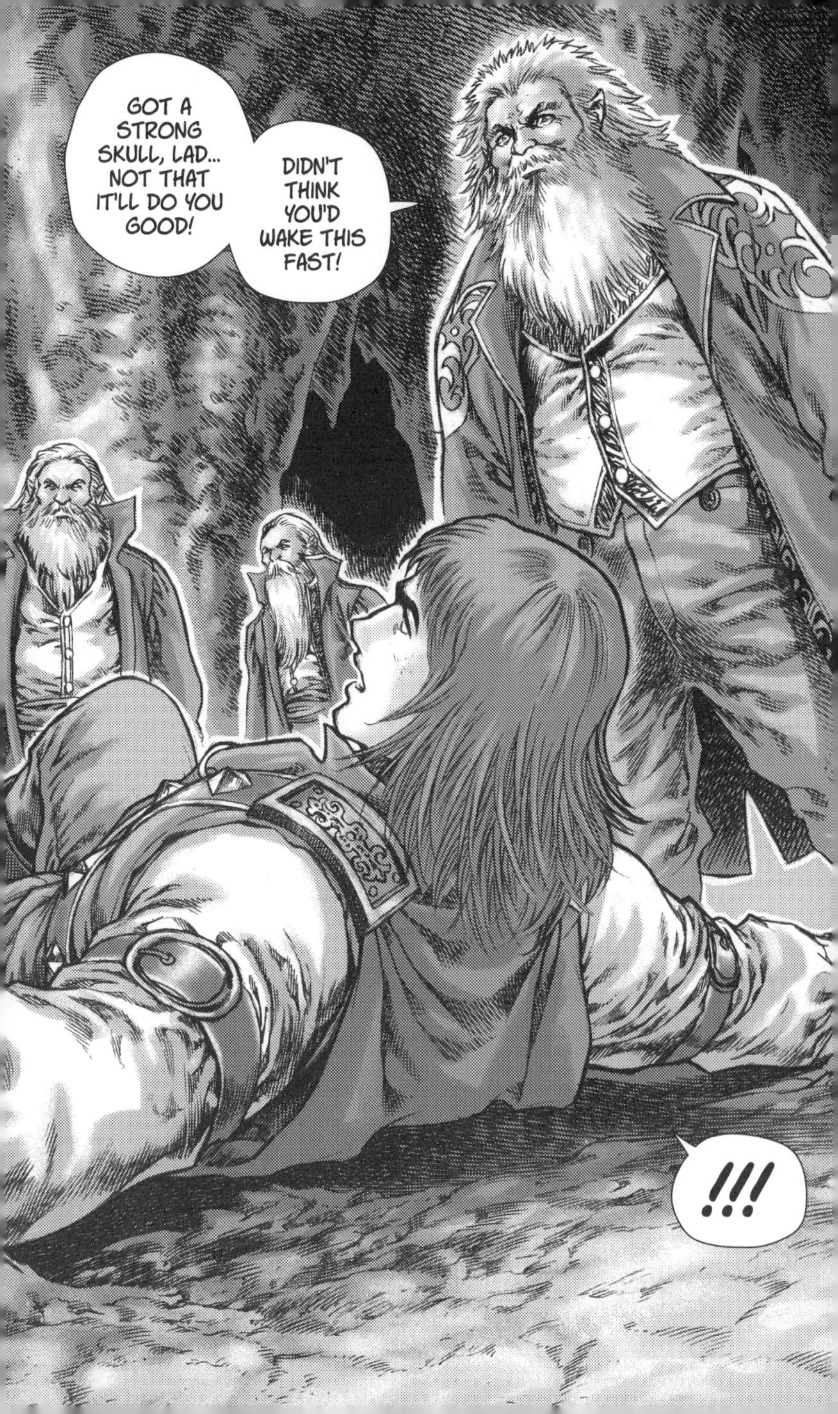
GOT A STRONG SKULL, LAD... NOT THAT IT'LL DO YOU GOOD!
DIDN'T THINK YOU'D WAKE THIS FAST!
!!!

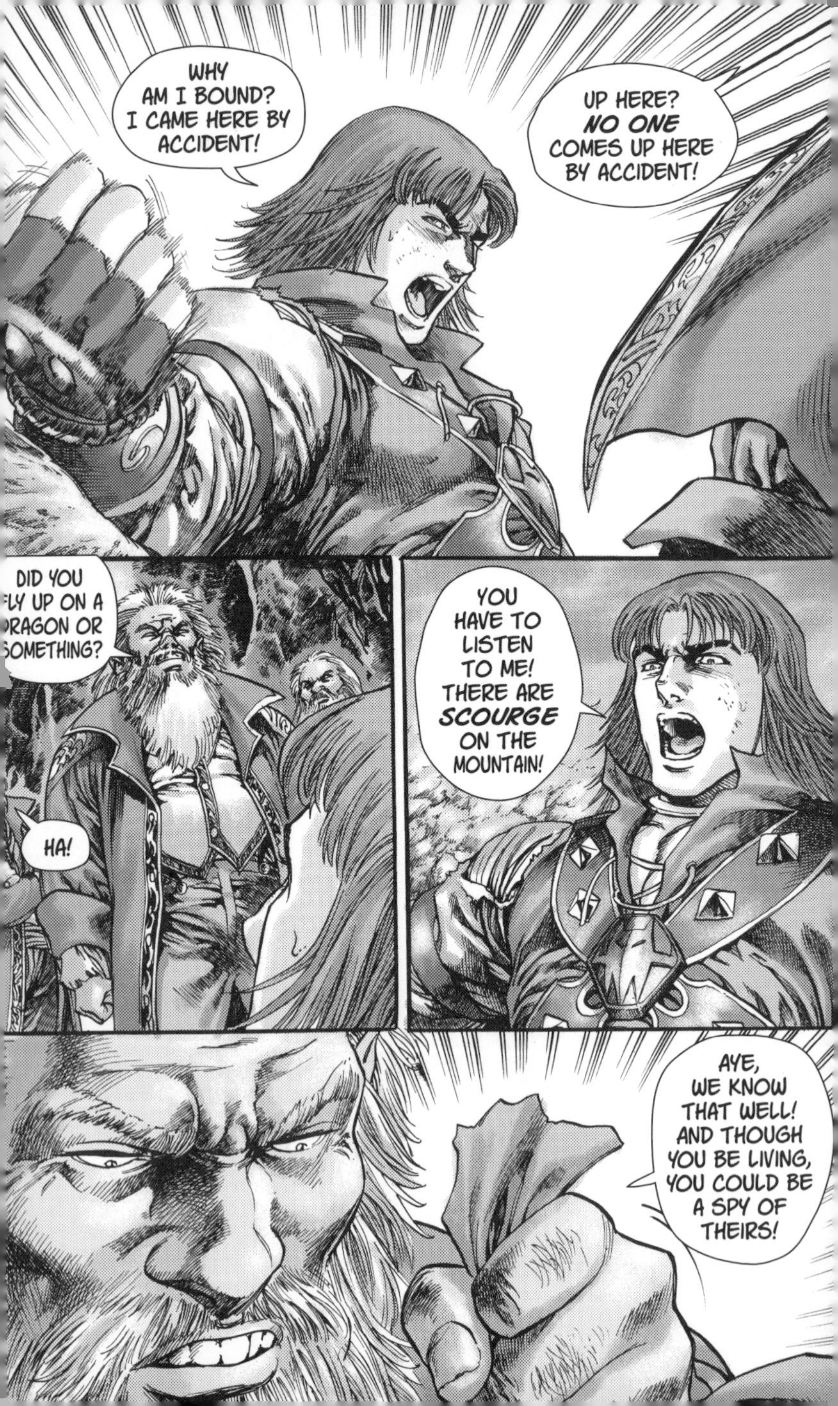
WHY AM I BOUND? I CAME HERE BY ACCIDENT!
UP HERE? *NO ONE* COMES UP HERE BY ACCIDENT!
DID YOU FLY UP ON A DRAGON OR SOMETHING?
HA!
YOU HAVE TO LISTEN TO ME! THERE ARE ***SCOURGE*** ON THE MOUNTAIN!
AYE, WE KNOW THAT WELL! AND THOUGH YOU BE LIVING, YOU COULD BE A SPY OF THEIRS!

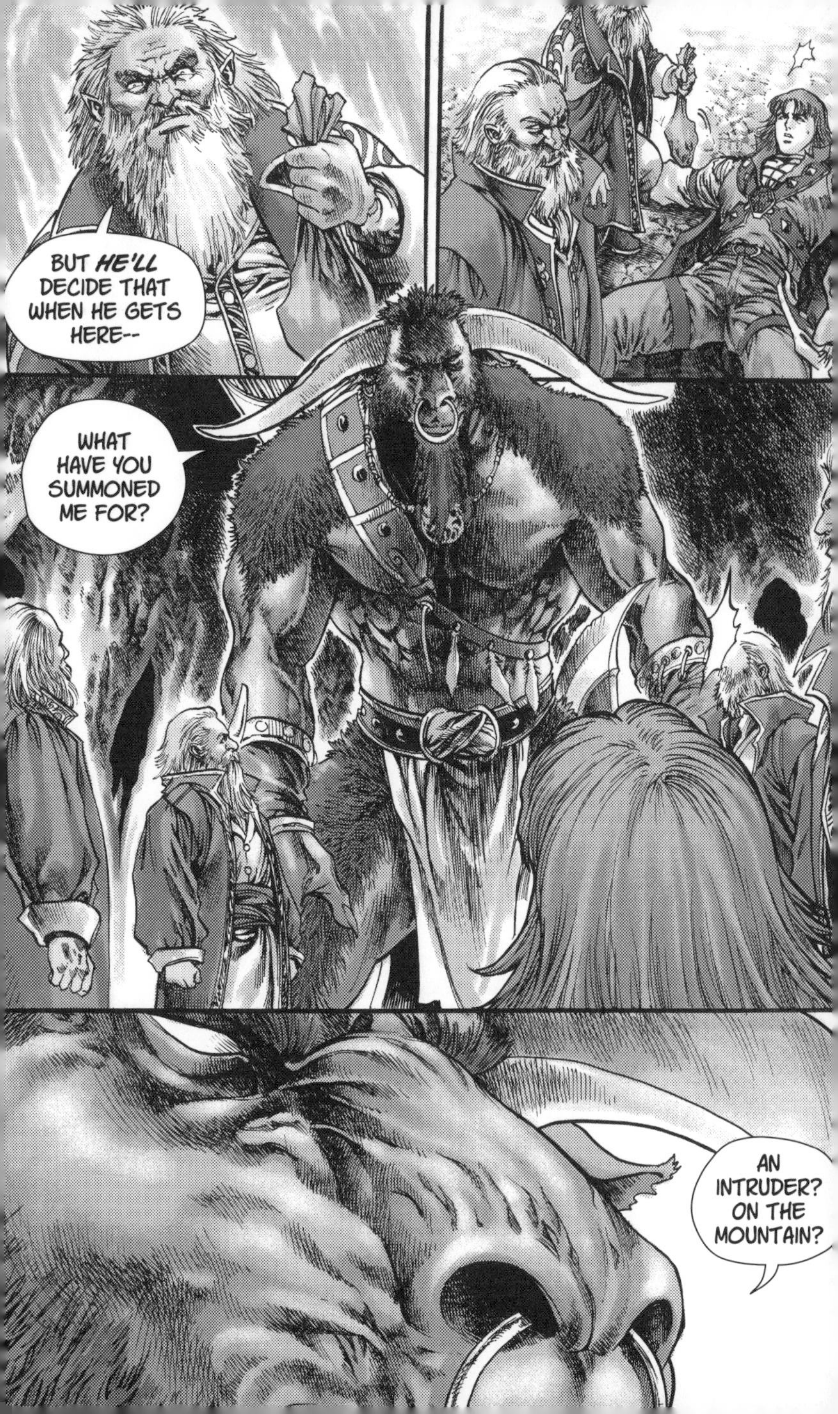
BUT *HE'LL* DECIDE THAT WHEN HE GETS HERE--
WHAT HAVE YOU SUMMONED ME FOR?
AN INTRUDER? ON THE MOUNTAIN?

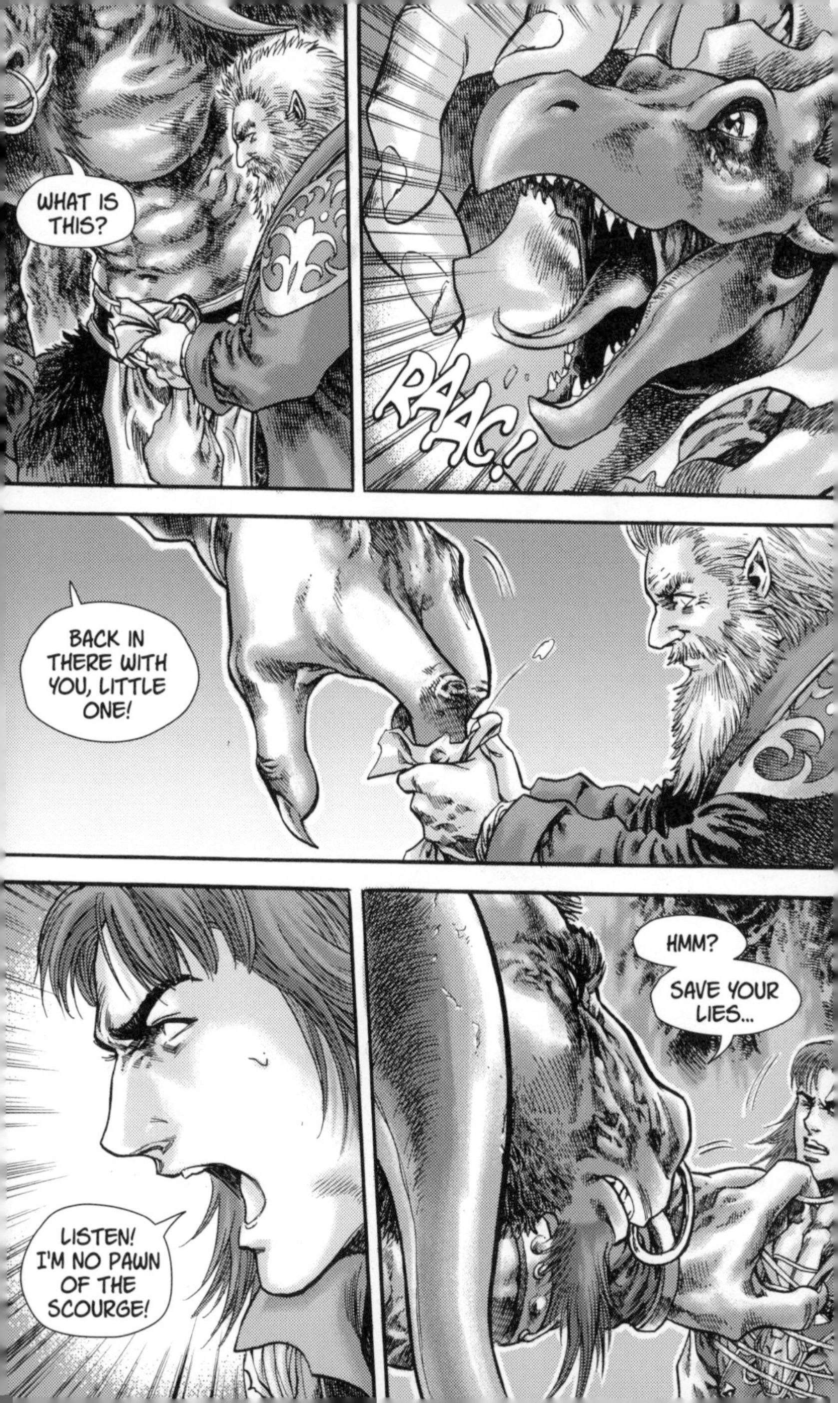
WHAT IS THIS?
RAAC!!
BACK IN THERE WITH YOU, LITTLE ONE!
LISTEN! I'M NO PAWN OF THE SCOURGE!
HMM?
SAVE YOUR LIES...

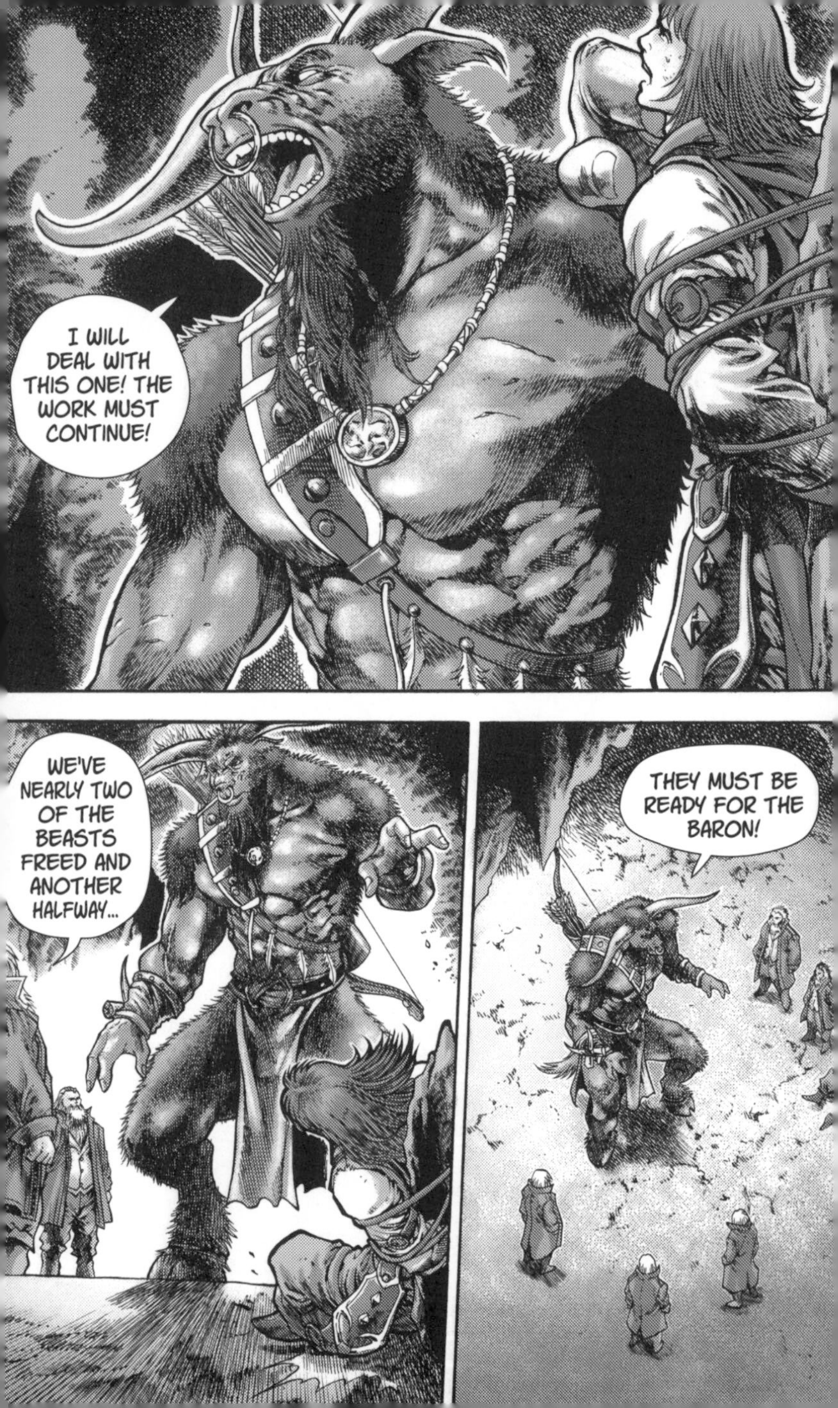
I WILL DEAL WITH THIS ONE! THE WORK MUST CONTINUE!
WE'VE NEARLY TWO OF THE BEASTS FREED AND ANOTHER HALFWAY...
THEY MUST BE READY FOR THE BARON!

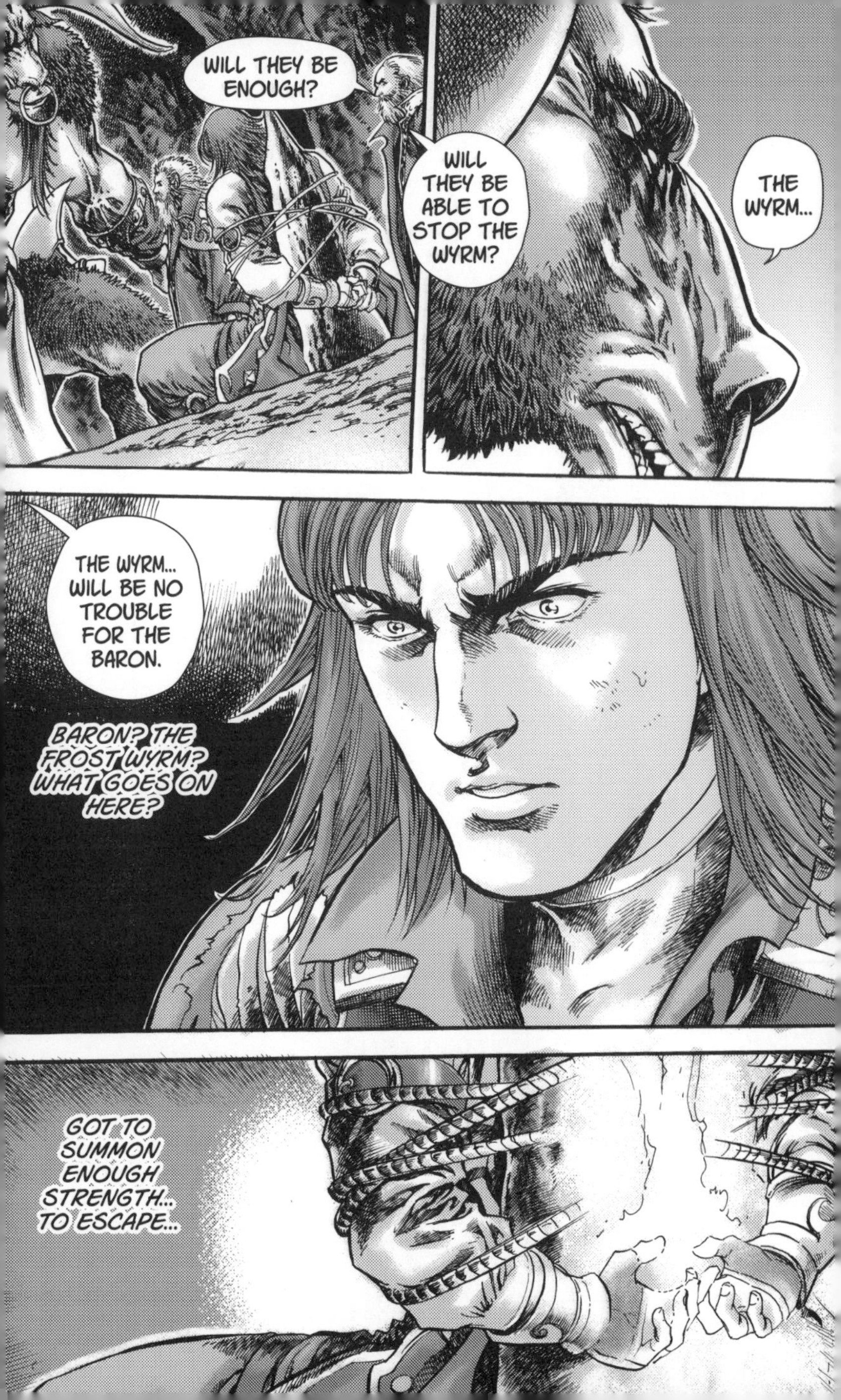
WILL THEY BE ENOUGH?
WILL THEY BE ABLE TO STOP THE WYRM?
THE WYRM...
THE WYRM... WILL BE NO TROUBLE FOR THE BARON.
BARON? THE FROST WYRM? WHAT GOES ON HERE?
GOT TO SUMMON ENOUGH STRENGTH... TO ESCAPE...

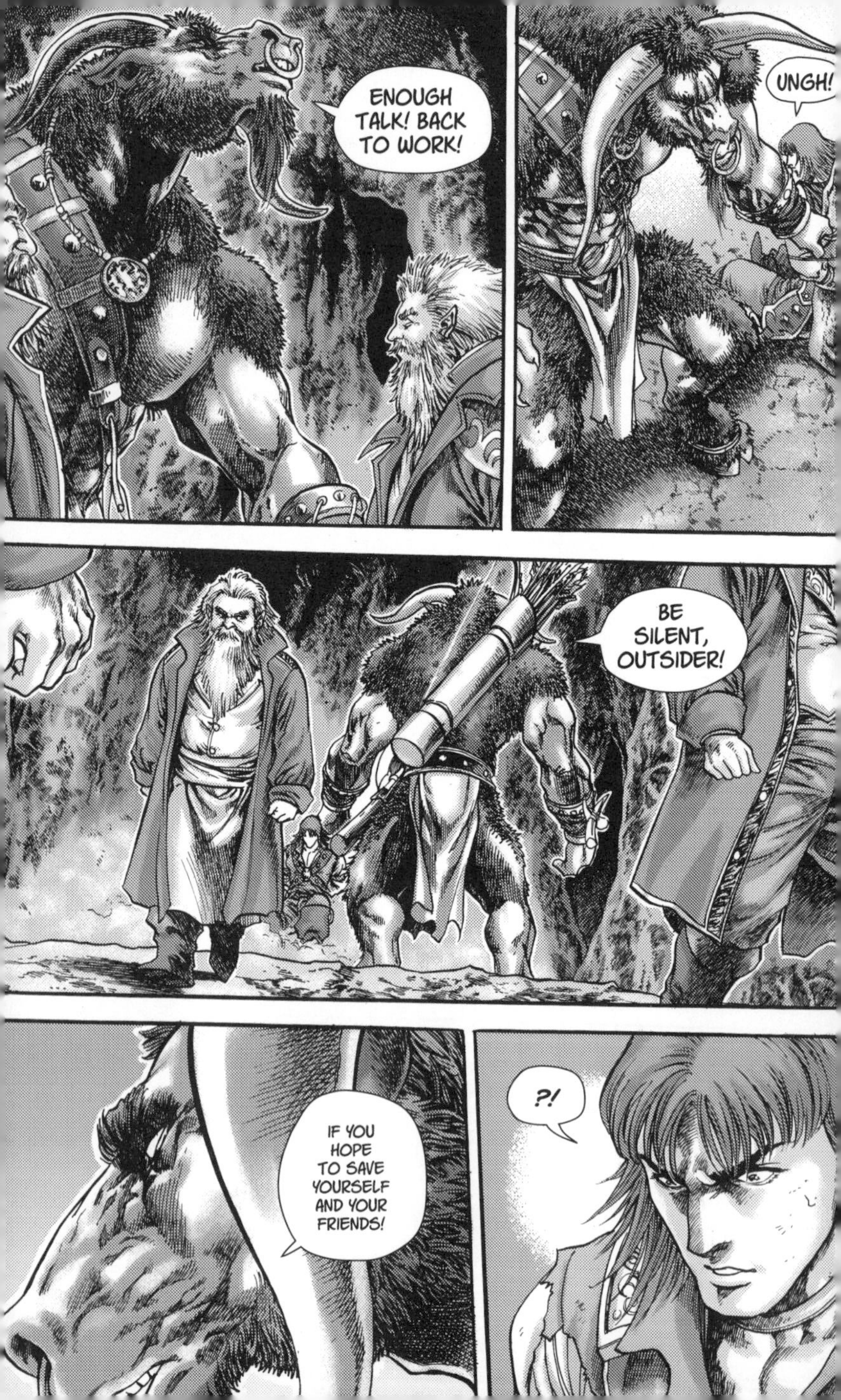
ENOUGH TALK! BACK TO WORK!
UNGH!
BE SILENT, OUTSIDER!
IF YOU HOPE TO SAVE YOURSELF AND YOUR FRIENDS!
?!

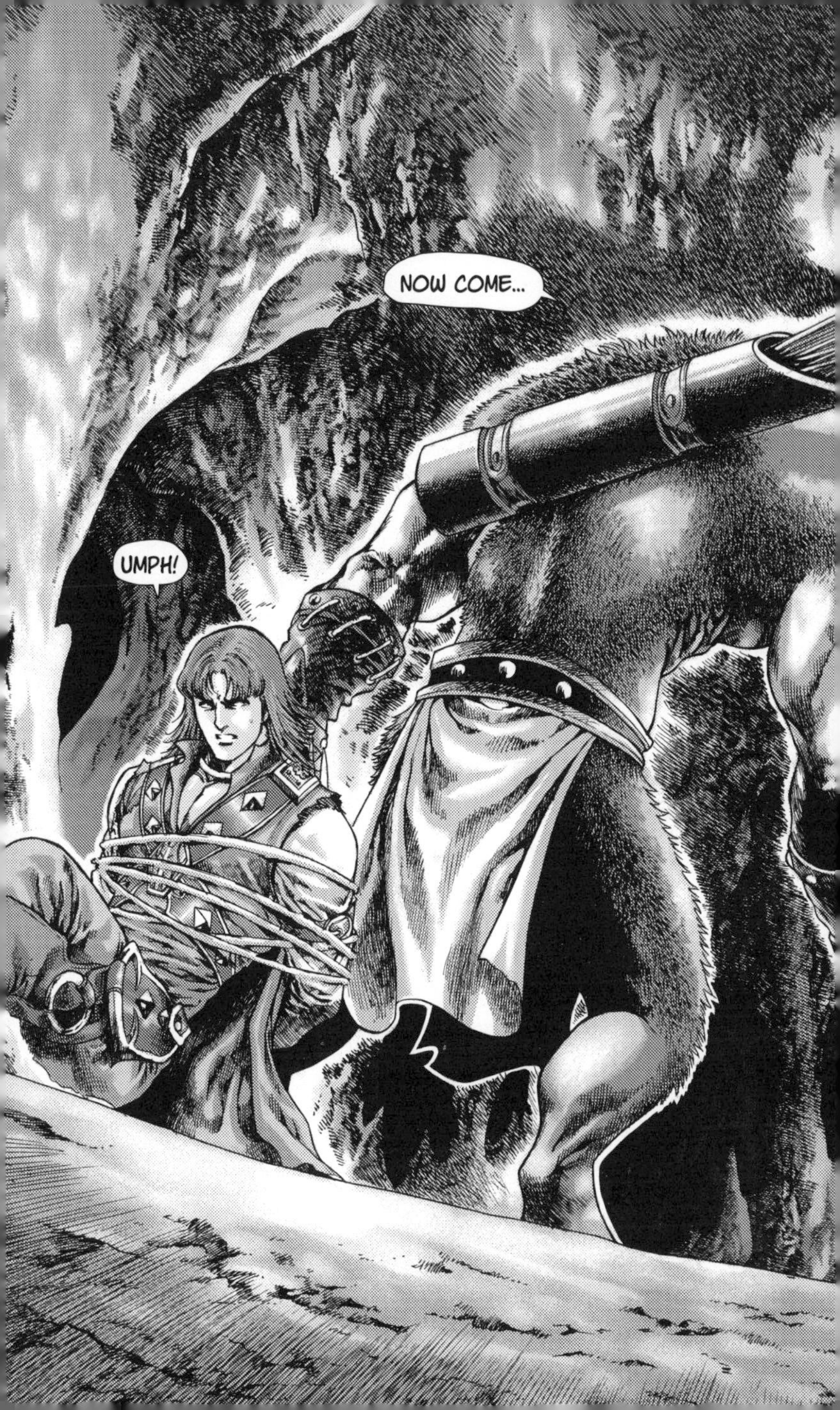
NOW COME...
UMPH!

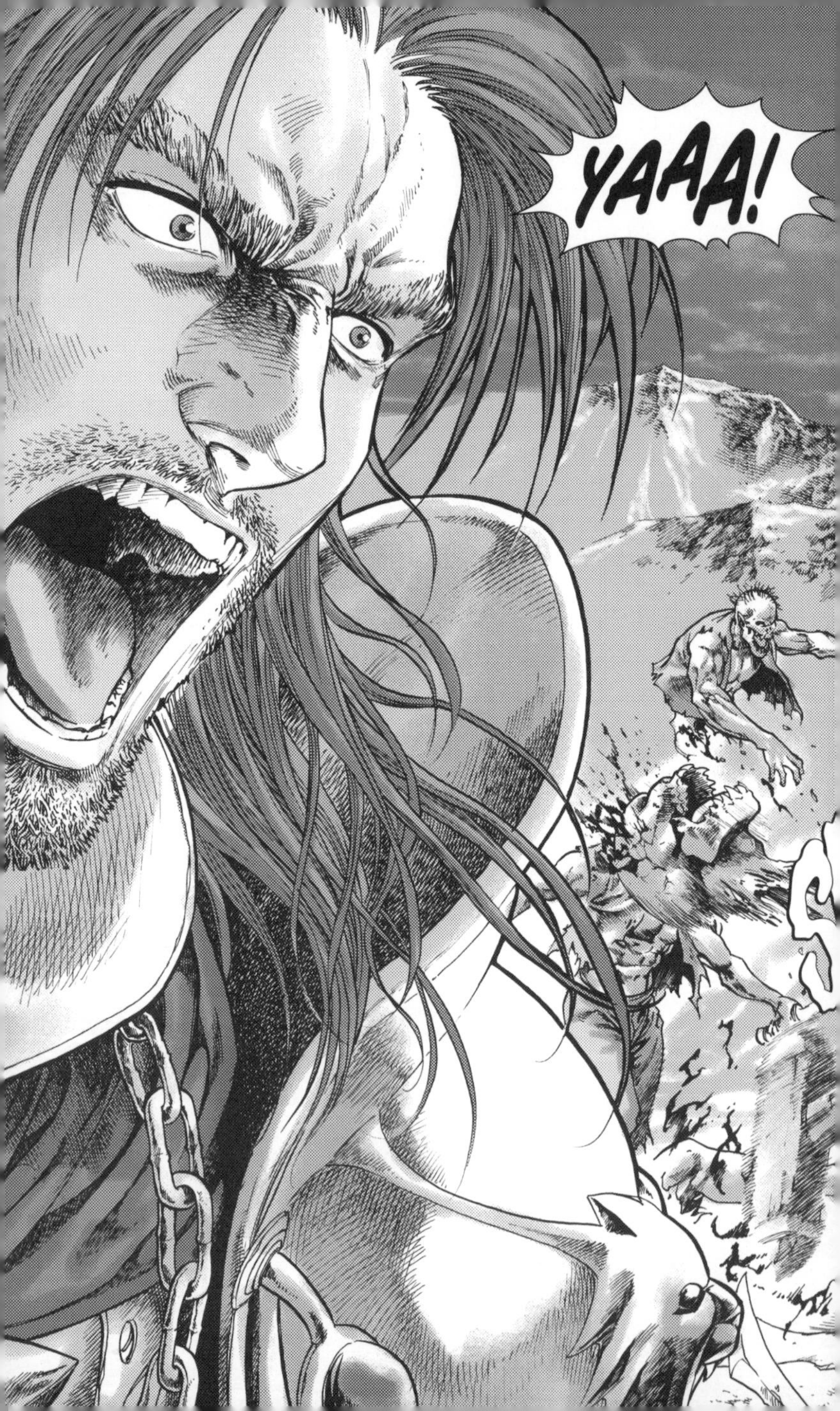
YAAA!

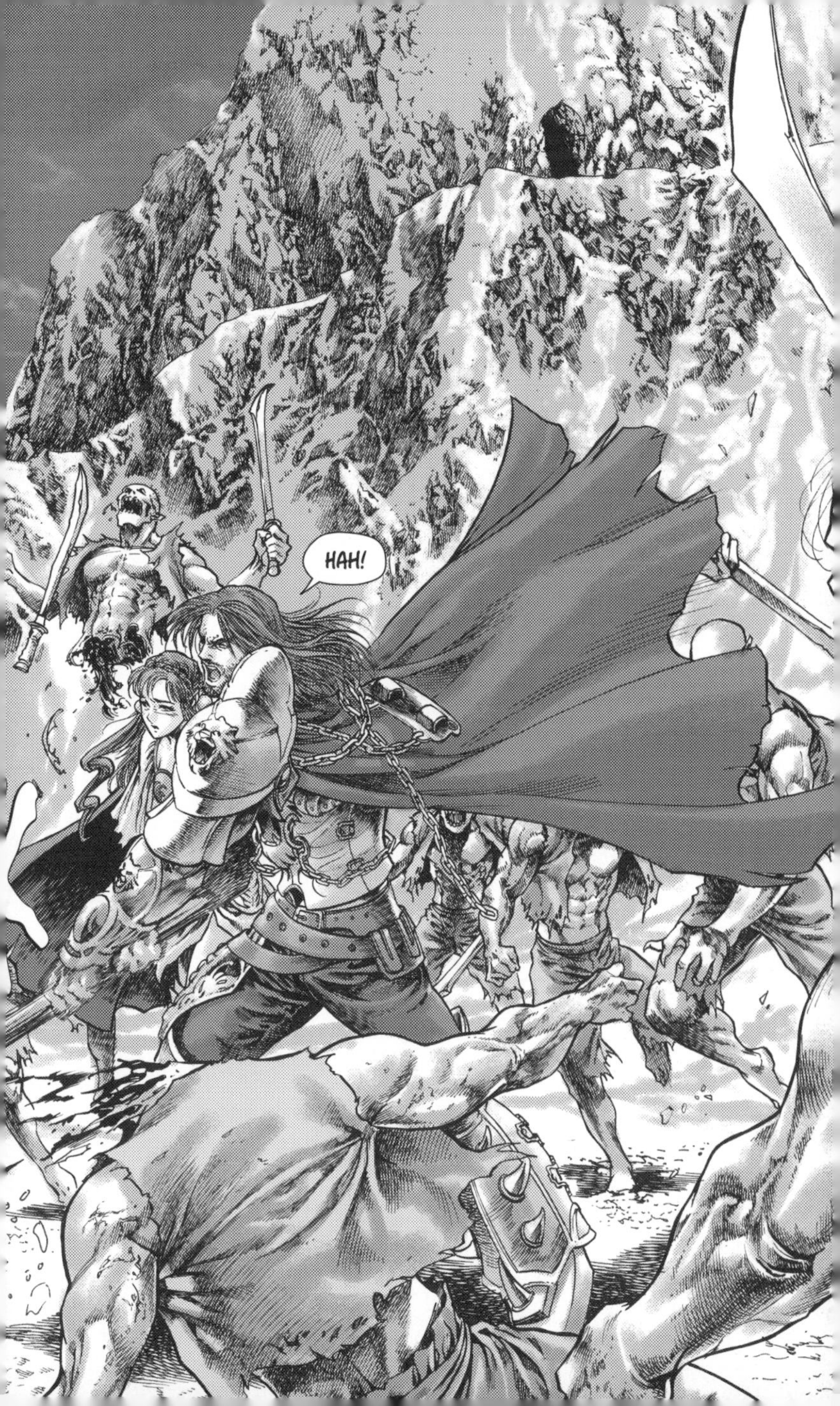
HAH!

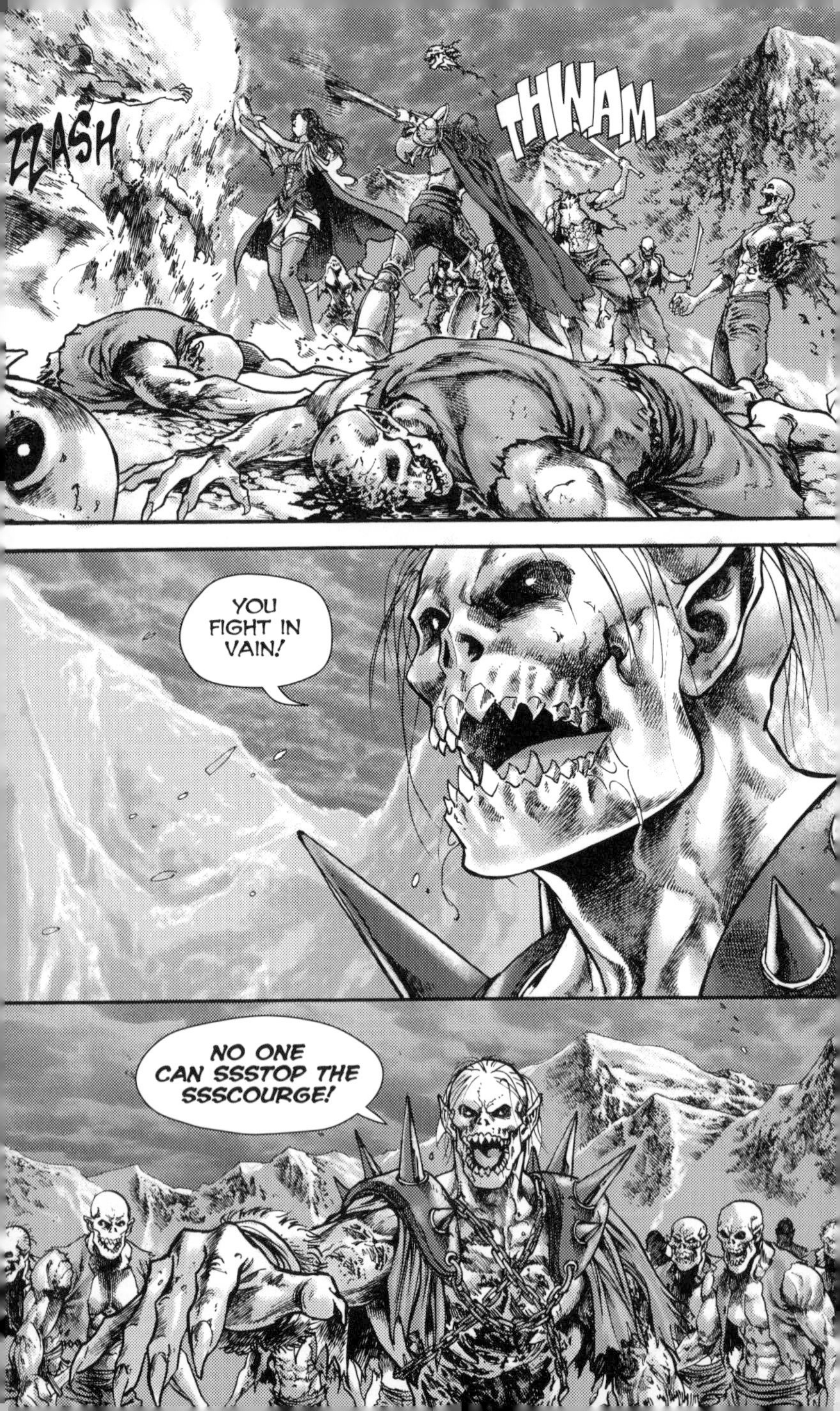
ZZASH
THWAM
YOU FIGHT IN VAIN!
NO ONE CAN SSSTOP THE SSSCOURGE!

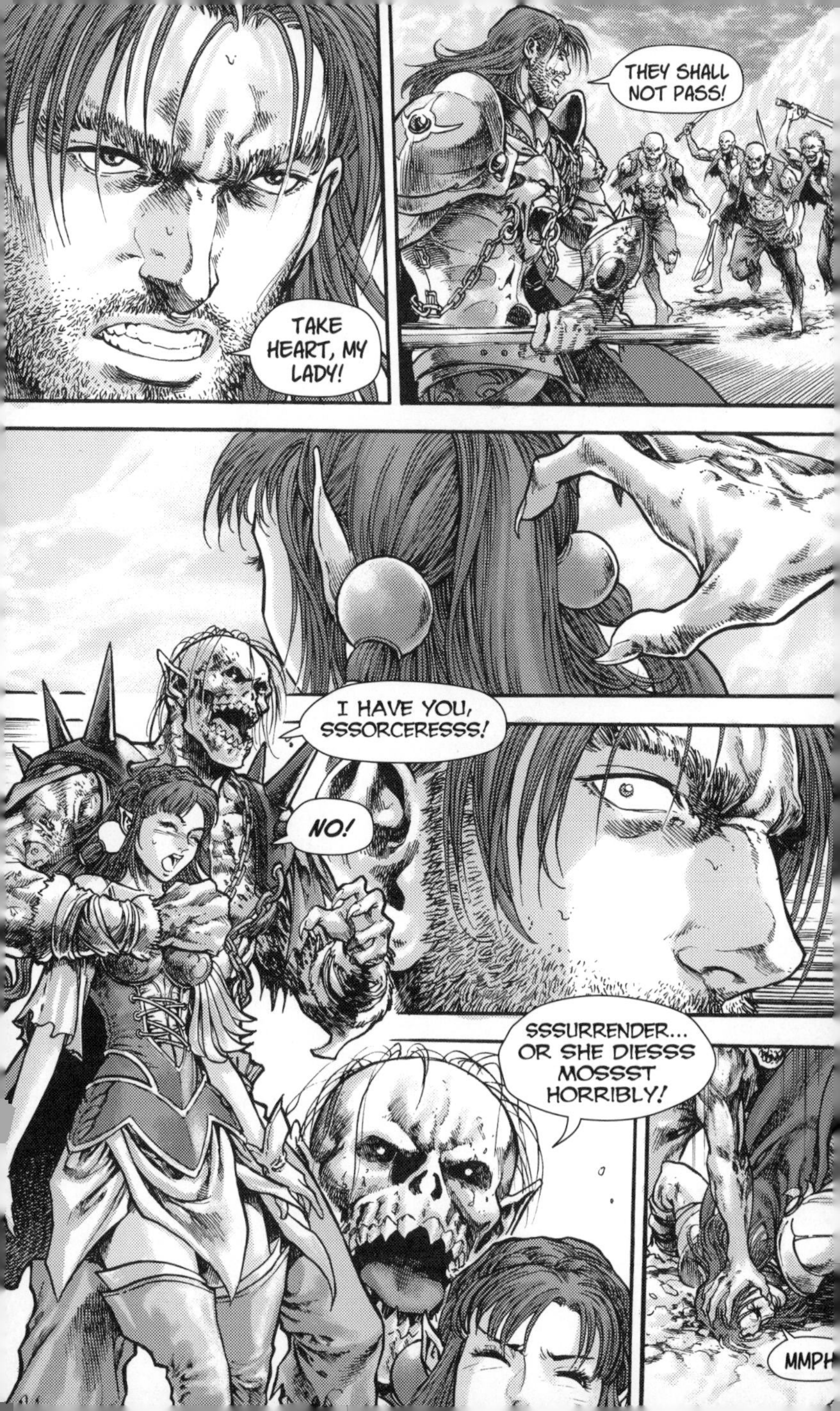
TAKE HEART, MY LADY!
THEY SHALL NOT PASS!
I HAVE YOU, SSSORCERESSS!
NO!
SSSURRENDER... OR SHE DIESSS MOSSST HORRIBLY!
MMPH

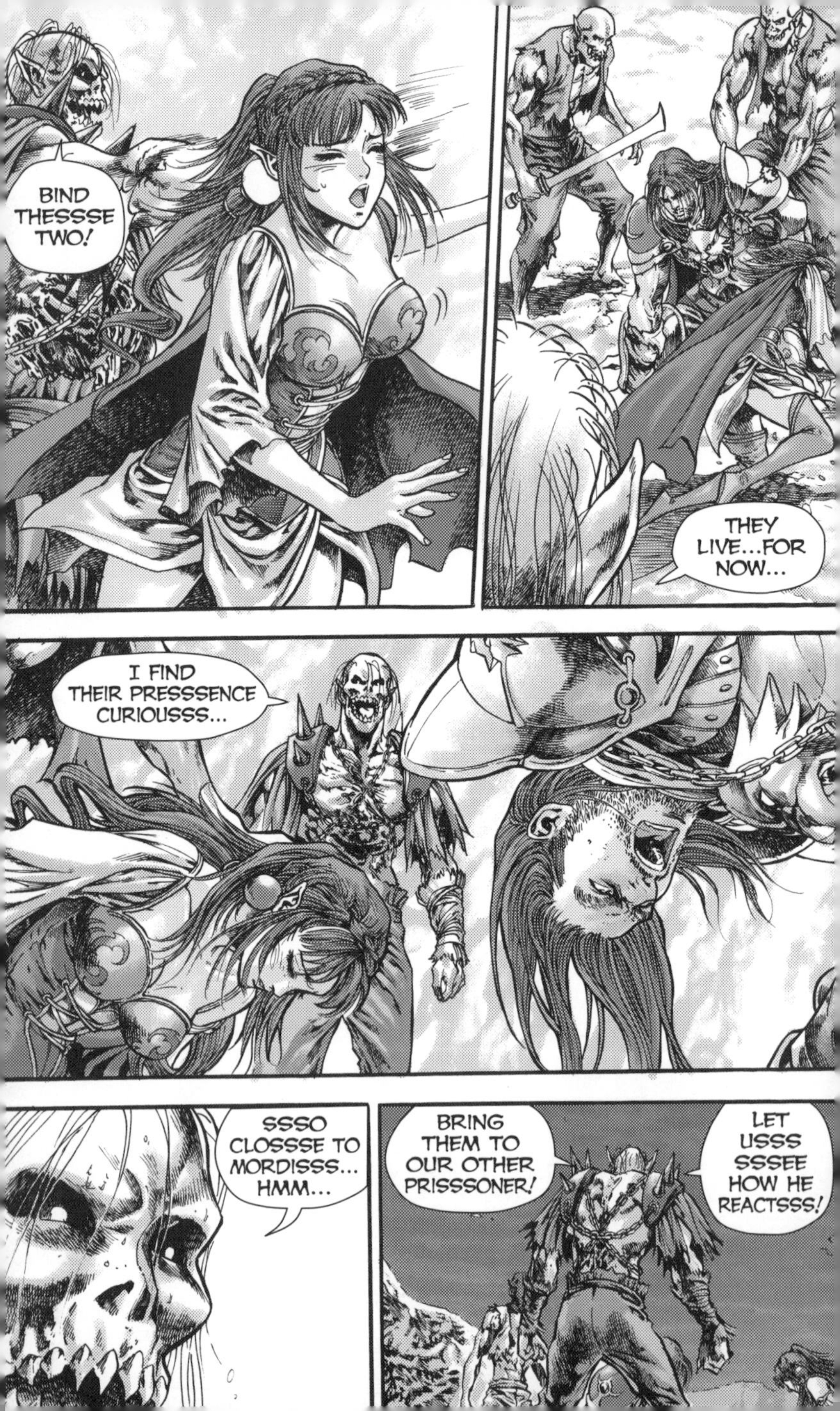
BIND THESSSE TWO!
THEY LIVE...FOR NOW...
I FIND THEIR PRESSSENCE CURIOUSSS...
SSSO CLOSSSE TO MORDISSS... HMM...
BRING THEM TO OUR OTHER PRISSSONER!
LET USSS SSSEE HOW HE REACTSSS!

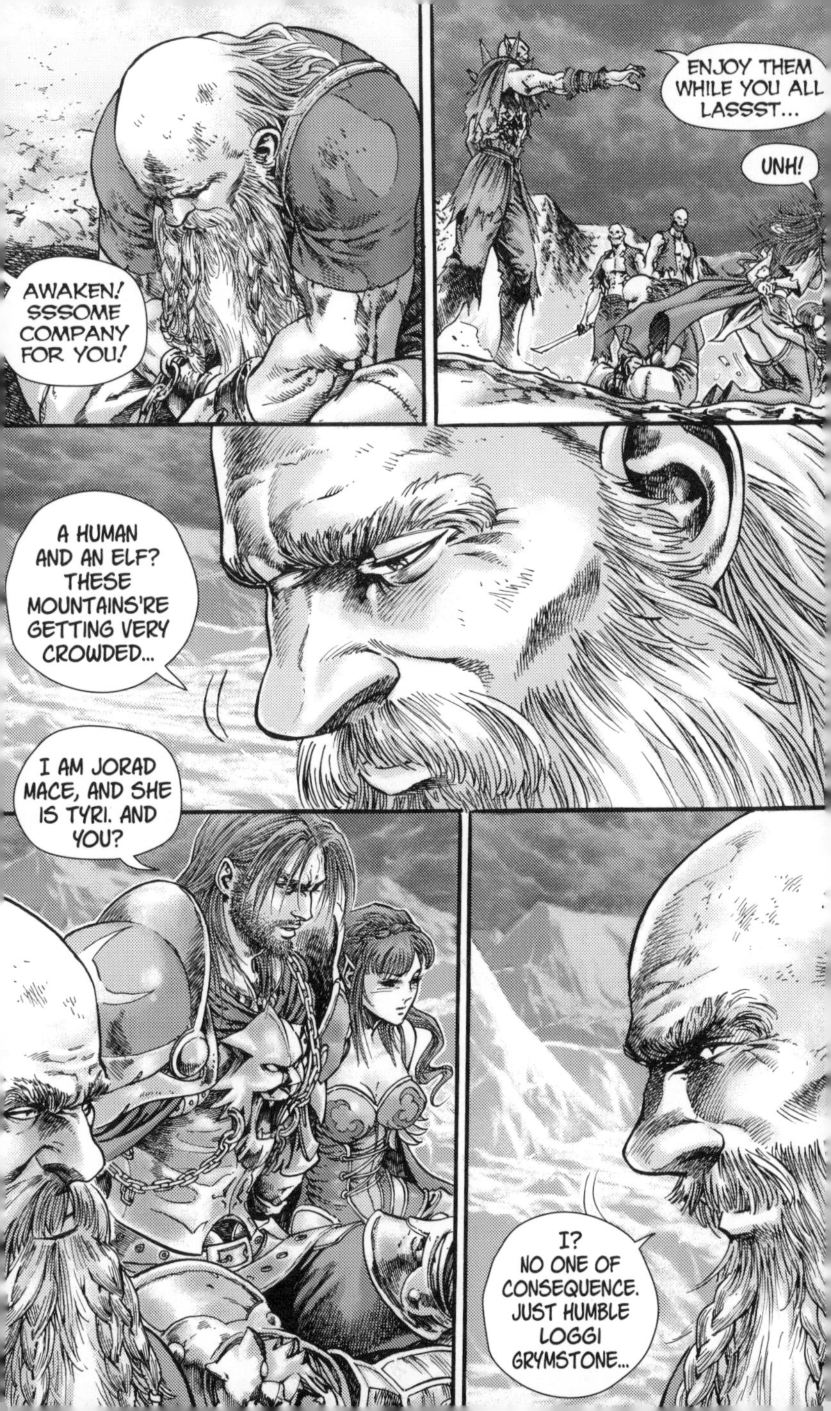
AWAKEN! SSSOME COMPANY FOR YOU!
ENJOY THEM WHILE YOU ALL LASSST...
UNH!
A HUMAN AND AN ELF? THESE MOUNTAINS'RE GETTING VERY CROWDED...
I AM JORAD MACE, AND SHE IS TYRI. AND YOU?
I? NO ONE OF CONSEQUENCE. JUST HUMBLE LOGGI GRYMSTONE...

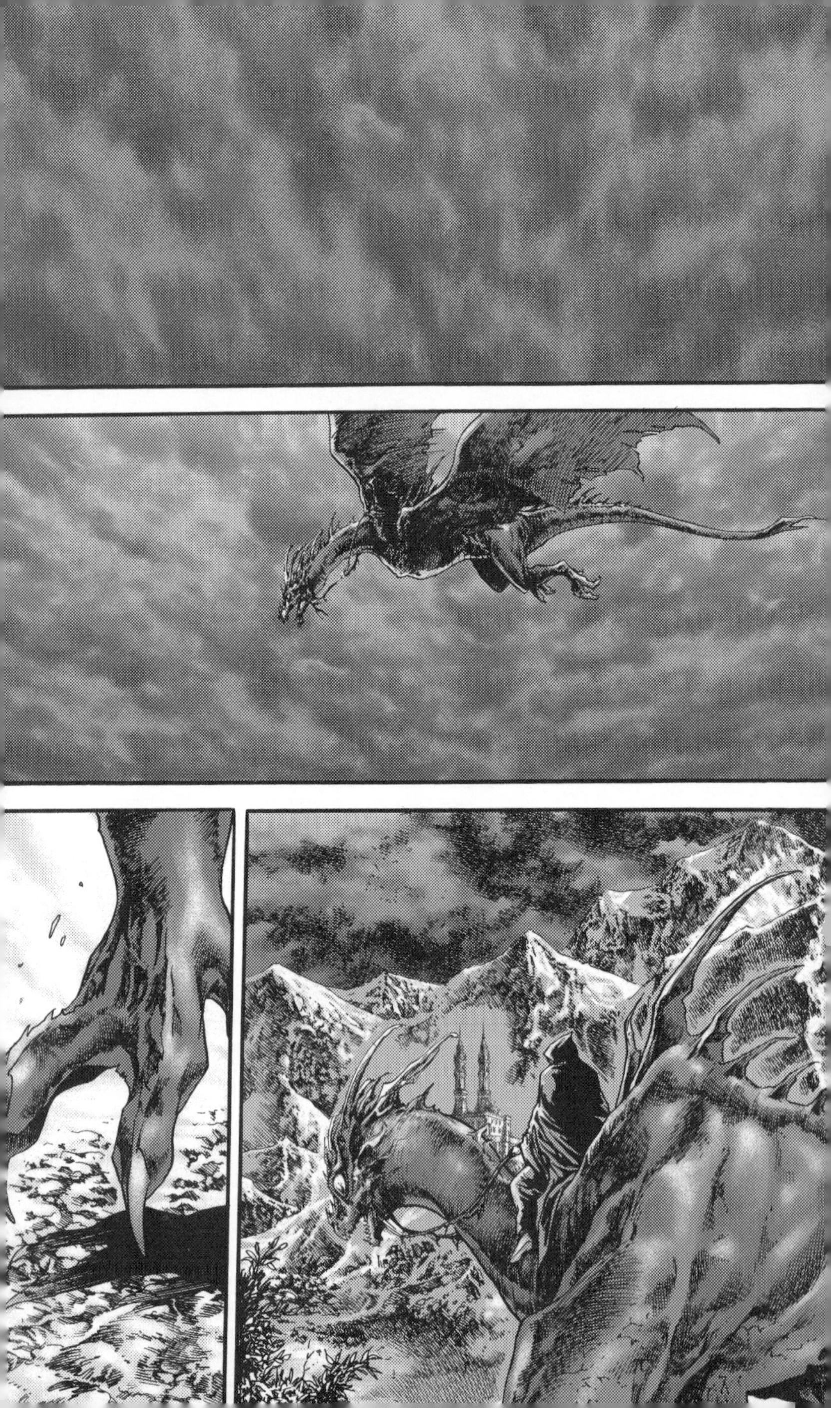

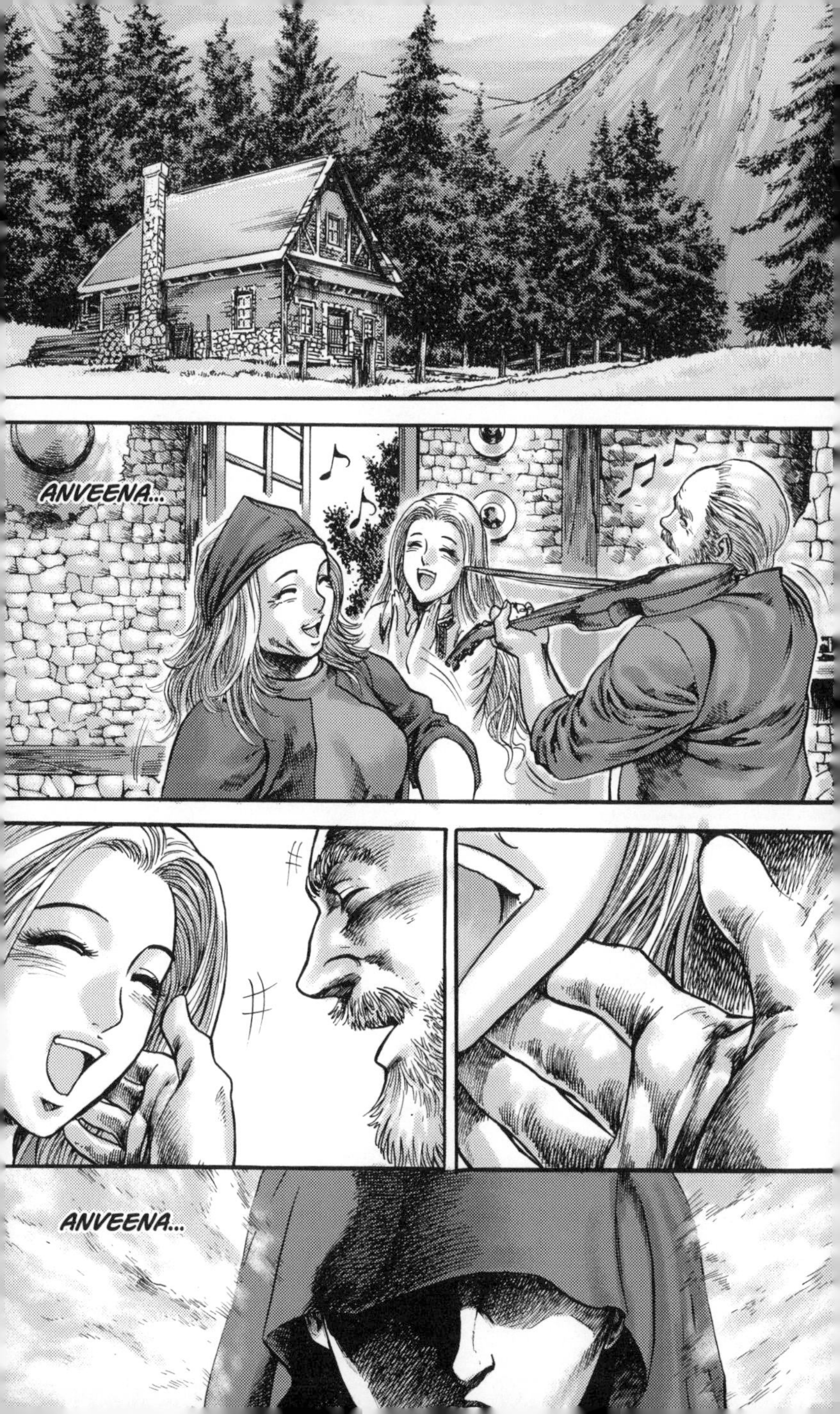
ANVEENA...
ANVEENA...

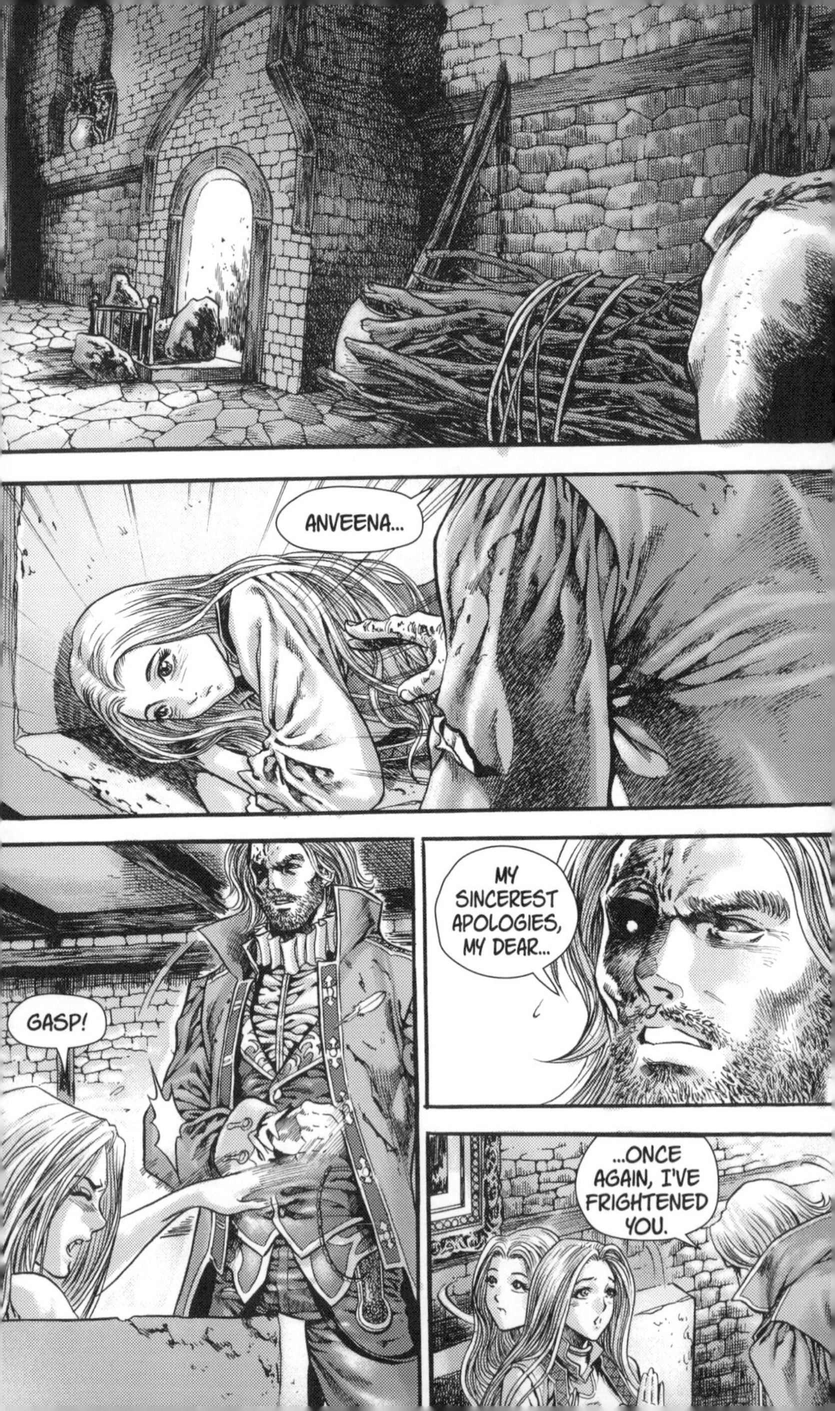
ANVEENA...
GASP!
MY SINCEREST APOLOGIES, MY DEAR...
...ONCE AGAIN, I'VE FRIGHTENED YOU.

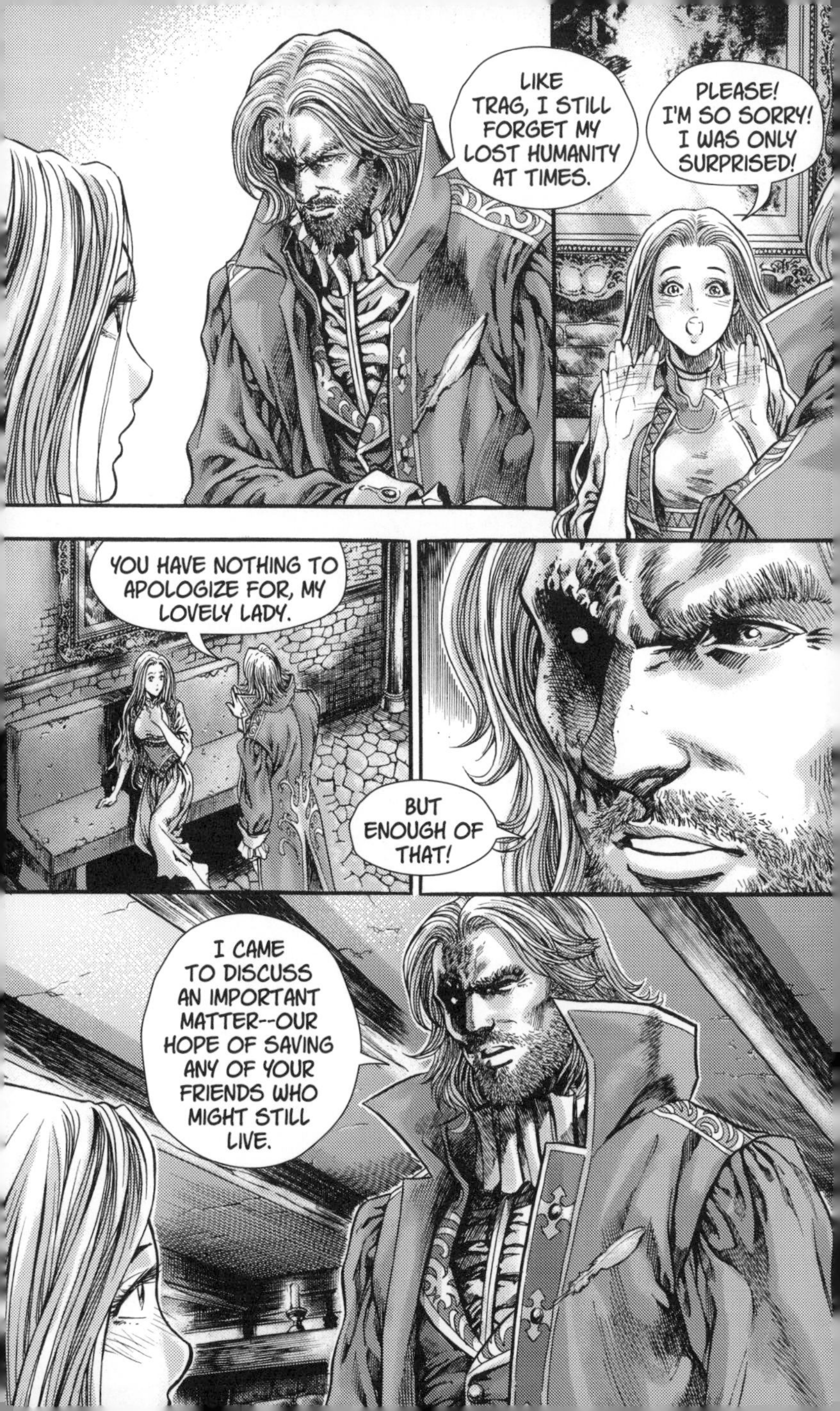
LIKE TRAG, I STILL FORGET MY LOST HUMANITY AT TIMES.
PLEASE! I'M SO SORRY! I WAS ONLY SURPRISED!
YOU HAVE NOTHING TO APOLOGIZE FOR, MY LOVELY LADY.
BUT ENOUGH OF THAT!
I CAME TO DISCUSS AN IMPORTANT MATTER--OUR HOPE OF SAVING ANY OF YOUR FRIENDS WHO MIGHT STILL LIVE.

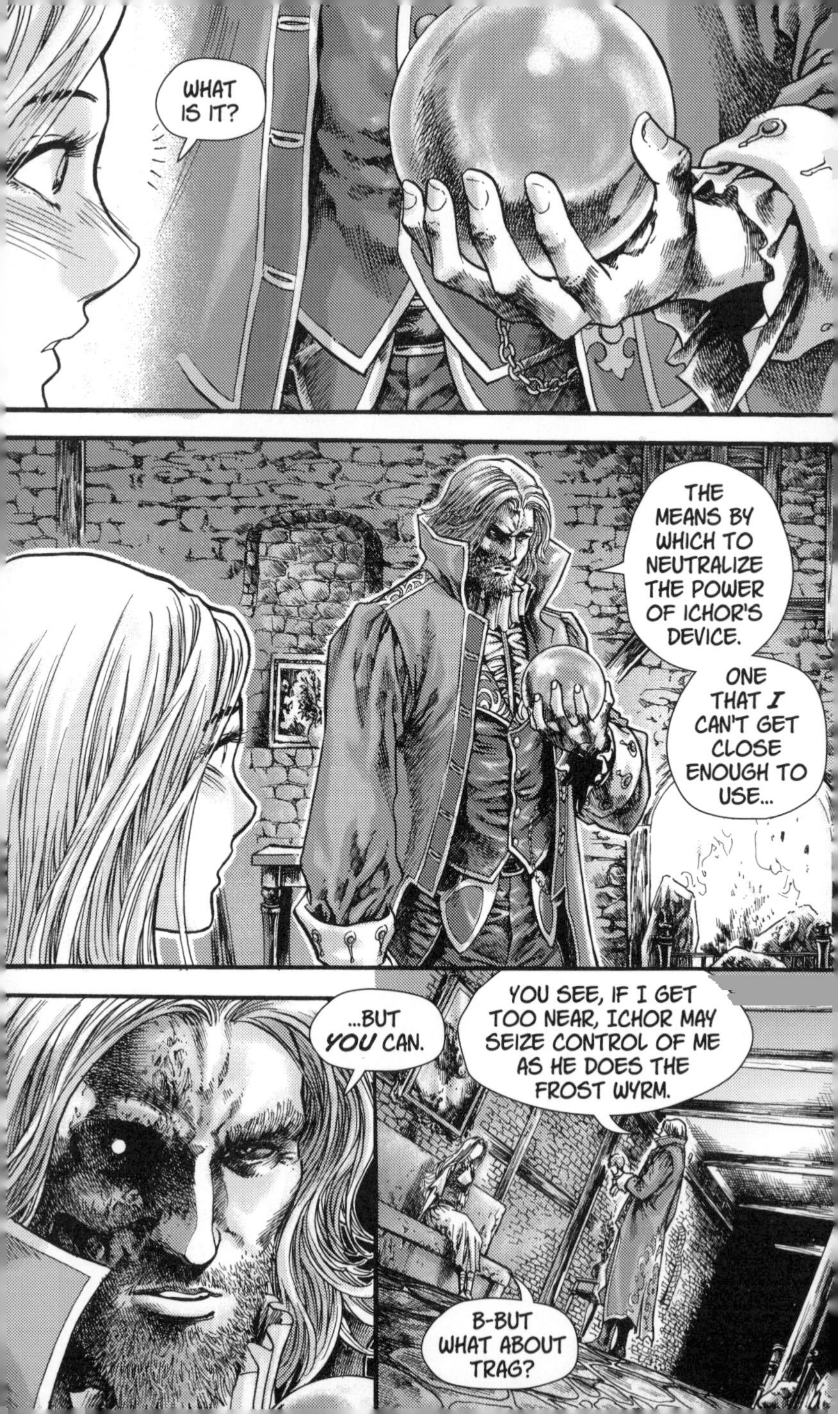
WHAT IS IT?
THE MEANS BY WHICH TO NEUTRALIZE THE POWER OF ICHOR'S DEVICE.
ONE THAT *I* CAN'T GET CLOSE ENOUGH TO USE...
...BUT *YOU* CAN.
YOU SEE, IF I GET TOO NEAR, ICHOR MAY SEIZE CONTROL OF ME AS HE DOES THE FROST WYRM.
B-BUT WHAT ABOUT TRAG?

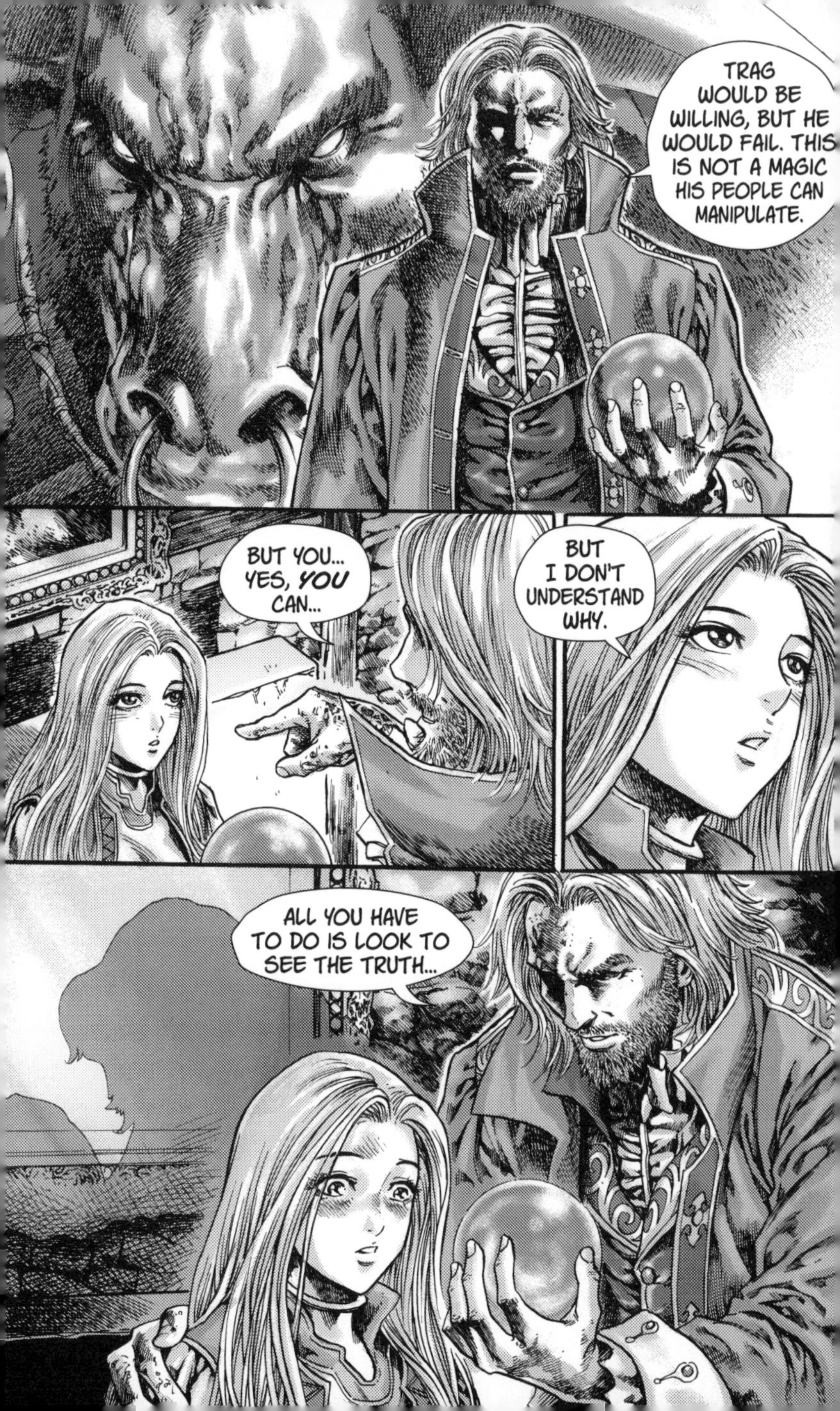
TRAG WOULD BE WILLING, BUT HE WOULD FAIL. THIS IS NOT A MAGIC HIS PEOPLE CAN MANIPULATE.
BUT YOU... YES, *YOU* CAN...
BUT I DON'T UNDERSTAND WHY.
ALL YOU HAVE TO DO IS LOOK TO SEE THE TRUTH...

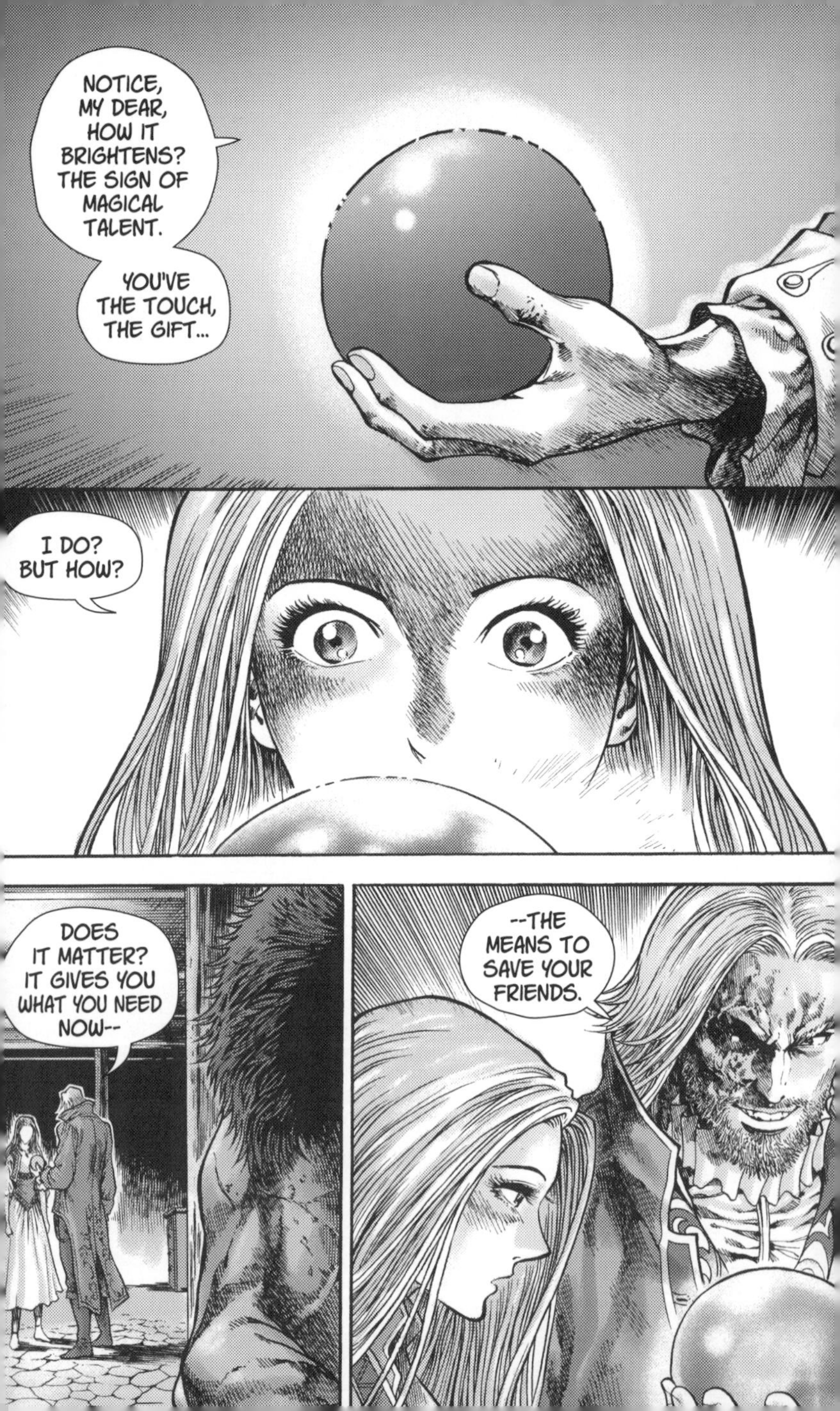
NOTICE, MY DEAR, HOW IT BRIGHTENS? THE SIGN OF MAGICAL TALENT.
YOU'VE THE TOUCH, THE GIFT...
I DO? BUT HOW?
DOES IT MATTER? IT GIVES YOU WHAT YOU NEED NOW--
--THE MEANS TO SAVE YOUR FRIENDS.

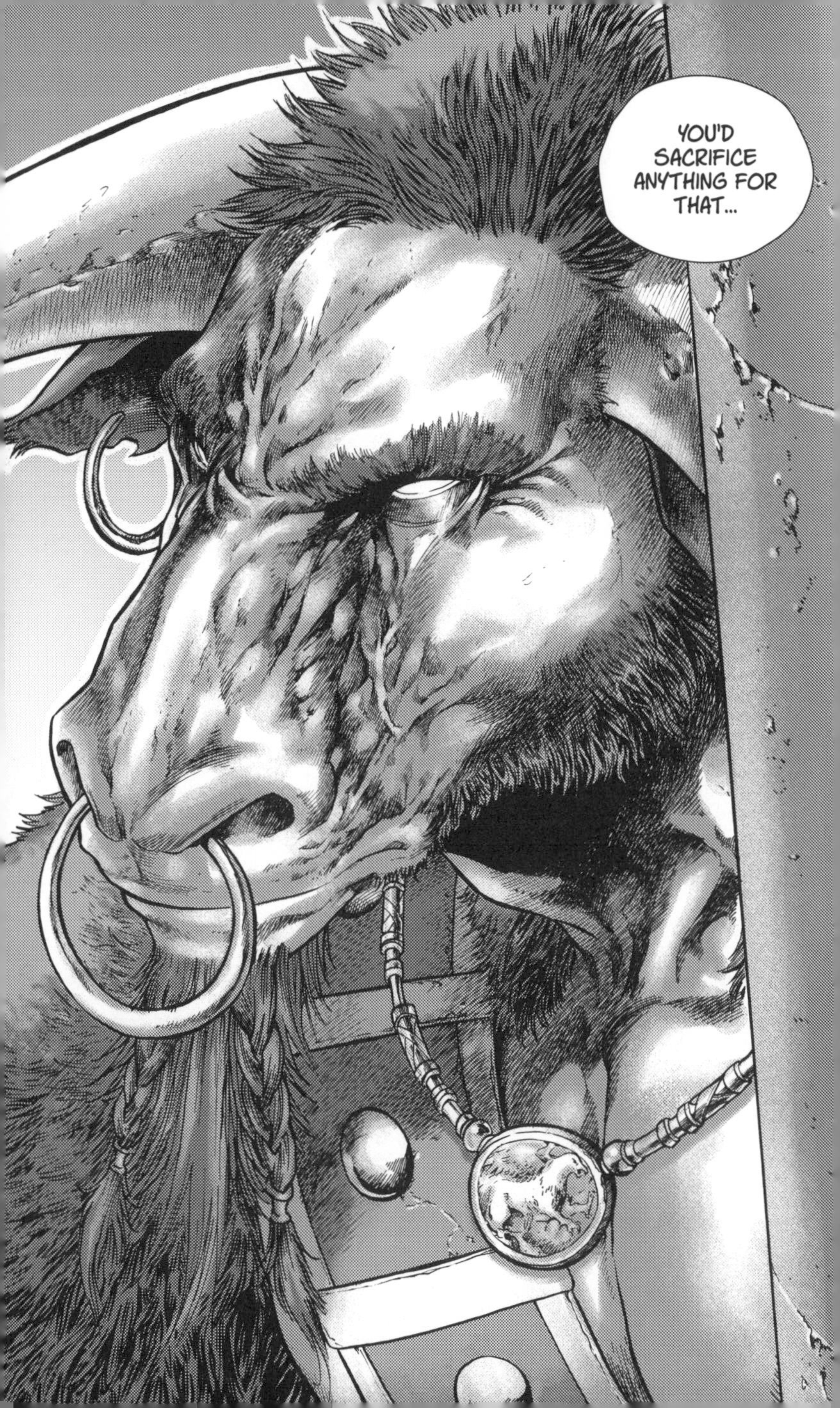
YOU'D SACRIFICE ANYTHING FOR THAT...

"...WOULDN'T YOU?"

CHAPTER FIVE
THE ORB OF NER'ZHUL

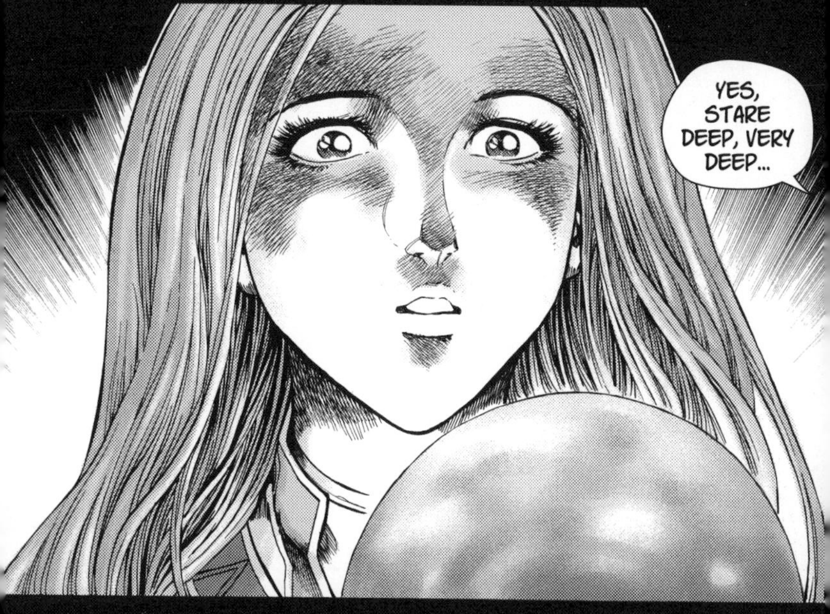
YES, STARE DEEP, VERY DEEP...

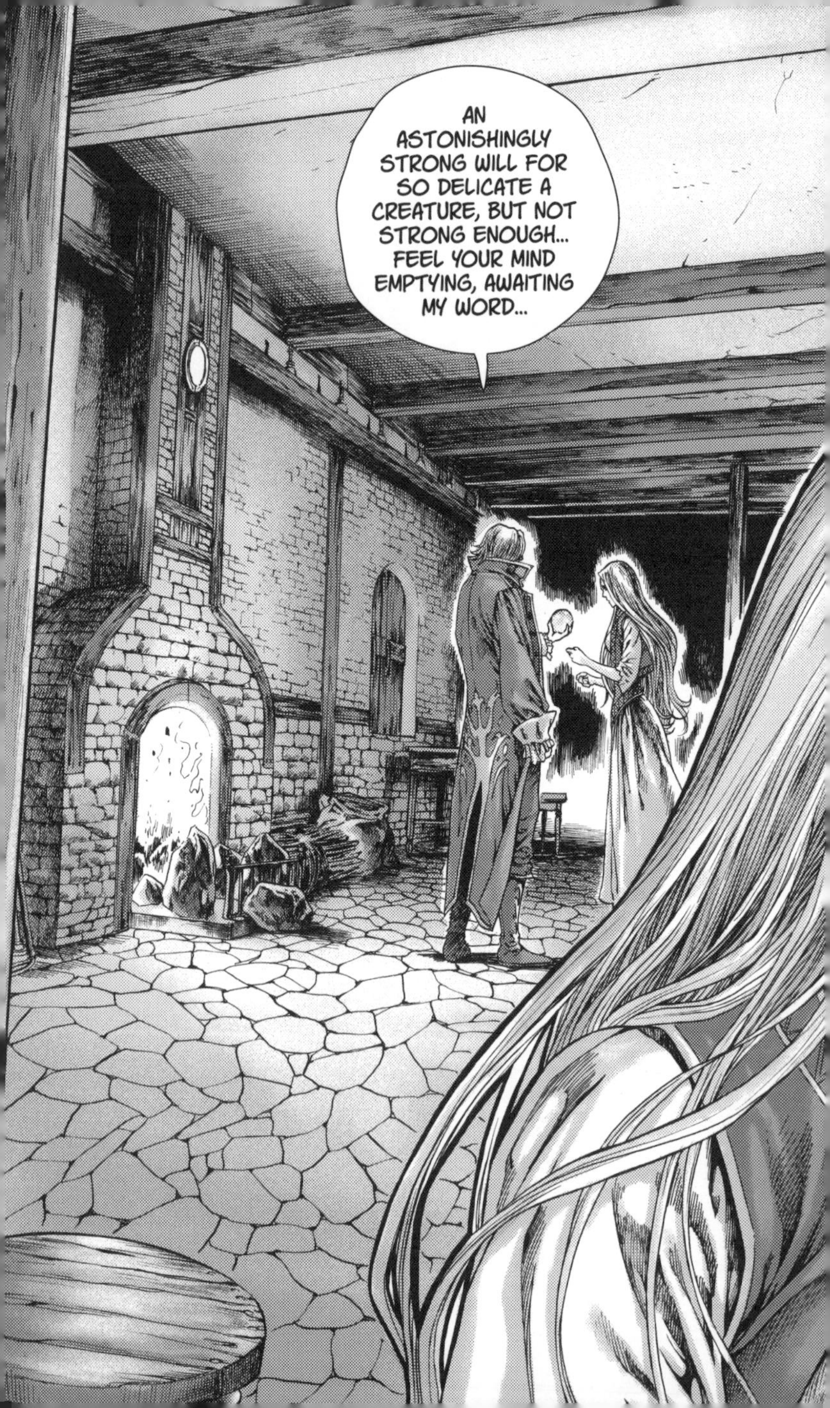
AN ASTONISHINGLY STRONG WILL FOR SO DELICATE A CREATURE, BUT NOT STRONG ENOUGH... FEEL YOUR MIND EMPTYING, AWAITING MY WORD...

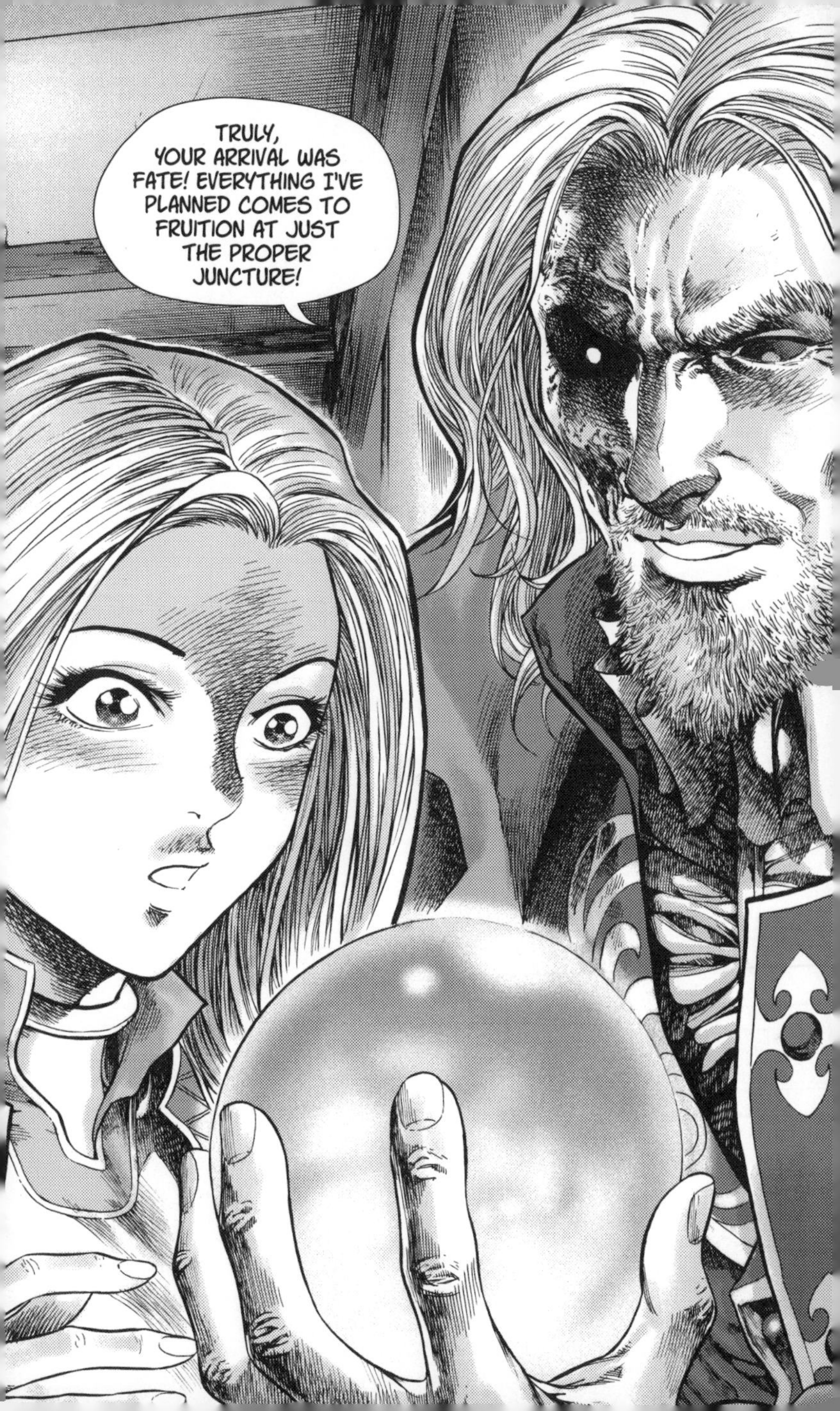
TRULY, YOUR ARRIVAL WAS FATE! EVERYTHING I'VE PLANNED COMES TO FRUITION AT JUST THE PROPER JUNCTURE!

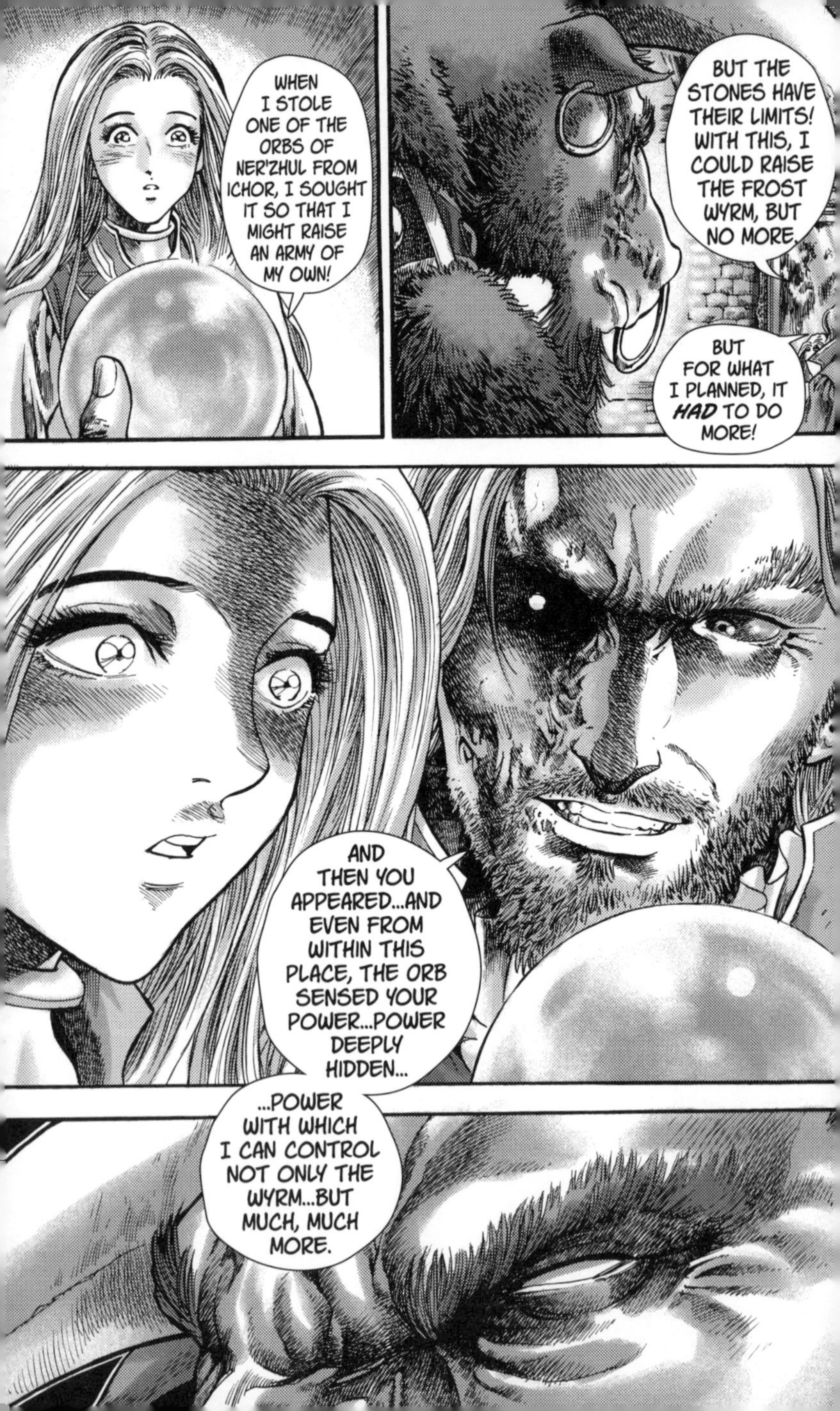
WHEN I STOLE ONE OF THE ORBS OF NER'ZHUL FROM ICHOR, I SOUGHT IT SO THAT I MIGHT RAISE AN ARMY OF MY OWN!
BUT THE STONES HAVE THEIR LIMITS! WITH THIS, I COULD RAISE THE FROST WYRM, BUT NO MORE.
BUT FOR WHAT I PLANNED, IT *HAD* TO DO MORE!
AND THEN YOU APPEARED...AND EVEN FROM WITHIN THIS PLACE, THE ORB SENSED YOUR POWER...POWER DEEPLY HIDDEN...
...POWER WITH WHICH I CAN CONTROL NOT ONLY THE WYRM...BUT MUCH, MUCH MORE.

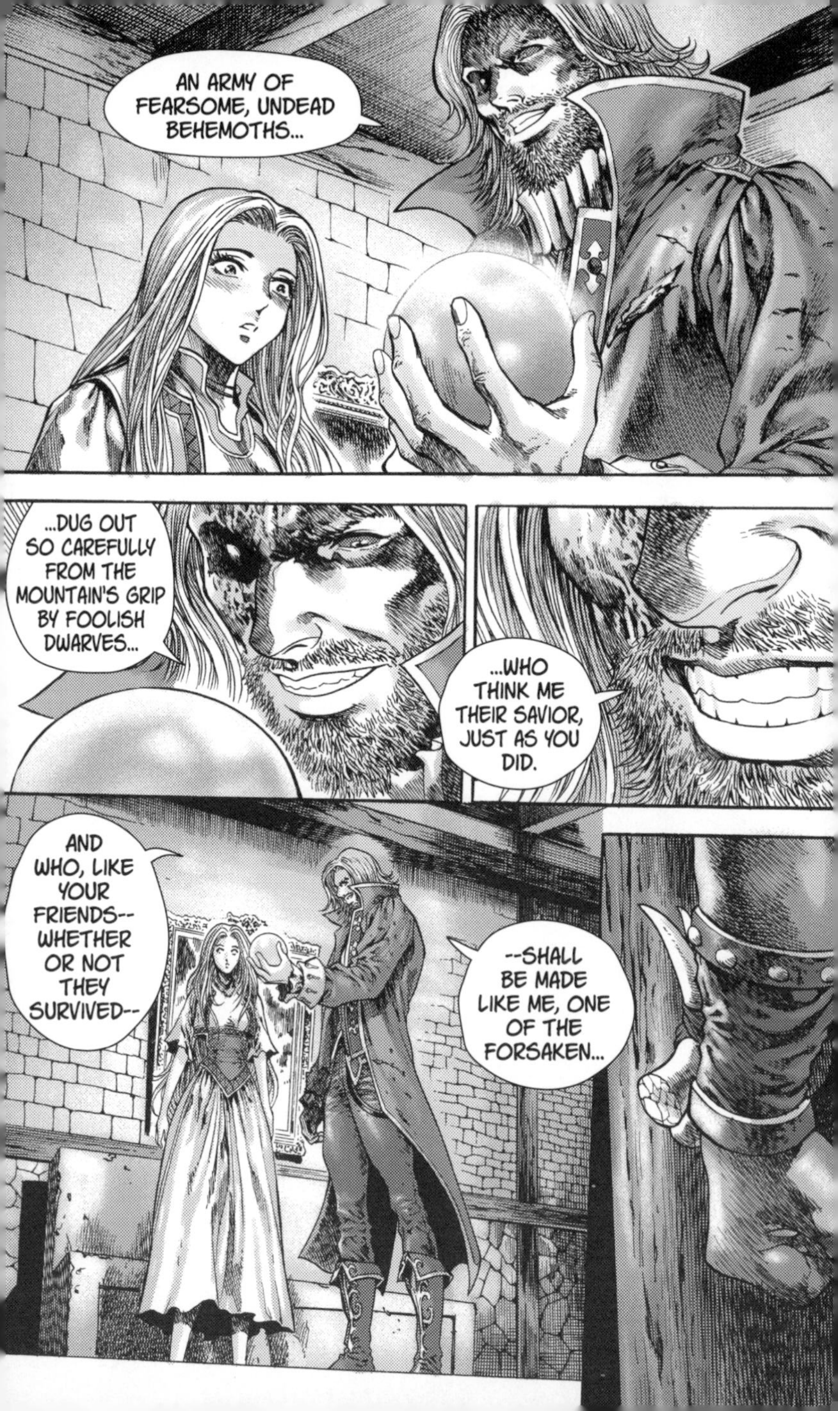
AN ARMY OF FEARSOME, UNDEAD BEHEMOTHS...
...DUG OUT SO CAREFULLY FROM THE MOUNTAIN'S GRIP BY FOOLISH DWARVES...
...WHO THINK ME THEIR SAVIOR, JUST AS YOU DID.
AND WHO, LIKE YOUR FRIENDS-- WHETHER OR NOT THEY SURVIVED--
--SHALL BE MADE LIKE ME, ONE OF THE FORSAKEN...

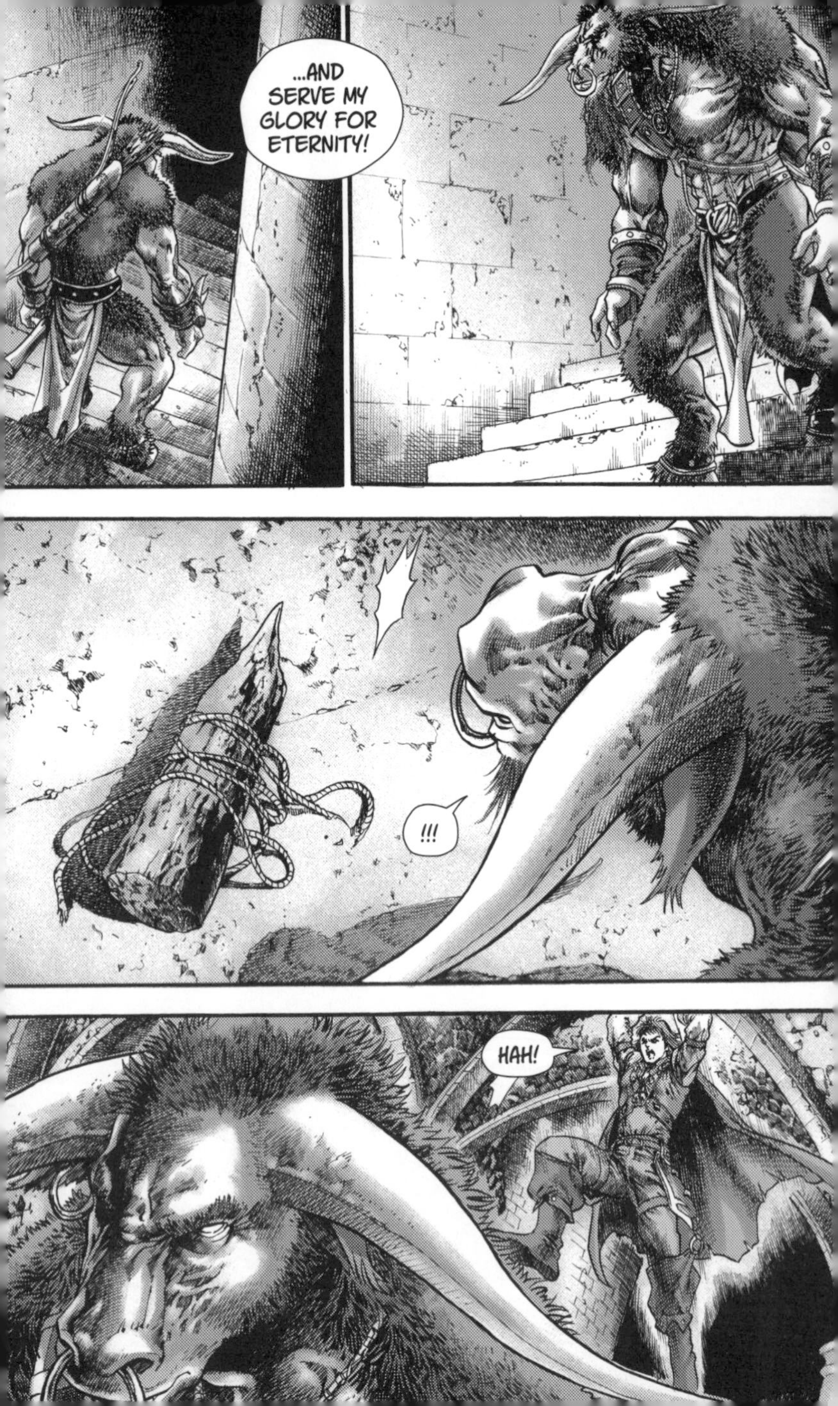
...AND SERVE MY GLORY FOR ETERNITY!
!!!
HAH!

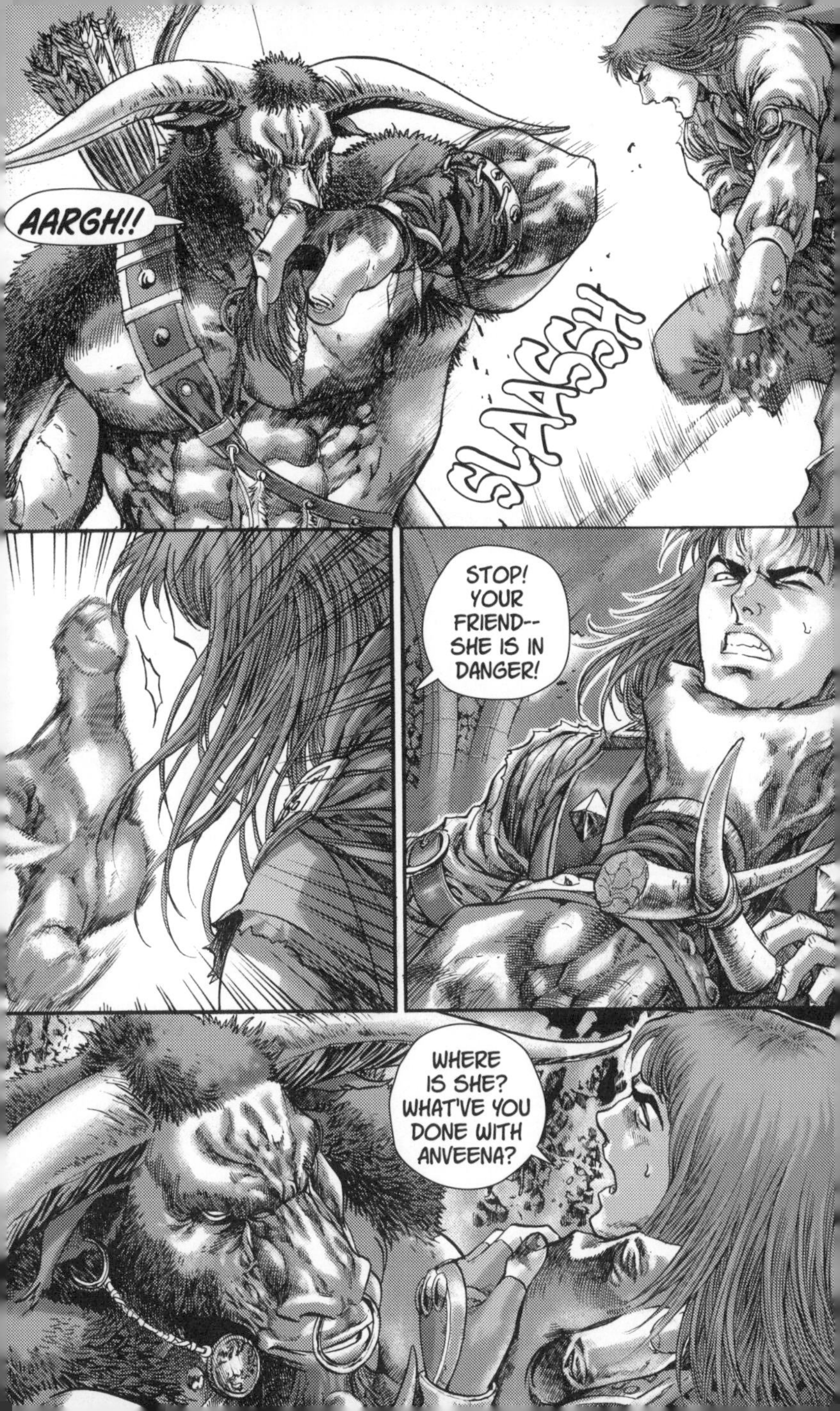
AARGH!!
SLAASSH
STOP! YOUR FRIEND-- SHE IS IN DANGER!
WHERE IS SHE? WHAT'VE YOU DONE WITH ANVEENA?

I TRIED TO BRING HER HERE, BUT THE BARON IS WITH HER!

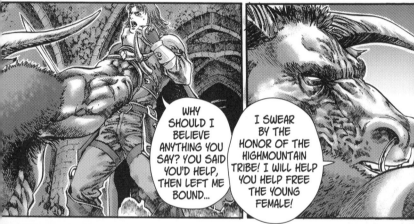

WHY SHOULD I BELIEVE ANYTHING YOU SAY? YOU SAID YOU'D HELP, THEN LEFT ME BOUND...

I SWEAR BY THE HONOR OF THE HIGHMOUNTAIN TRIBE! I WILL HELP YOU HELP FREE THE YOUNG FEMALE!

I STILL DON'T UNDERSTAND HOW SHE COULD BE ANY HELP WITH THIS ORB YOU SPOKE OF! SHE CAN'T USE MAGIC!

THE ORB OF NER'ZHUL TELLS THE BARON IT IS SO... NOTHING ELSE MATTERS...

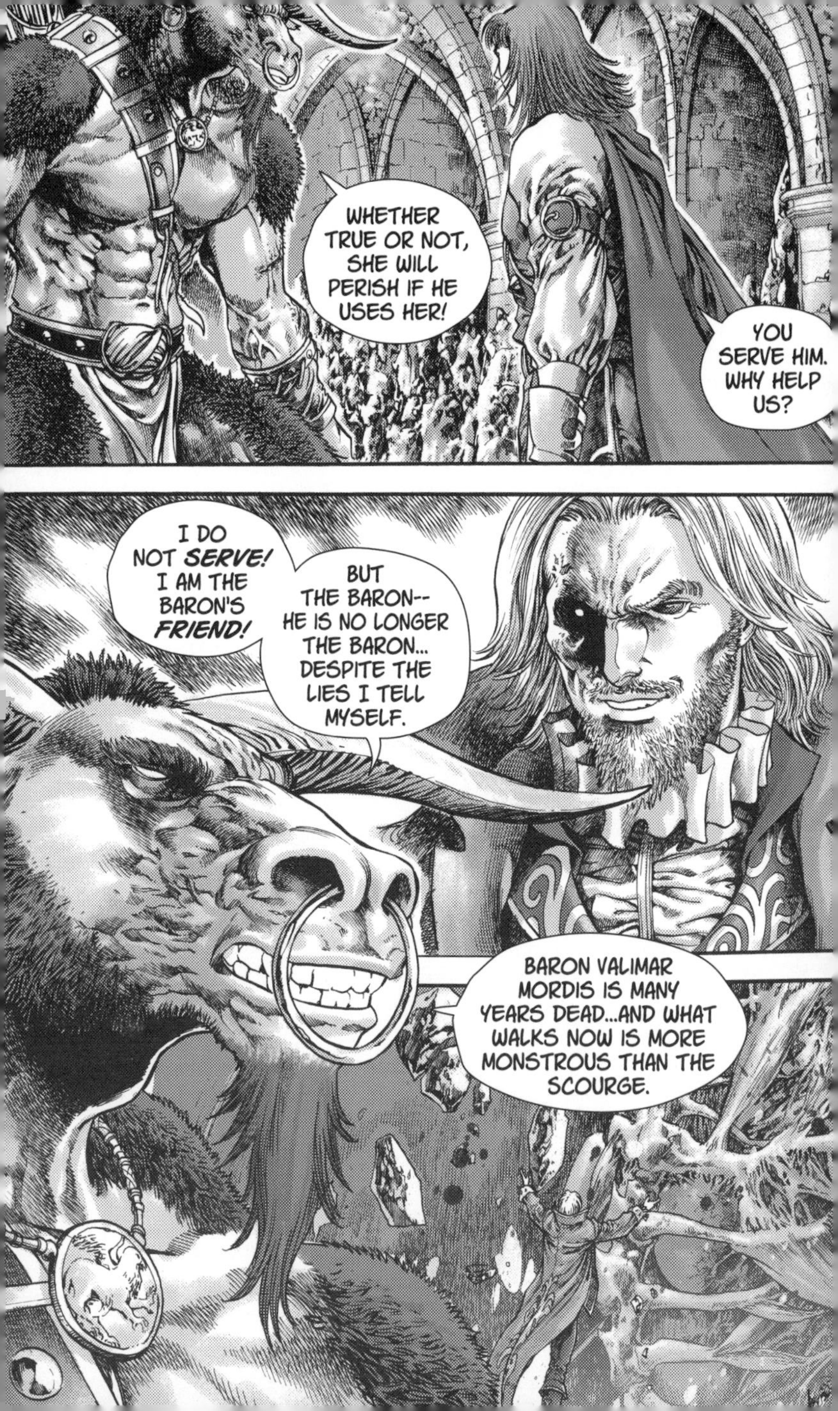
WHETHER TRUE OR NOT, SHE WILL PERISH IF HE USES HER!
YOU SERVE HIM. WHY HELP US?
I DO NOT *SERVE!* I AM THE BARON'S *FRIEND!*
BUT THE BARON-- HE IS NO LONGER THE BARON... DESPITE THE LIES I TELL MYSELF.
BARON VALIMAR MORDIS IS MANY YEARS DEAD...AND WHAT WALKS NOW IS MORE MONSTROUS THAN THE SCOURGE.

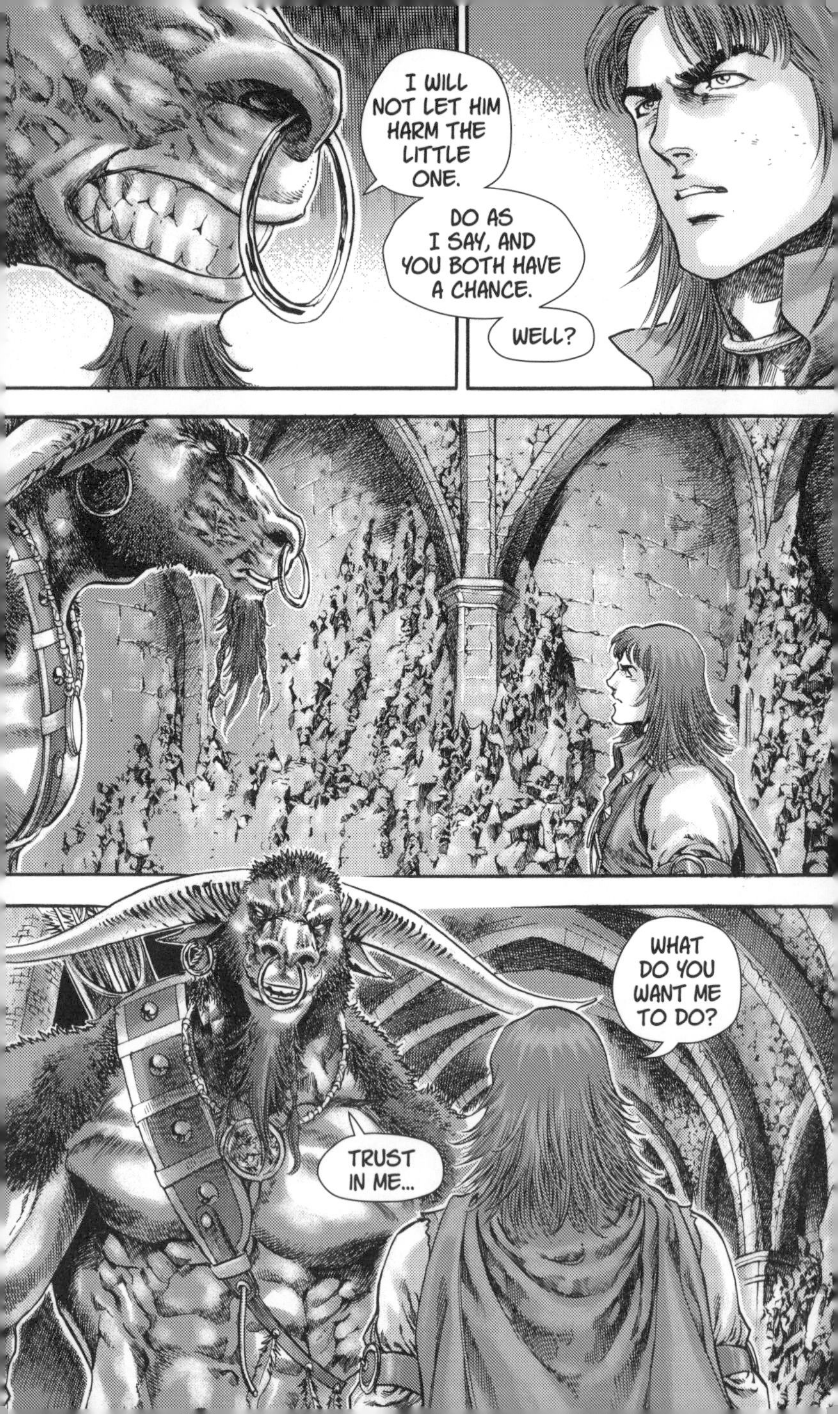
I WILL NOT LET HIM HARM THE LITTLE ONE.
DO AS I SAY, AND YOU BOTH HAVE A CHANCE.
WELL?
WHAT DO YOU WANT ME TO DO?
TRUST IN ME...

WE CAME SEEKING METALS BADLY NEEDED FOR WEAPONS AGAINST THE SCOURGE, BUT WE FOUND INSTEAD THE BARON MORDIS.

THERE WERE SCOURGE IN THE MOUNTAINS, HE SAID, BUT HE HAD A WAY TO WIPE THEM OUT... AND MAYBE HELP BRING THE WAR TO THE PLAGUELANDS.

HE HAD AN ARTIFACT, STOLEN FROM THAT ONE, AND COULD RAISE GIANTS FROM THE DEAD.

THEY'D COME FOR MORDIS AND THE ORB, BUT I KEPT MUM. WOULDN'T BETRAY MY LADS OR THE BARON.

WE DUG 'EM UP, BUT I WENT OUT ONE DAY FOR AIR... AND WAS CAUGHT.

BUT THEN I SAW THE WYRM ATTACK YOU AND YOURS...AND I KNEW THAT THE BARON WAS FRIEND TO NO ONE.

THE SCOURGE HE MIGHT HATE, BUT SO DOES HE ALL LIFE.

A TERRIBLE TALE, MUCH LIKE OURS, WHICH YOU KNOW NOW. HERE WE CAME IN SEARCH OF YOU...

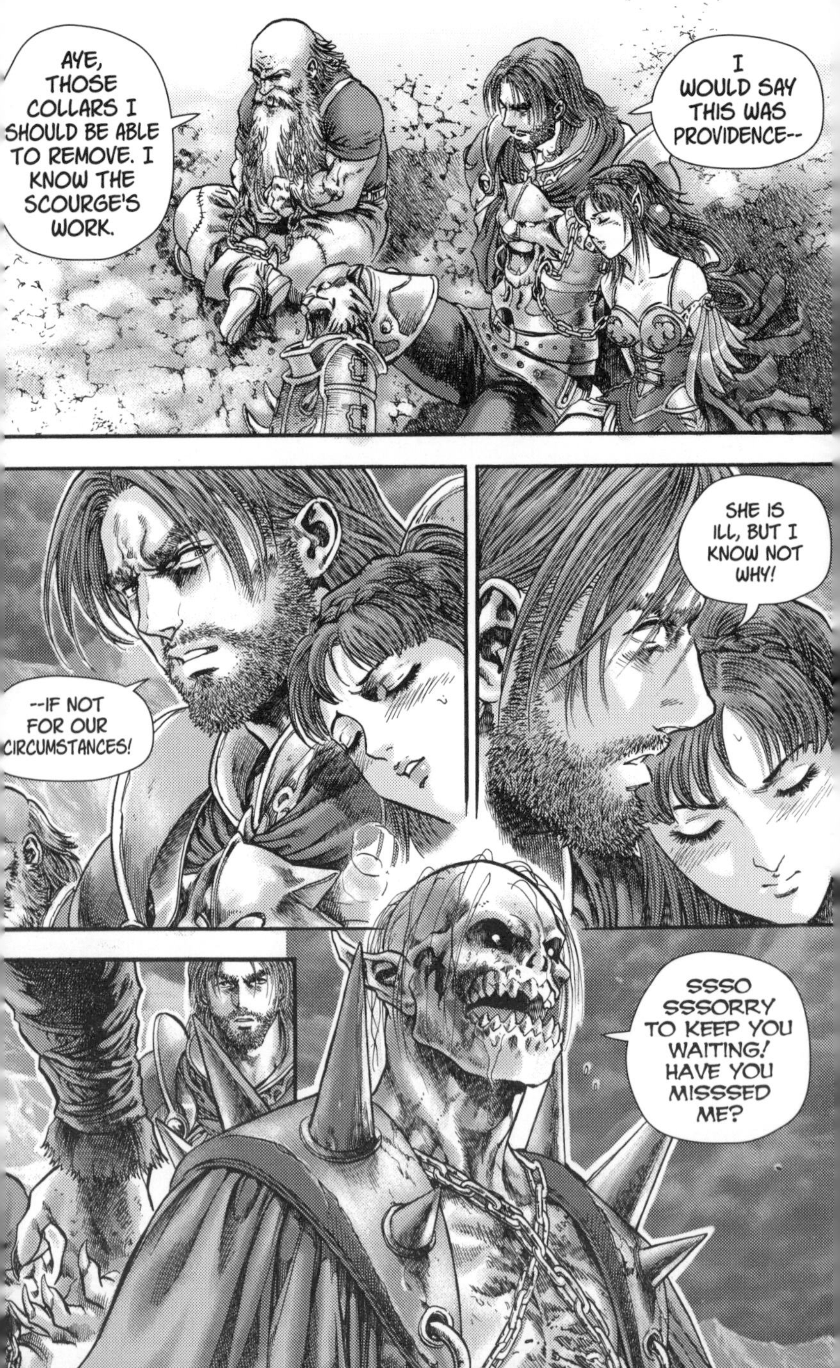
AYE, THOSE COLLARS I SHOULD BE ABLE TO REMOVE. I KNOW THE SCOURGE'S WORK.
I WOULD SAY THIS WAS PROVIDENCE--
--IF NOT FOR OUR CIRCUMSTANCES!
SHE IS ILL, BUT I KNOW NOT WHY!
SSSO SSSORRY TO KEEP YOU WAITING! HAVE YOU MISSSED ME?

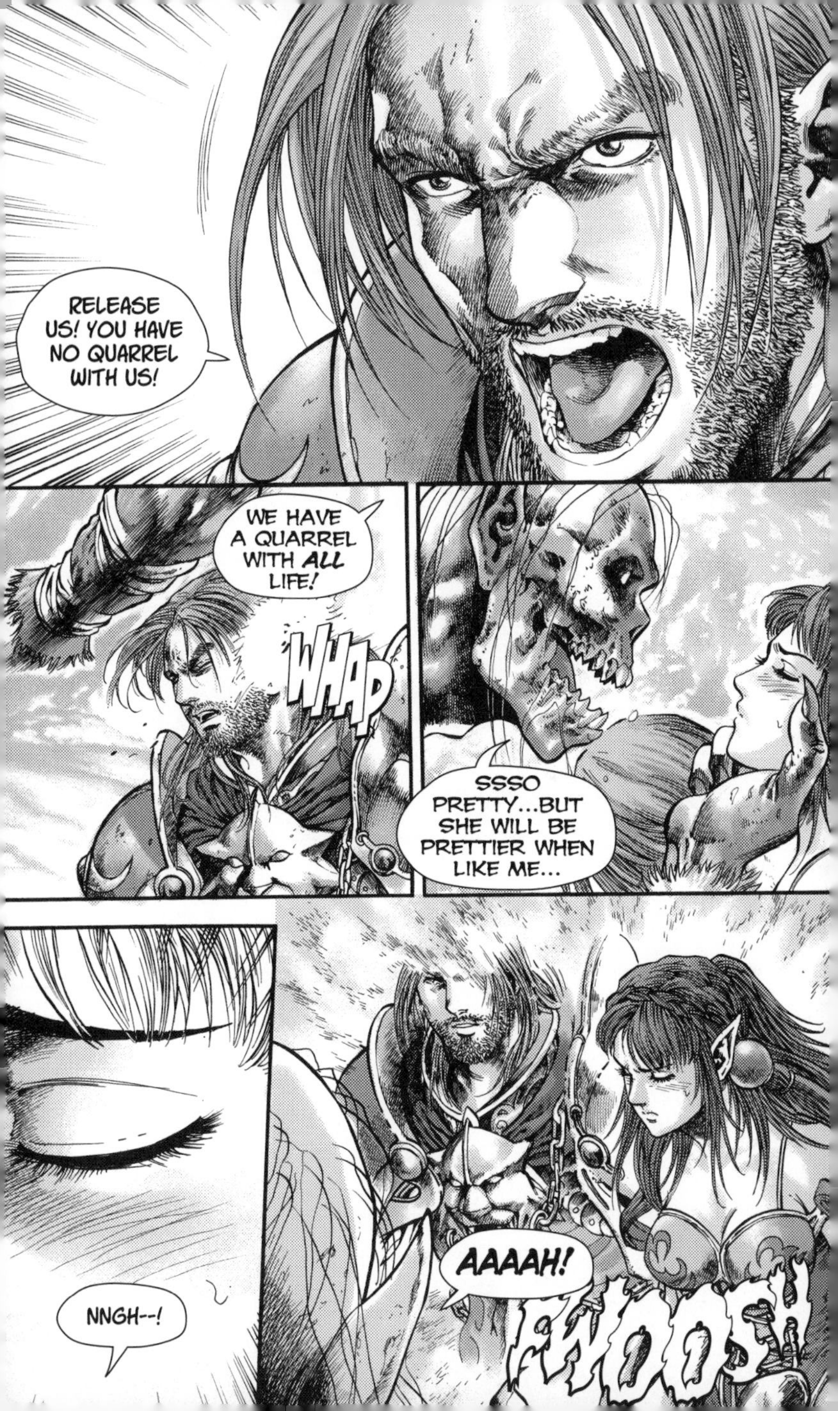
RELEASE US! YOU HAVE NO QUARREL WITH US!
WE HAVE A QUARREL WITH **ALL** LIFE!
WHAP
SSSO PRETTY...BUT SHE WILL BE PRETTIER WHEN LIKE ME...
NNGH--!
AAAAH!
FWOOSH

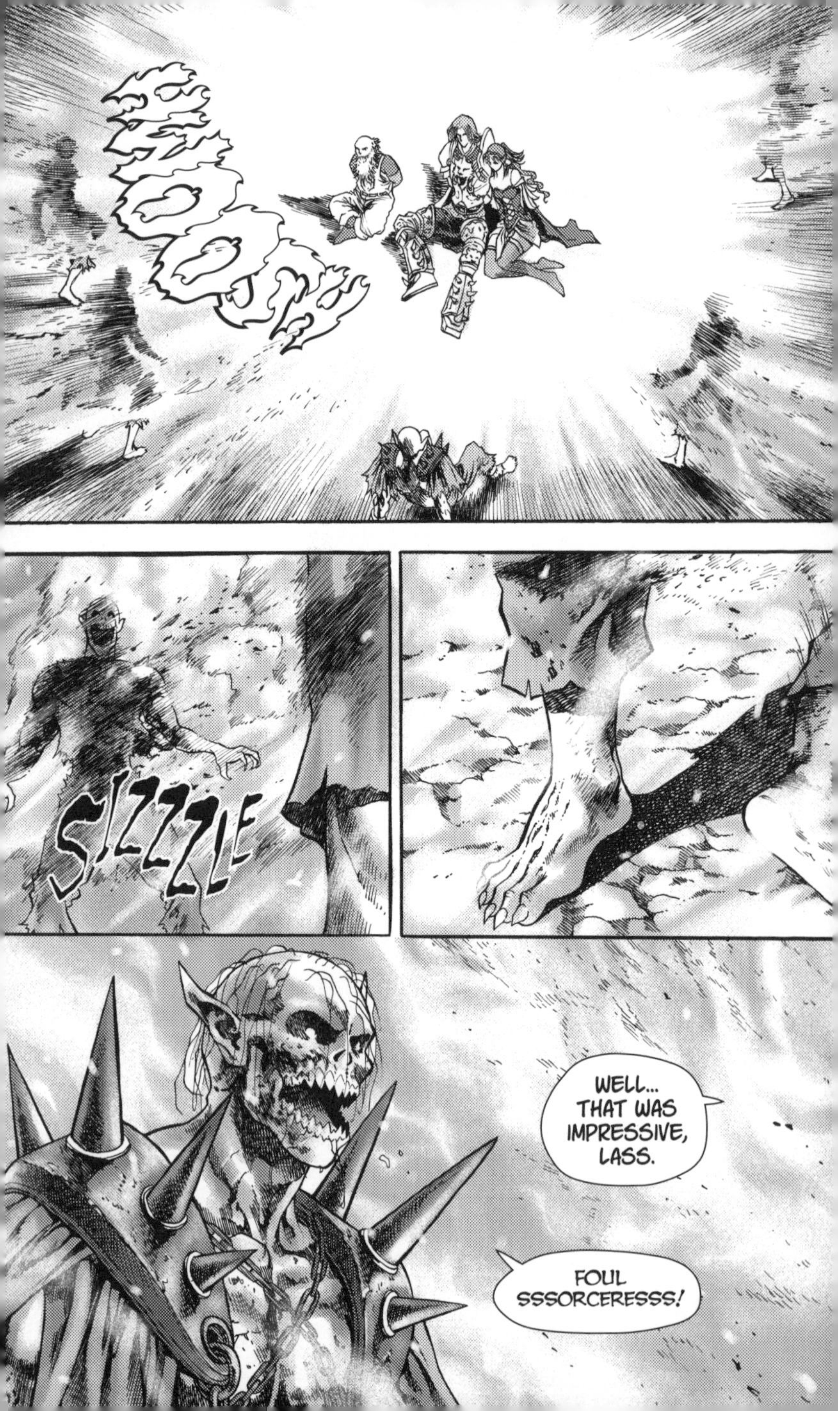
FZOOOSH
SIZZZLE
WELL... THAT WAS IMPRESSIVE, LASS.
FOUL SSSORCERESSS!

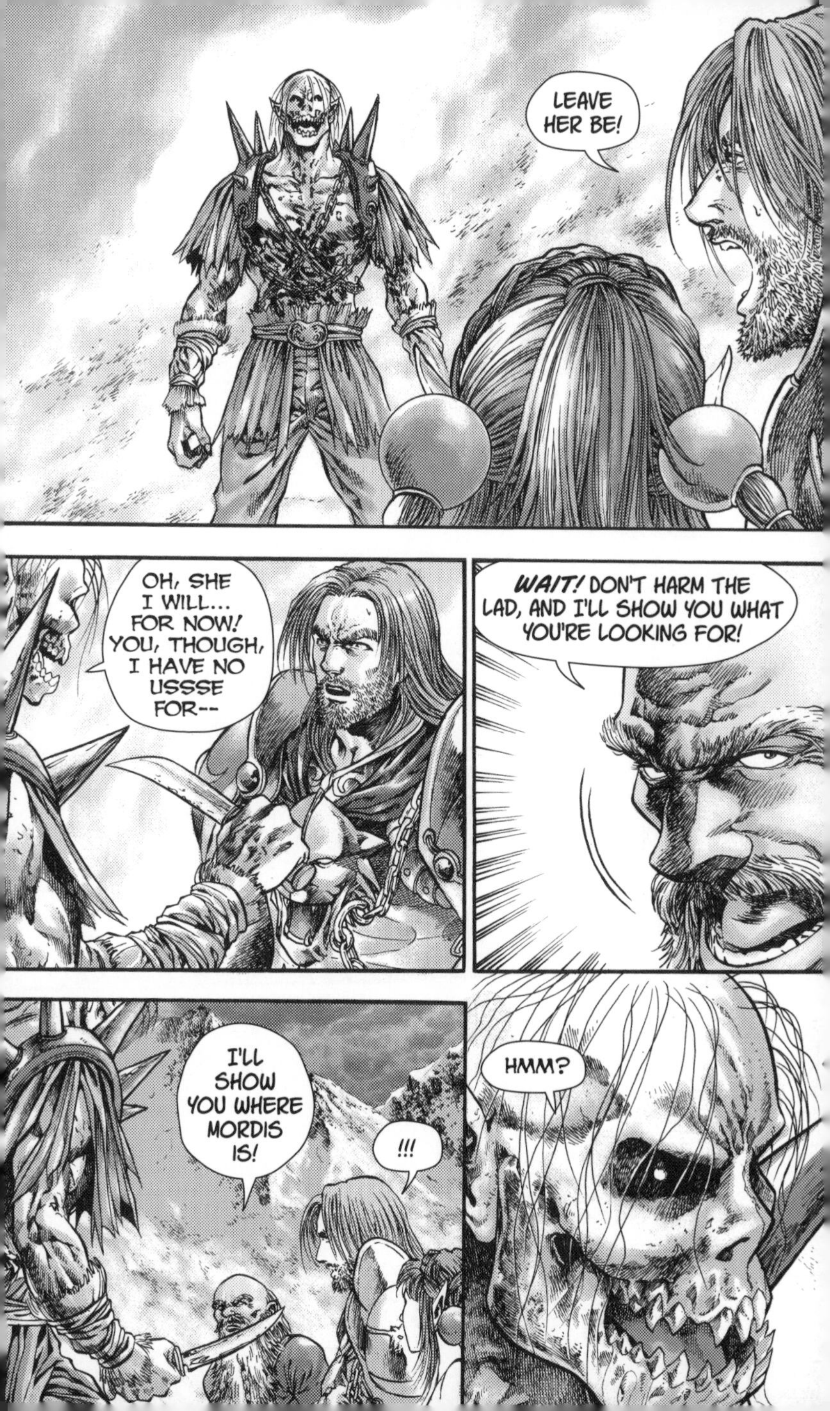
LEAVE HER BE!
OH, SHE I WILL... FOR NOW! YOU, THOUGH, I HAVE NO USSSE FOR--
WAIT! DON'T HARM THE LAD, AND I'LL SHOW YOU WHAT YOU'RE LOOKING FOR!
I'LL SHOW YOU WHERE MORDIS IS!
!!!
HMM?

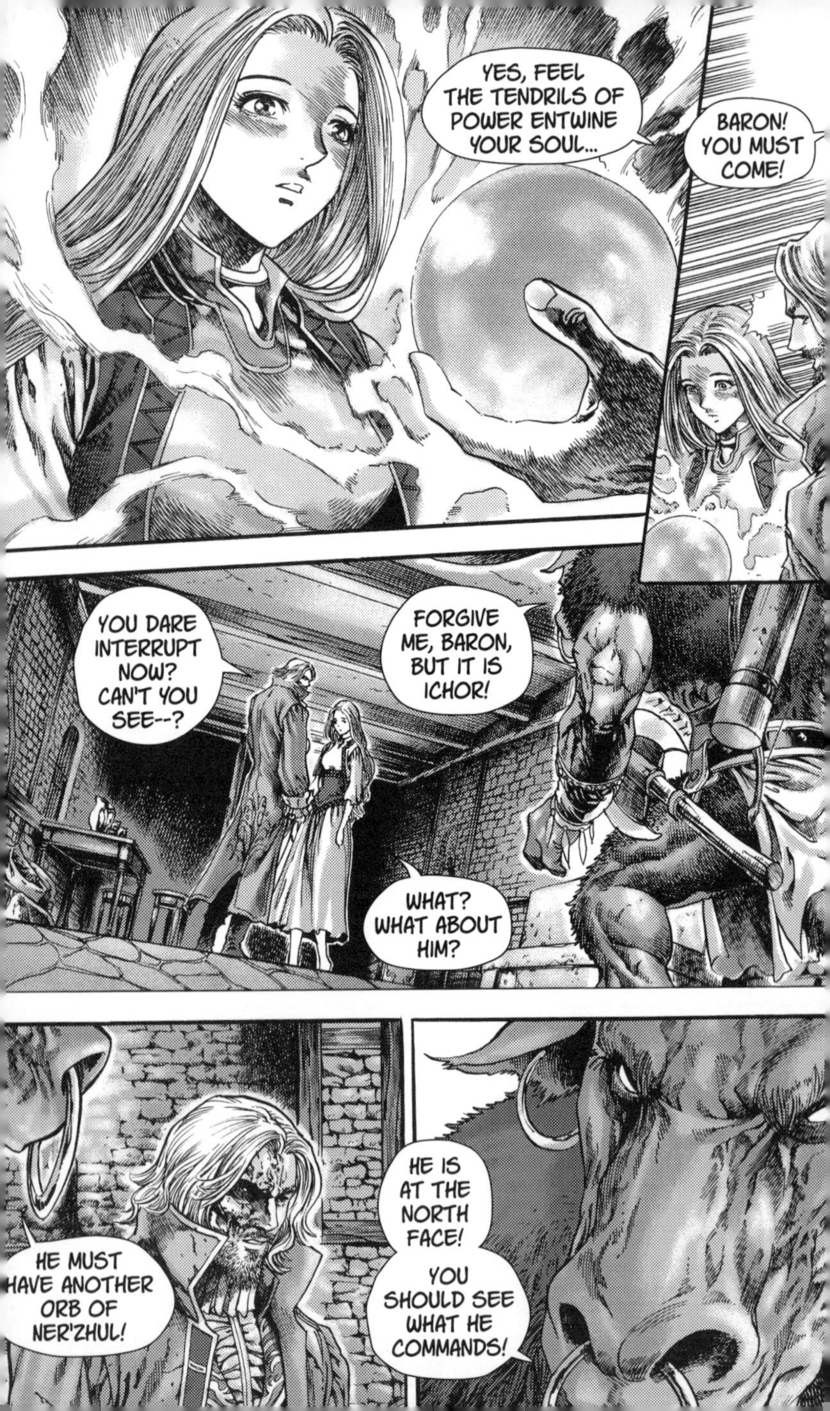
YES, FEEL THE TENDRILS OF POWER ENTWINE YOUR SOUL...
BARON! YOU MUST COME!
YOU DARE INTERRUPT NOW? CAN'T YOU SEE--?
FORGIVE ME, BARON, BUT IT IS ICHOR!
WHAT? WHAT ABOUT HIM?
HE MUST HAVE ANOTHER ORB OF NER'ZHUL!
HE IS AT THE NORTH FACE!
YOU SHOULD SEE WHAT HE COMMANDS!

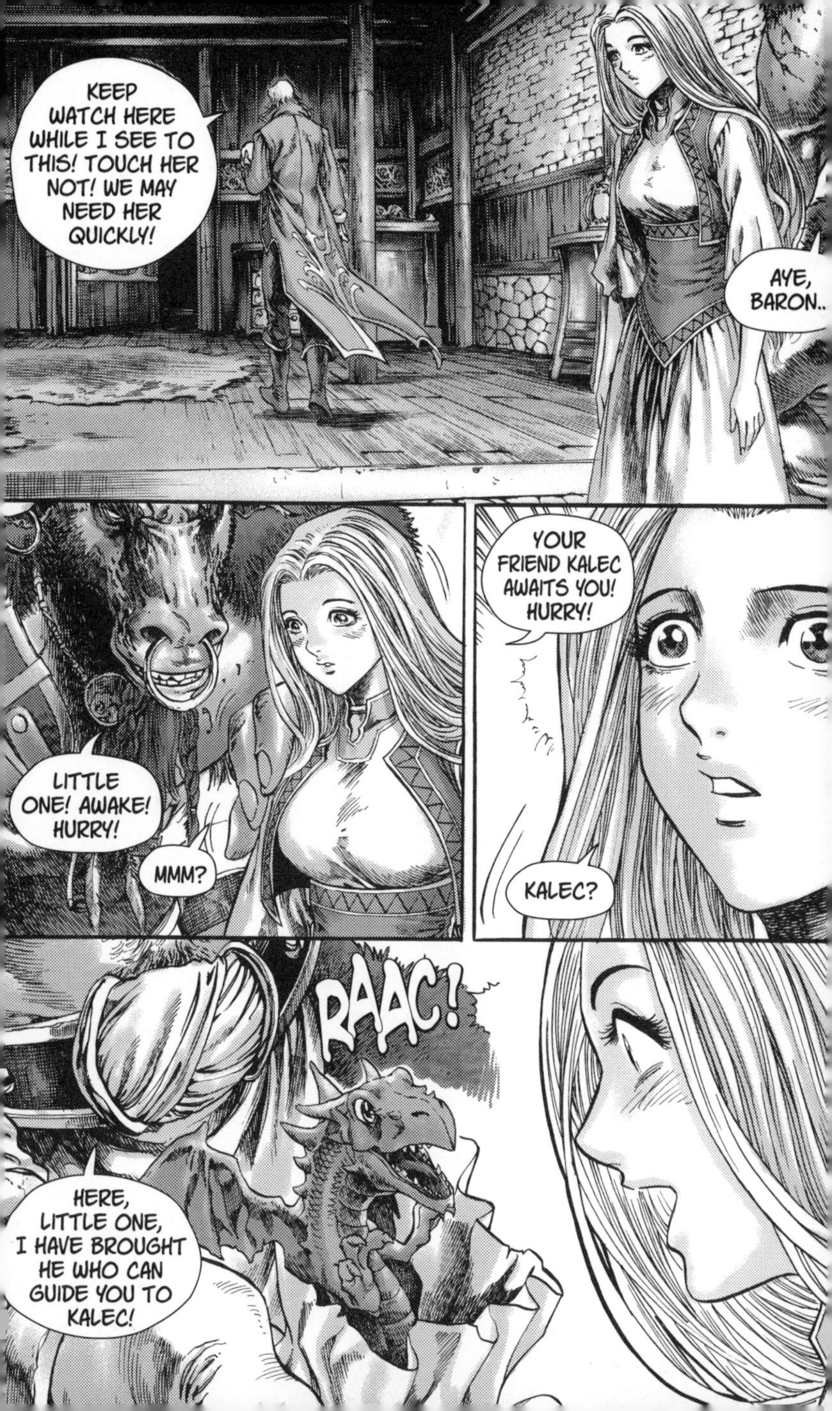
KEEP WATCH HERE WHILE I SEE TO THIS! TOUCH HER NOT! WE MAY NEED HER QUICKLY!
AYE, BARON..
LITTLE ONE! AWAKE! HURRY!
MMM?
YOUR FRIEND KALEC AWAITS YOU! HURRY!
KALEC?
RAAC!
HERE, LITTLE ONE, I HAVE BROUGHT HE WHO CAN GUIDE YOU TO KALEC!

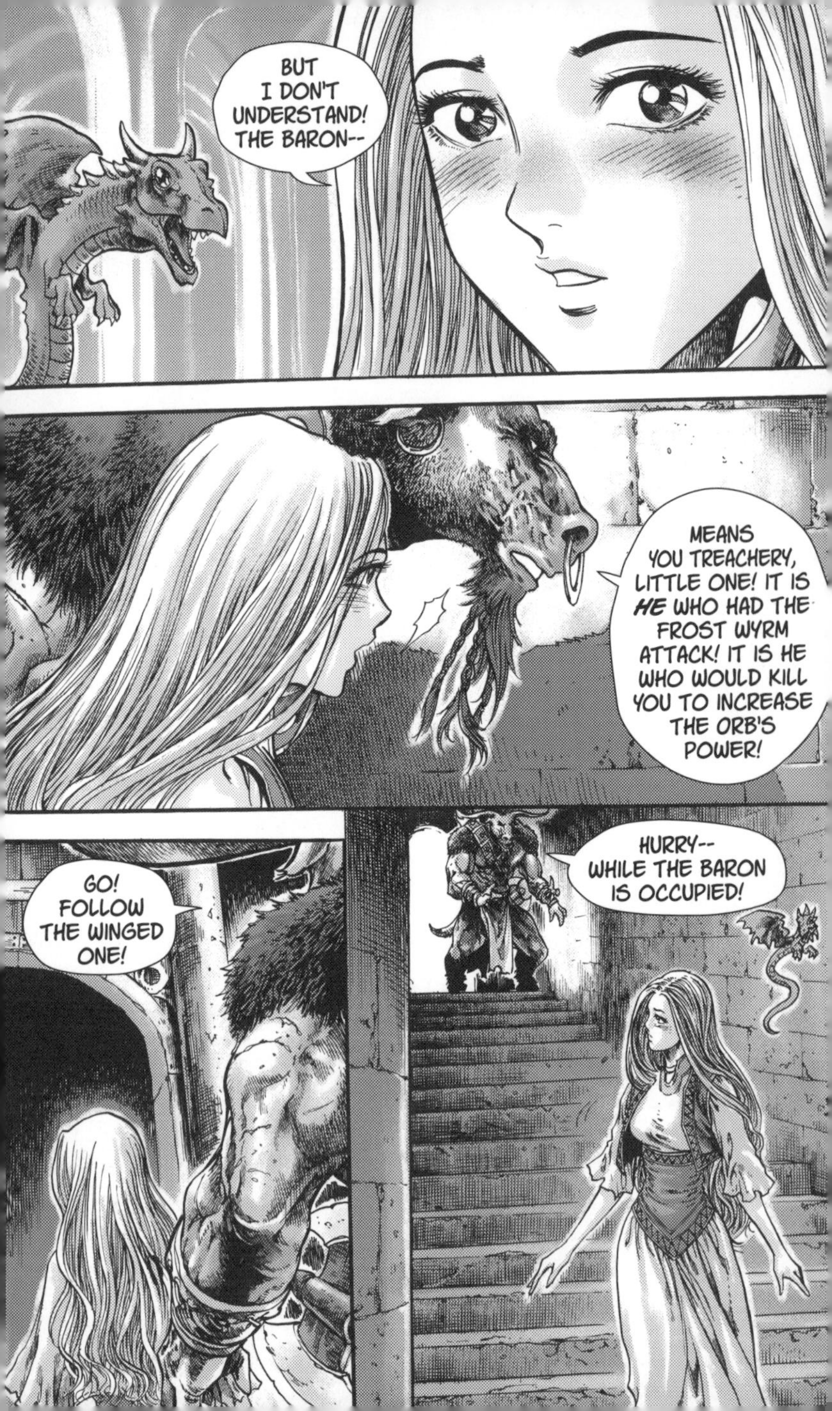
BUT I DON'T UNDERSTAND! THE BARON--
MEANS YOU TREACHERY, LITTLE ONE! IT IS *HE* WHO HAD THE FROST WYRM ATTACK! IT IS HE WHO WOULD KILL YOU TO INCREASE THE ORB'S POWER!
GO! FOLLOW THE WINGED ONE!
HURRY-- WHILE THE BARON IS OCCUPIED!

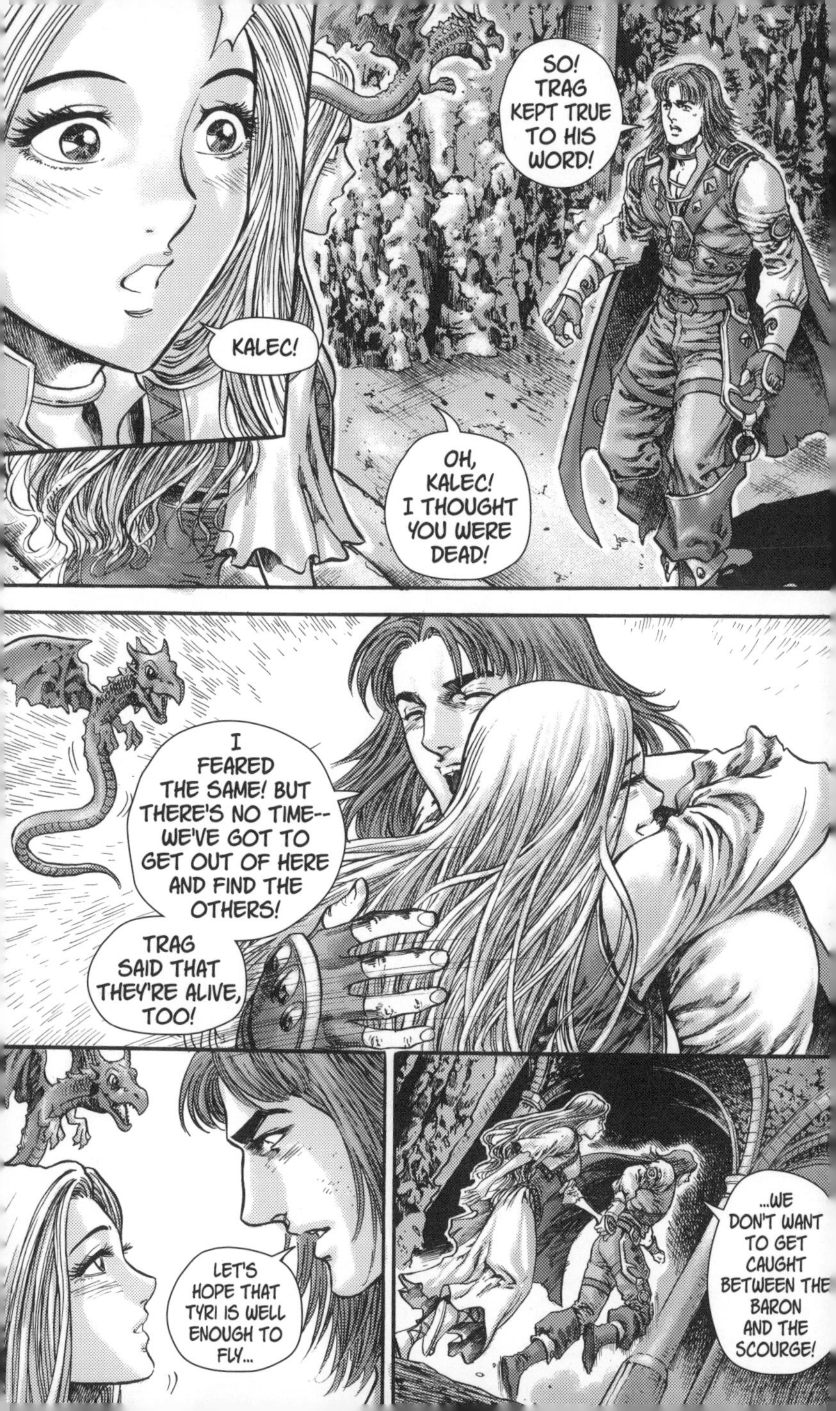
KALEC!
SO! TRAG KEPT TRUE TO HIS WORD!
OH, KALEC! I THOUGHT YOU WERE DEAD!
I FEARED THE SAME! BUT THERE'S NO TIME-- WE'VE GOT TO GET OUT OF HERE AND FIND THE OTHERS!
TRAG SAID THAT THEY'RE ALIVE, TOO!
LET'S HOPE THAT TYRI IS WELL ENOUGH TO FLY...
...WE DON'T WANT TO GET CAUGHT BETWEEN THE BARON AND THE SCOURGE!

I THINK... IF I JUST HAVE A LITTLE MORE TIME--

HOW FARE YOU NOW, TYRI?

I FEAR WE MAY NOT HAVE THAT...

!SSS THAT IT AHEAD? IF YOU LIE--!

I'VE NOT LIED, BAG O' BONES. THE END OF YOUR HUNT LIES THERE.

CHAPTER SIX
Death on the Mountain

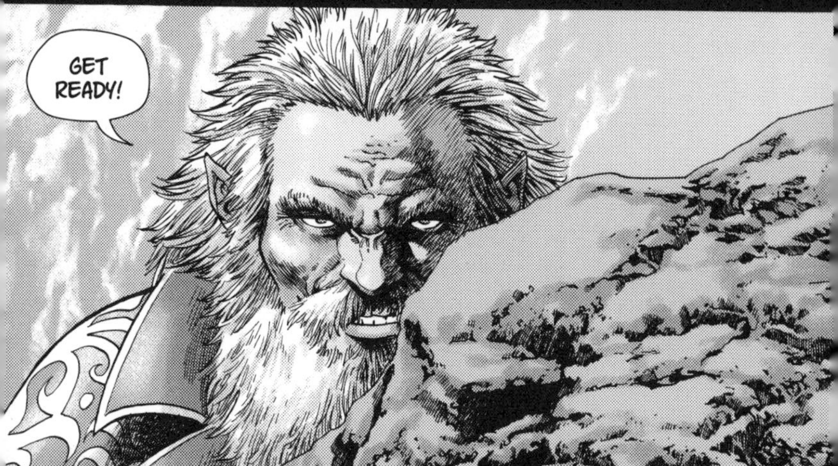
GET READY!

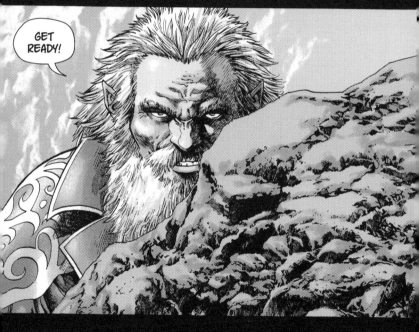

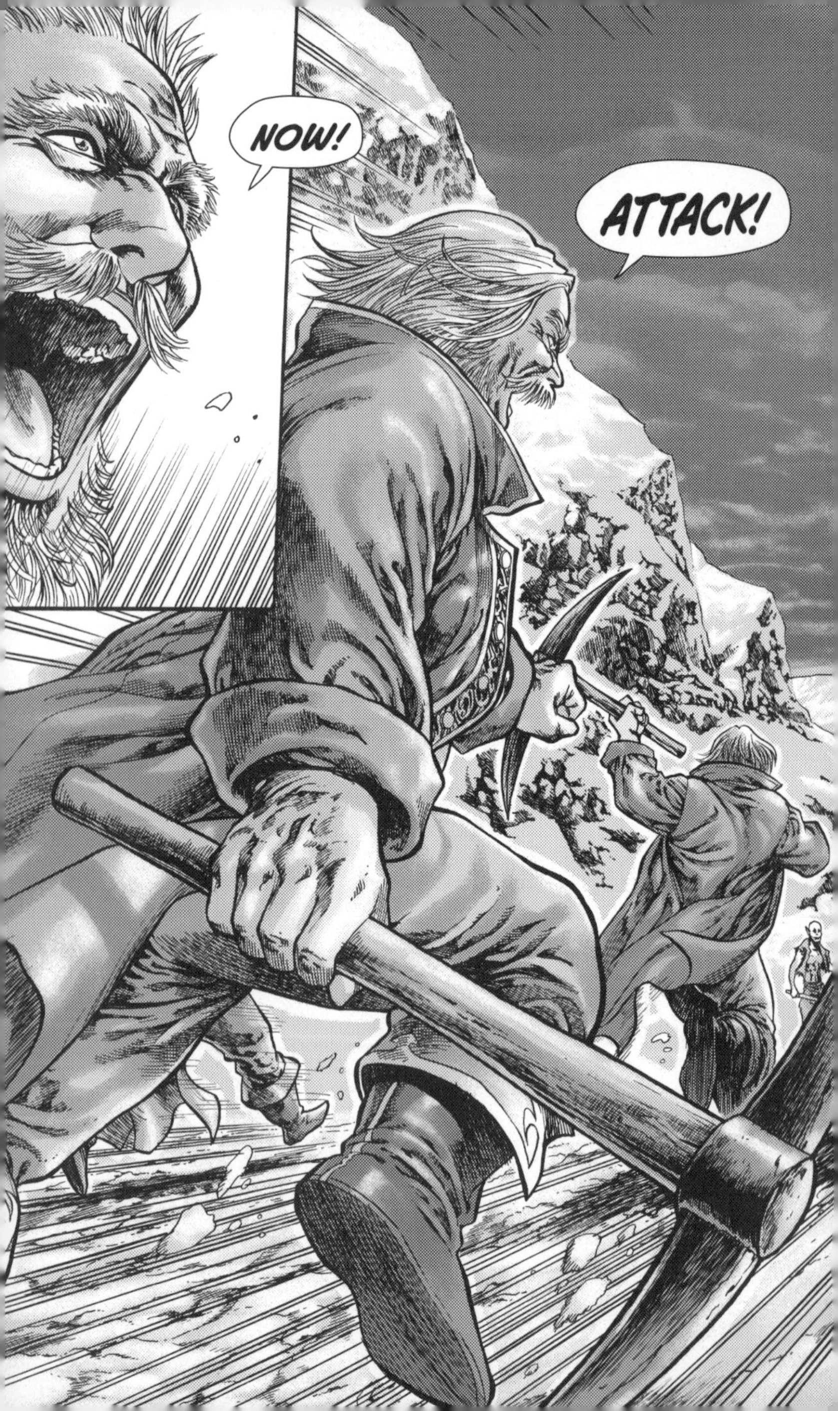
NOW!
ATTACK!

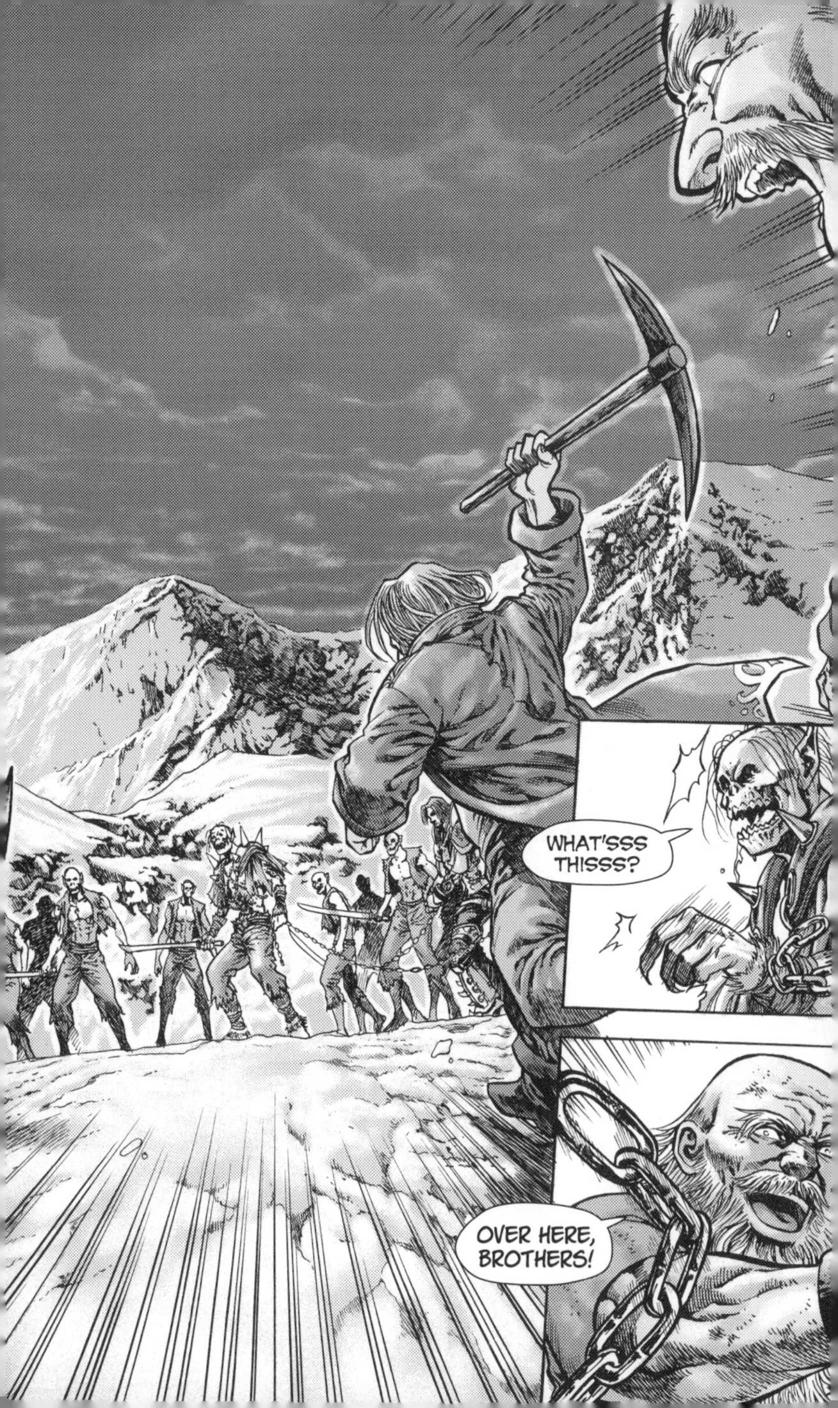
WHAT'SSS THISSS?
OVER HERE, BROTHERS!

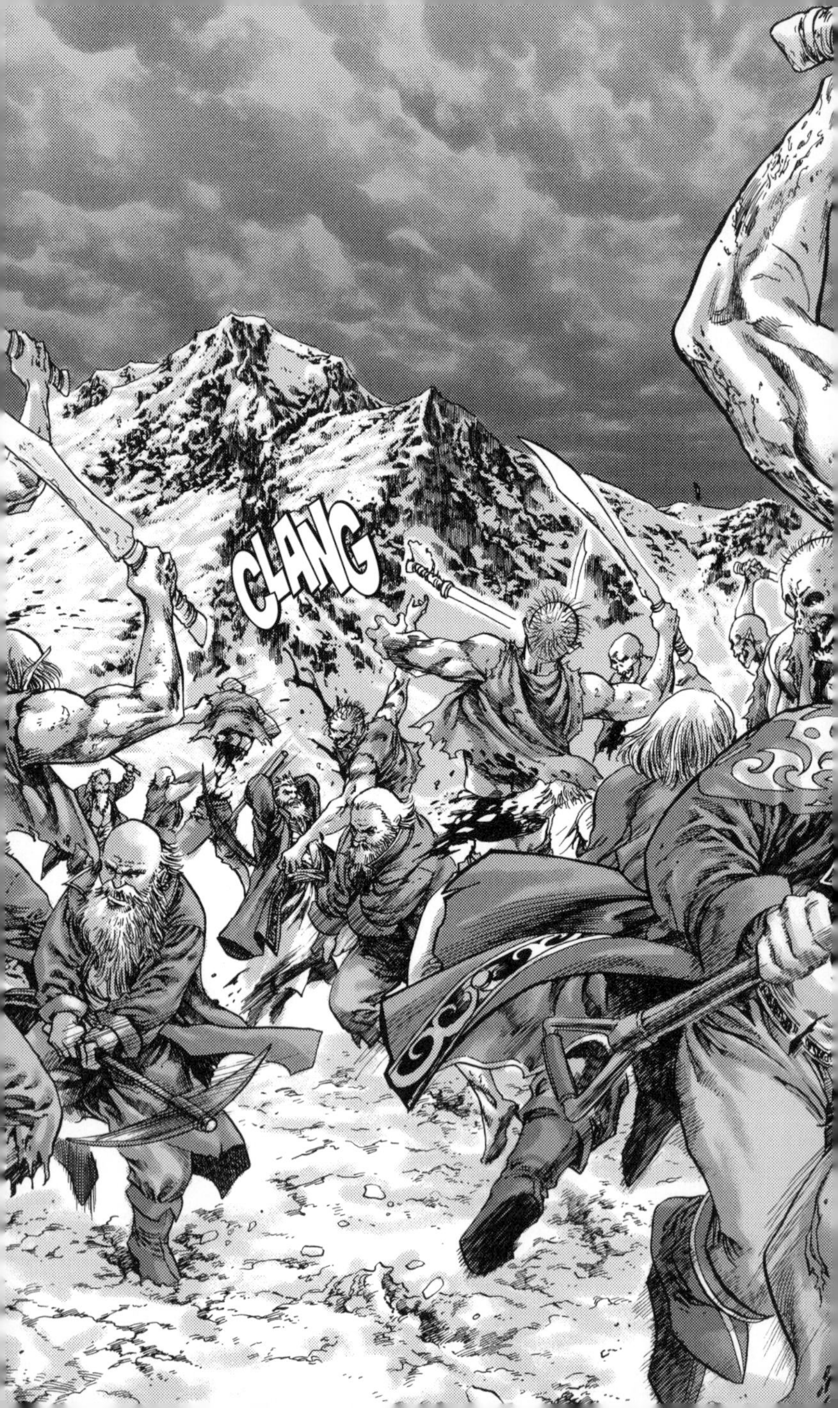
CLANG

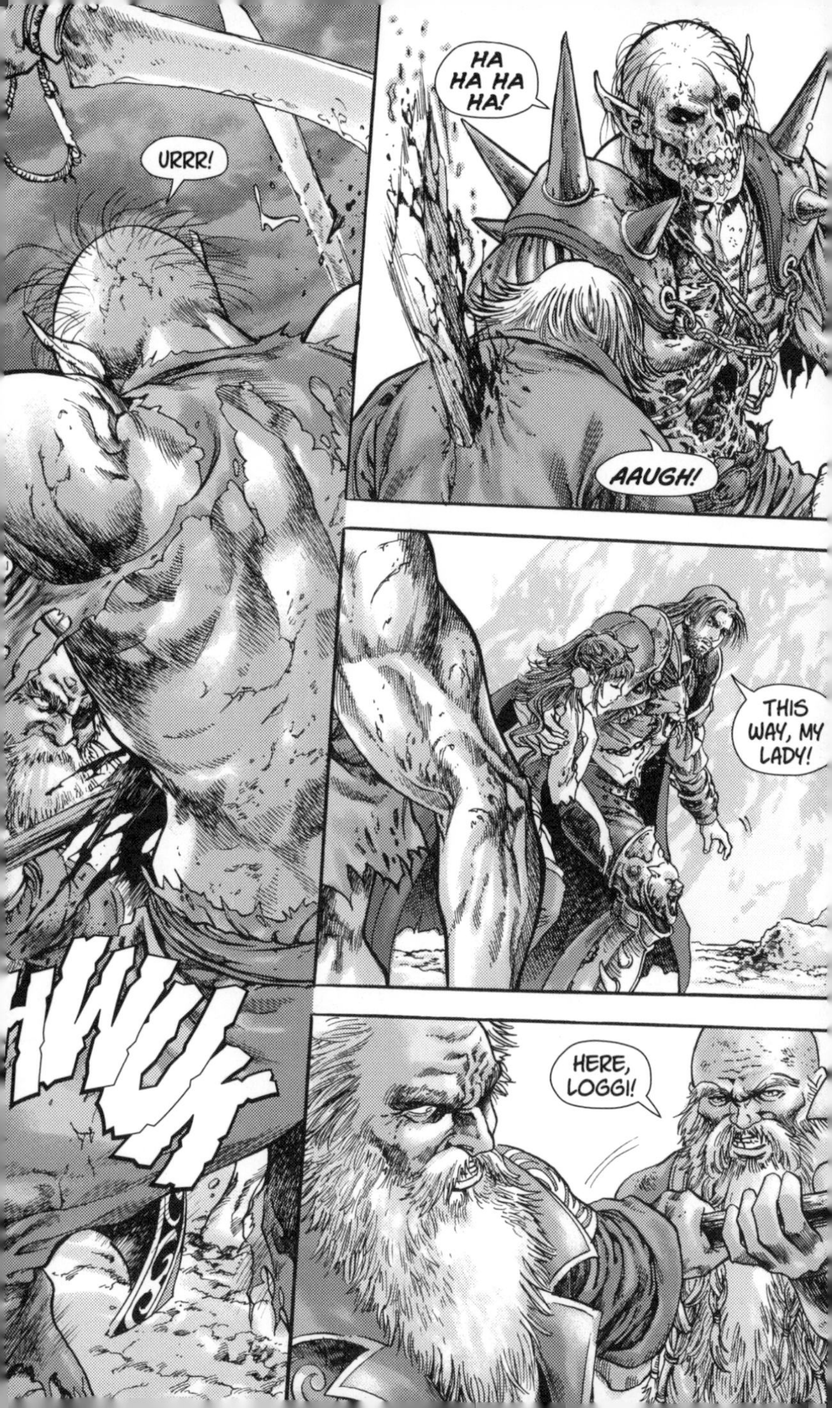
URRR!
HWUK
HA HA HA HA!
AAUGH!
THIS WAY, MY LADY!
HERE, LOGGI!

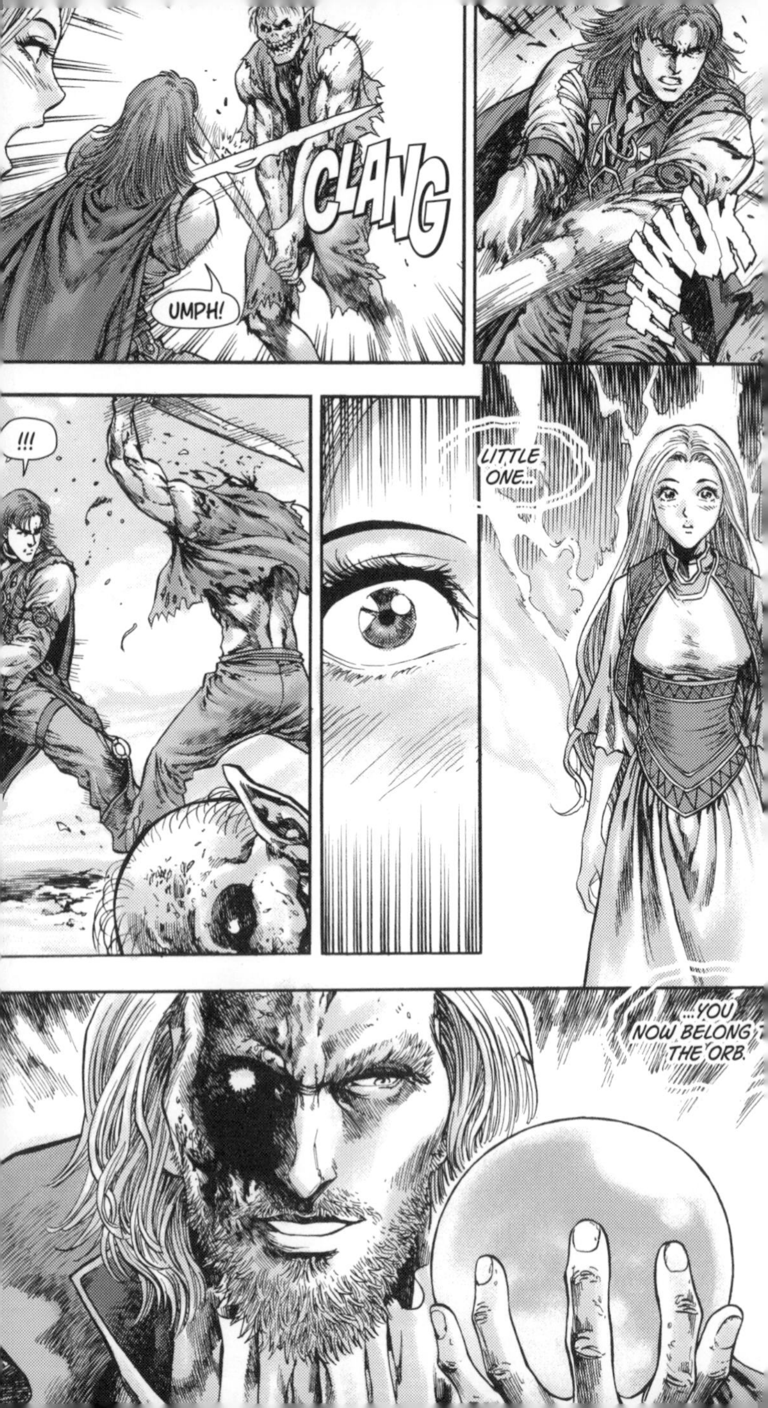
CLANG
UMPH!
THUNK
!!!
LITTLE ONE...
...YOU NOW BELONG THE ORB.

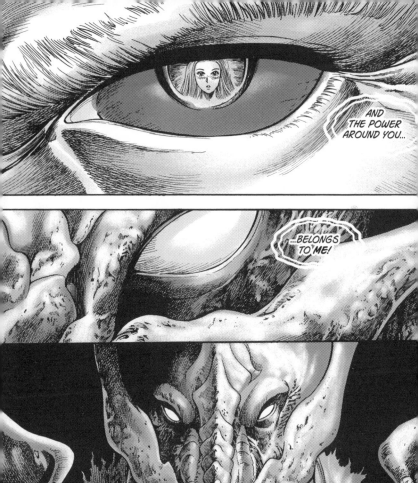

AND THE POWER AROUND YOU...

...BELONGS TO ME!

HISSSSSSAAA

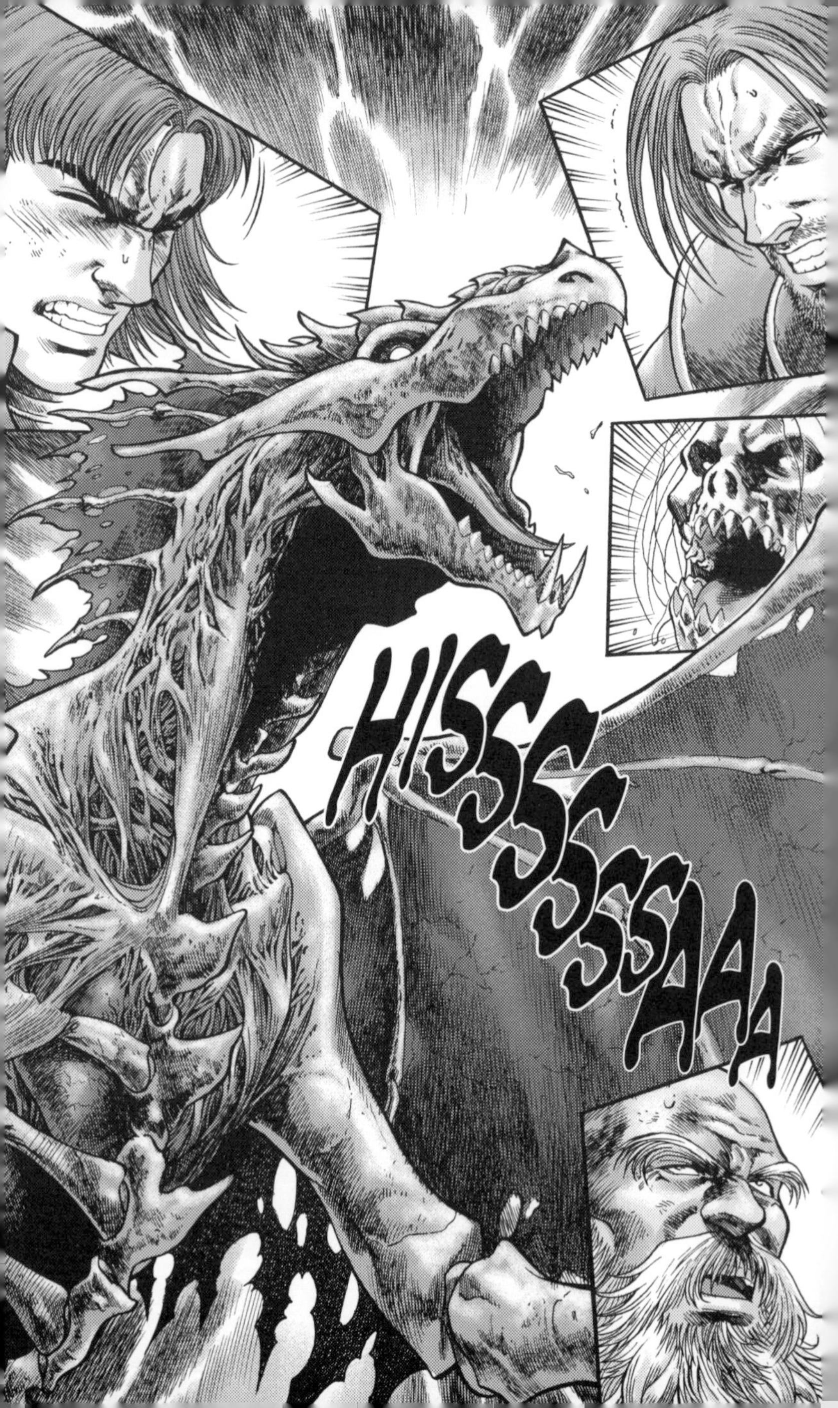
HISSSSSSAAA

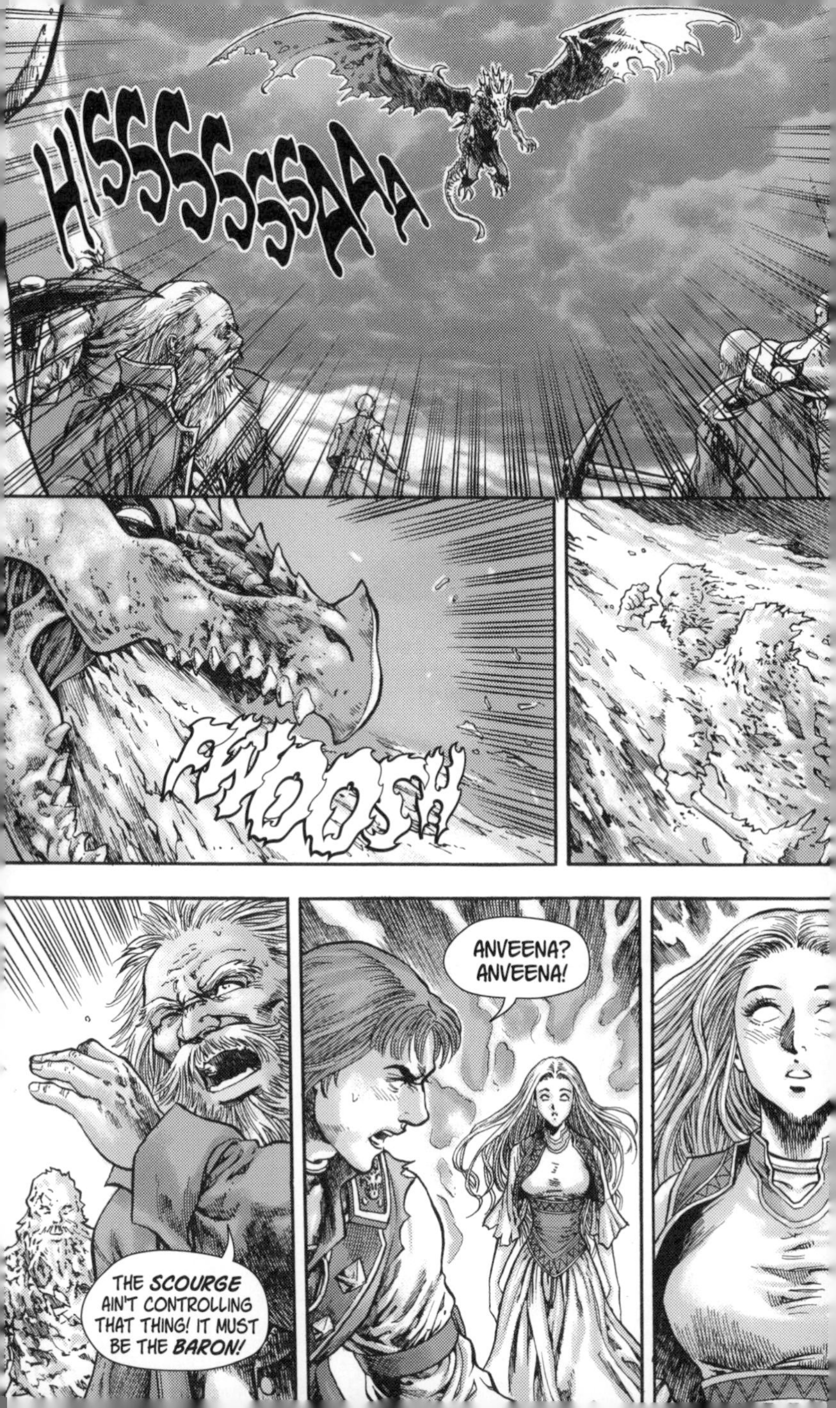
HISSSSSSSAAA
FWOOSH
THE SCOURGE AIN'T CONTROLLING THAT THING! IT MUST BE THE BARON!
ANVEENA? ANVEENA!

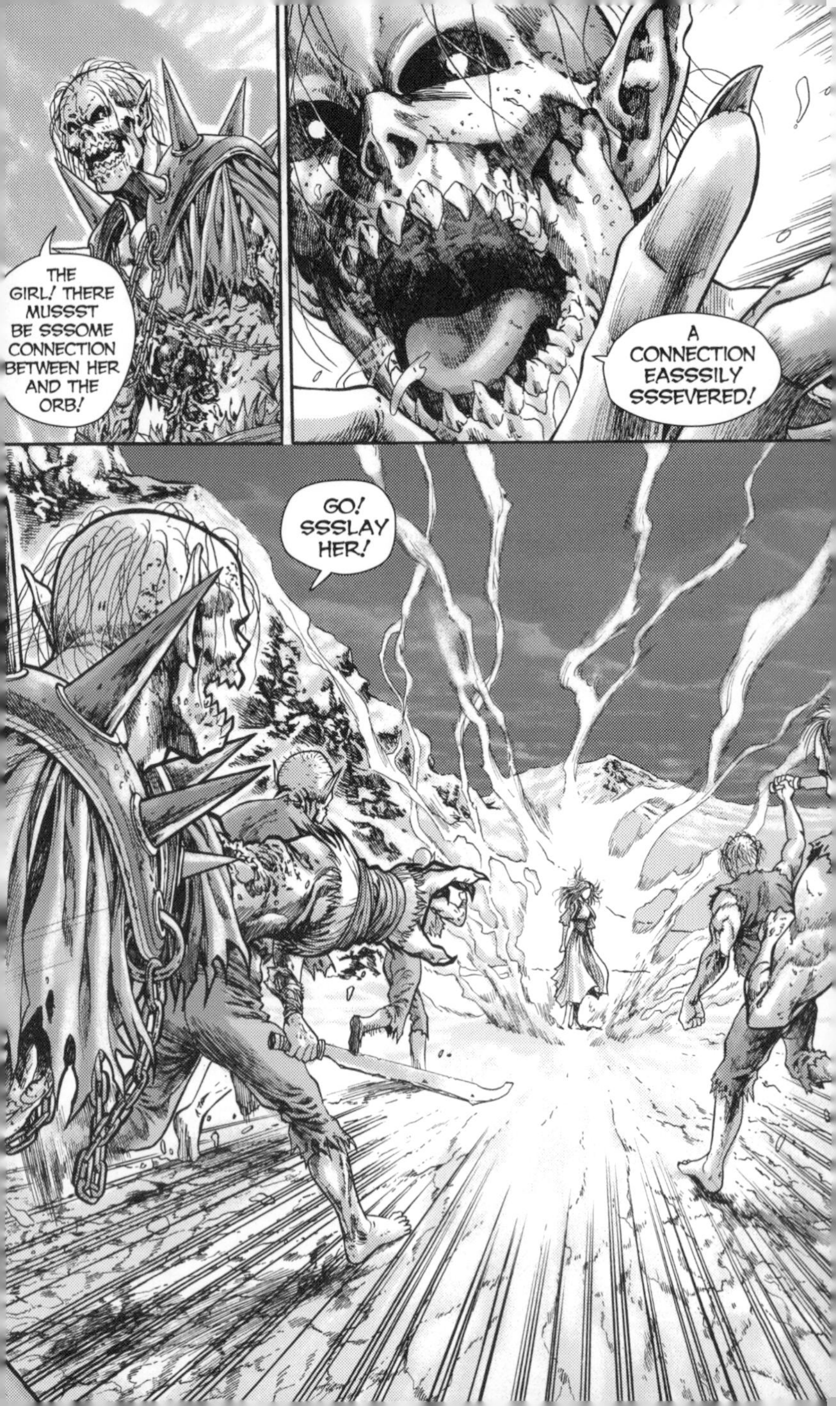
THE GIRL! THERE MUSSST BE SSSOME CONNECTION BETWEEN HER AND THE ORB!
A CONNECTION EASSSILY SSSEVERED!
GO! SSSLAY HER!

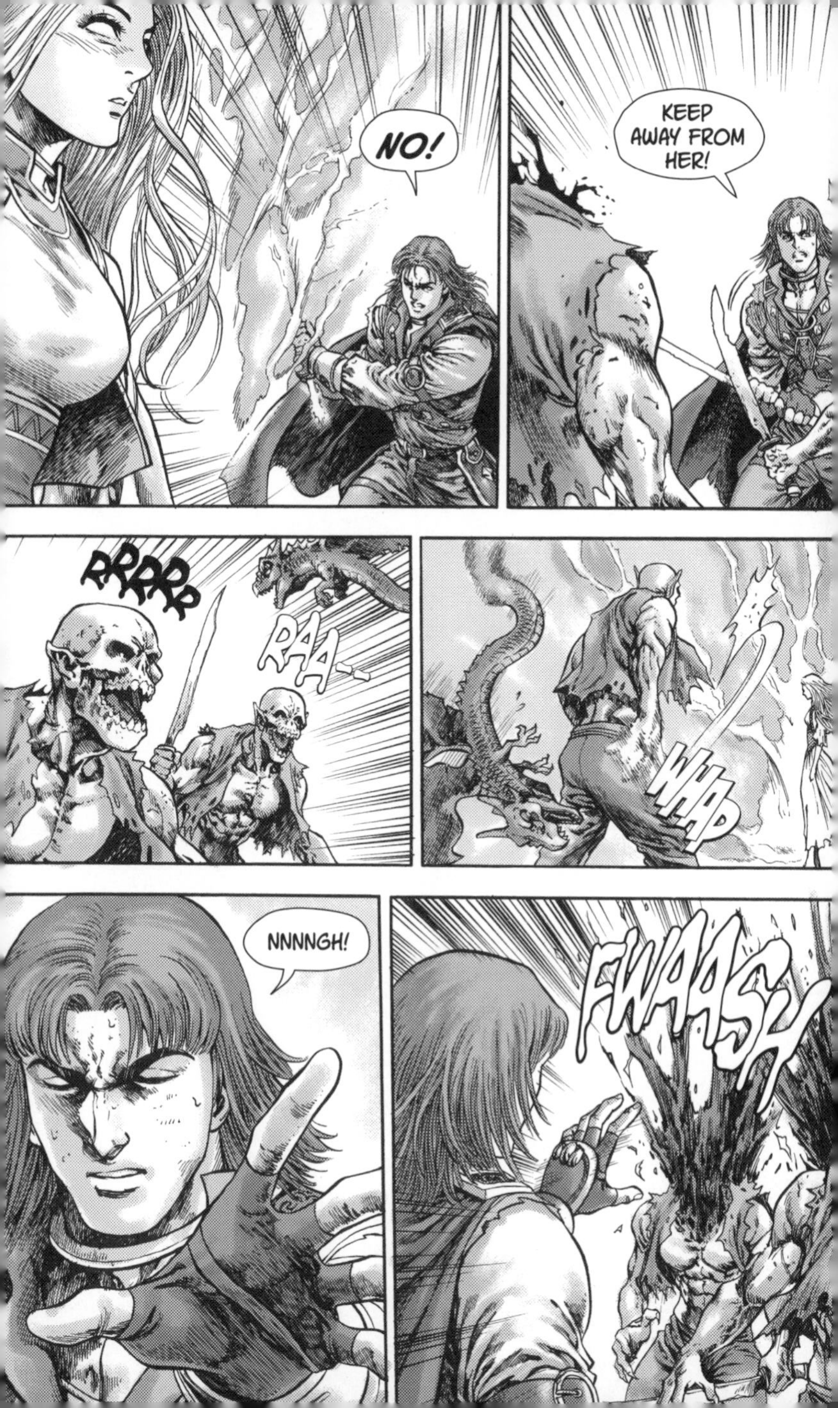
NO!
KEEP AWAY FROM HER!
RRRRR
RAA
WHAP
NNNNGH!
FWAASH

RRRR.OARR!

TYRI! NO! SHE LOOKS TOO WEAK!

THEN AT LEAST SHE'LL BUY YOU TIME! HURRY!

!!!

HISSSSSSAAA

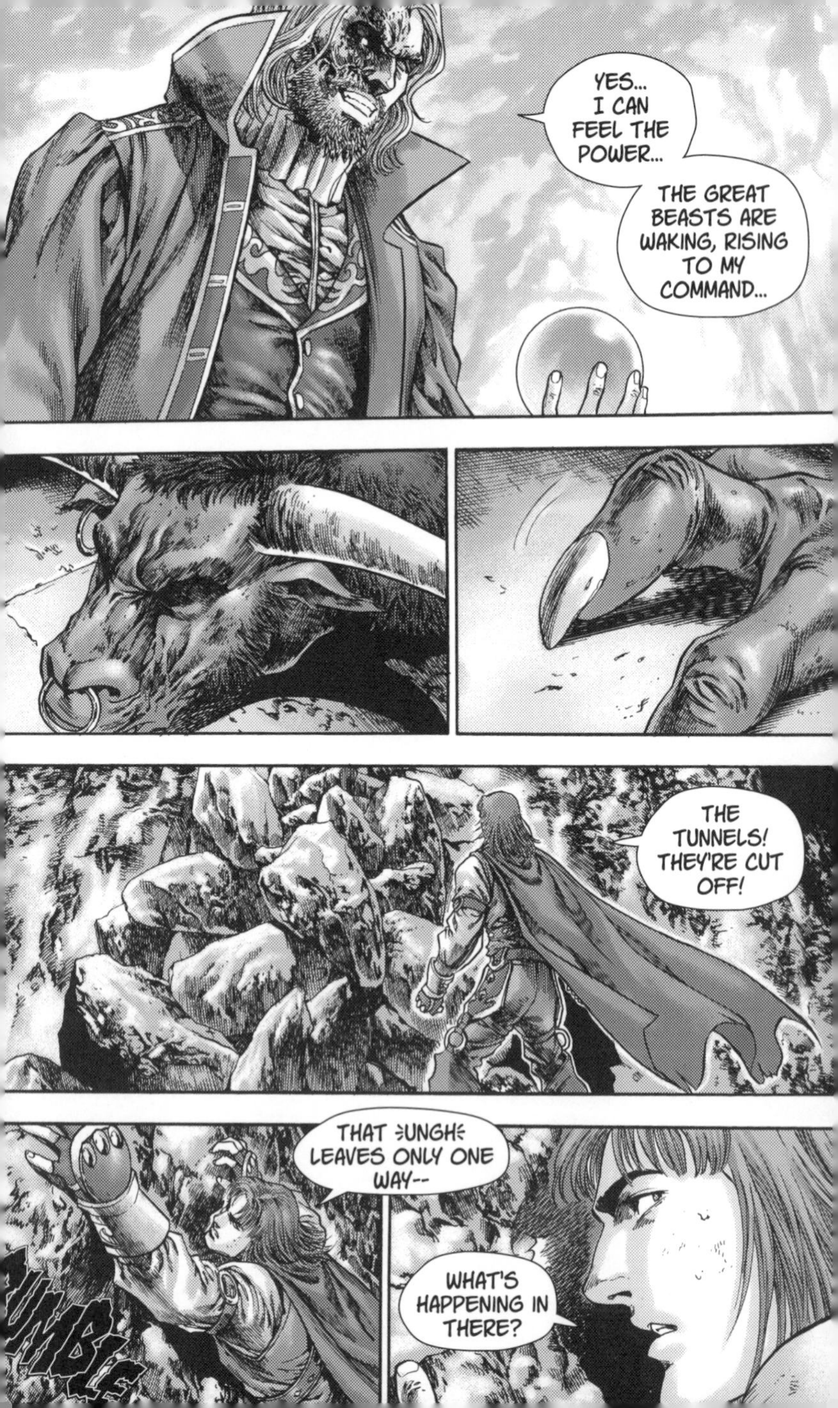
YES... I CAN FEEL THE POWER...
THE GREAT BEASTS ARE WAKING, RISING TO MY COMMAND...
THE TUNNELS! THEY'RE CUT OFF!
THAT ≡UNGH≡ LEAVES ONLY ONE WAY--
WHAT'S HAPPENING IN THERE?

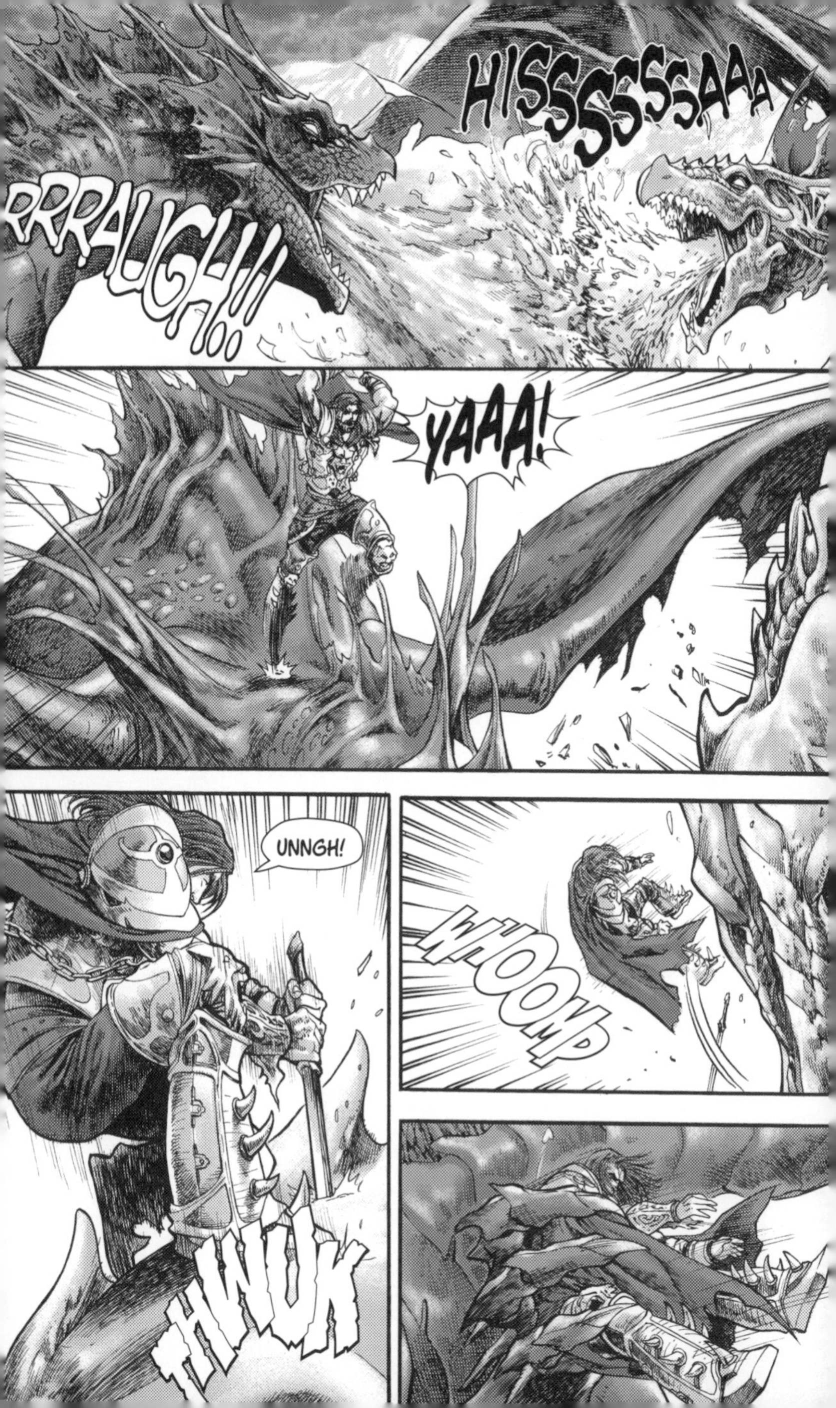
RRRRAUGH!!...
HISSSSSAAA
YAAA!
UNNGH!
THWUK
WHOOOMP

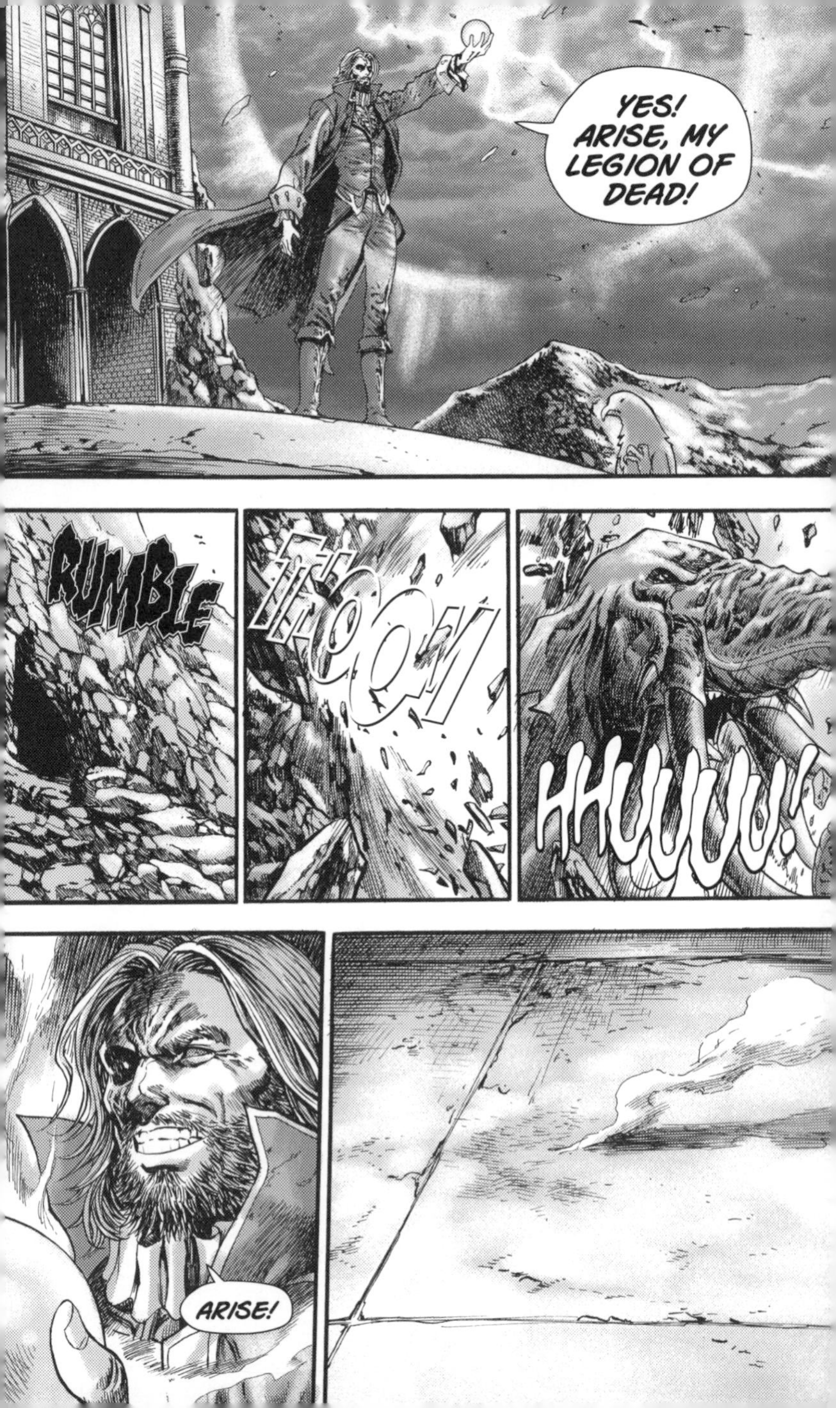
YES! ARISE, MY LEGION OF DEAD!
RUMBLE
HHUUUU!
ARISE!

THERE'S SOMETHING MOVING INSIDE THE MOUNTAIN! SOMETHING HUGE!

I'VE GOT TO HOLD ON--

STAB

AAUGH!

THE ORB OF NER'ZHUL ISSS MINE! NO ONE ELSSSE'SSS!

I WILL TAKE IT AND THE GIRL FROM MORDISSS!

IF I CAN JUS SUMMON ENOUGH POWER.

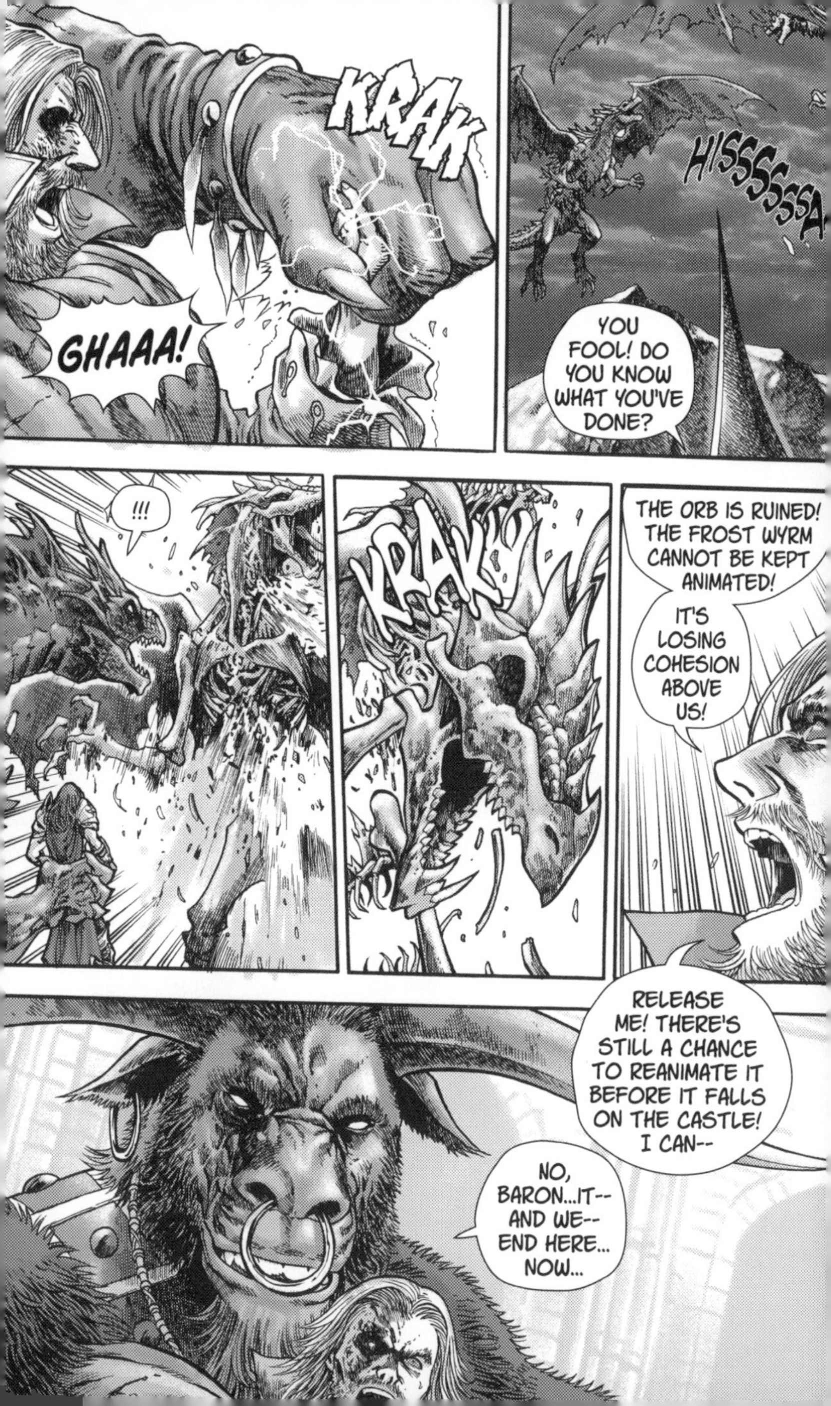
KRAK
GHAAA!
HISSSSSSSA
YOU FOOL! DO YOU KNOW WHAT YOU'VE DONE?
!!!
KRAK
THE ORB IS RUINED! THE FROST WYRM CANNOT BE KEPT ANIMATED!
IT'S LOSING COHESION ABOVE US!
RELEASE ME! THERE'S STILL A CHANCE TO REANIMATE IT BEFORE IT FALLS ON THE CASTLE! I CAN--
NO, BARON...IT--AND WE--END HERE... NOW...

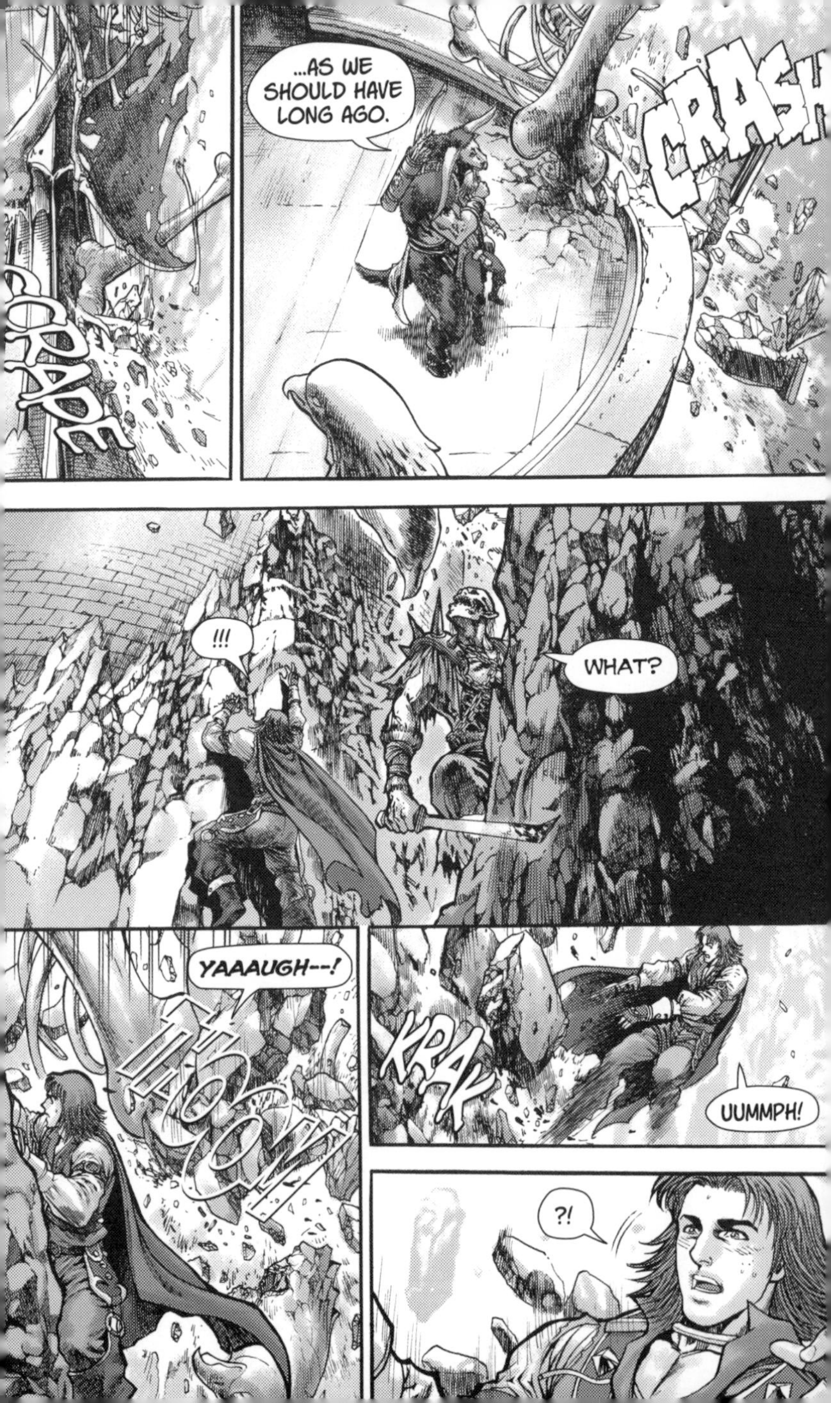
SCRAPE
...AS WE SHOULD HAVE LONG AGO.
CRASH
!!!
WHAT?
YAAAUGH--!
THOOOM
KRAK
UUMMPH!
?!

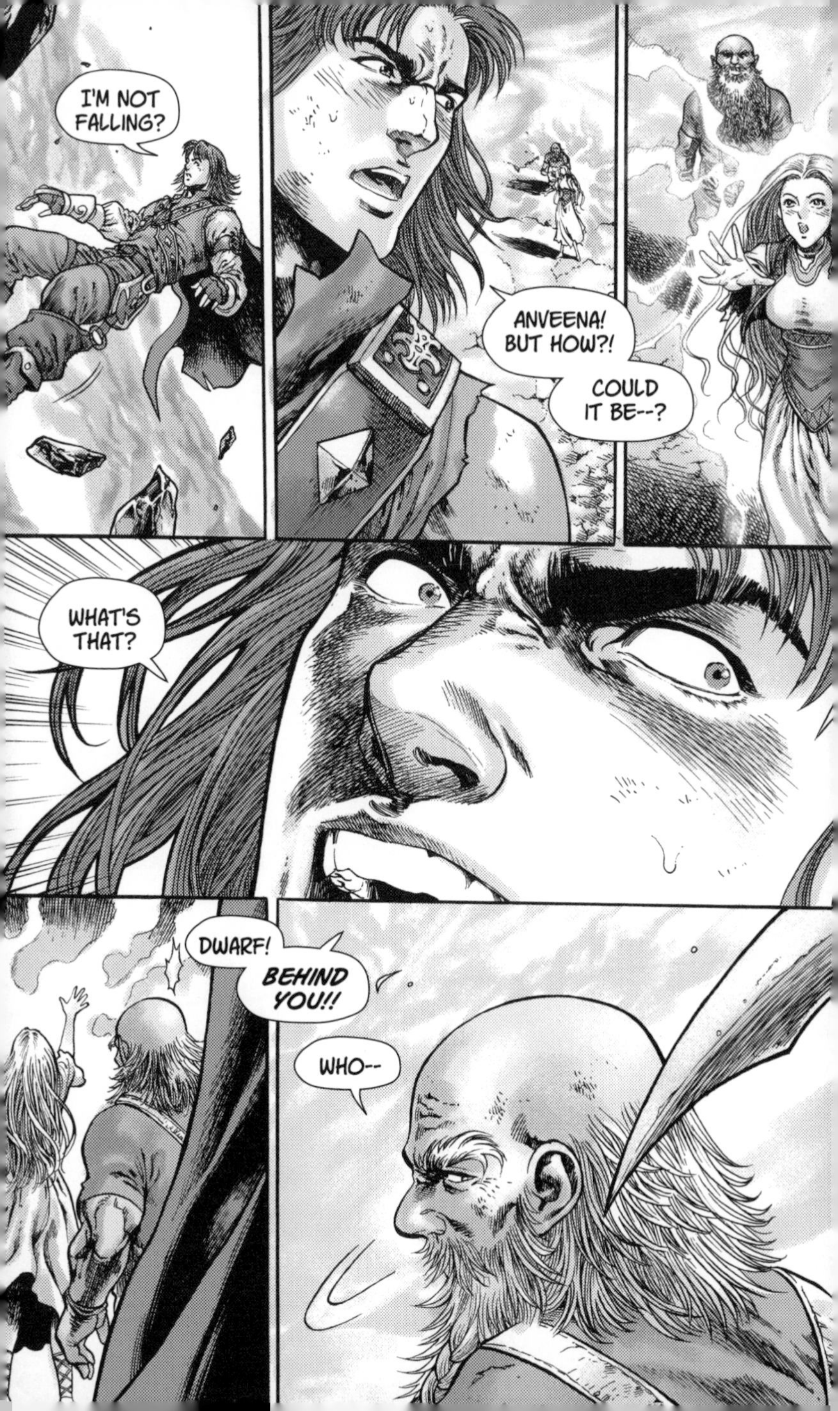
I'M NOT FALLING?
ANVEENA! BUT HOW?!
COULD IT BE--?
WHAT'S THAT?
DWARF!
BEHIND YOU!!
WHO--

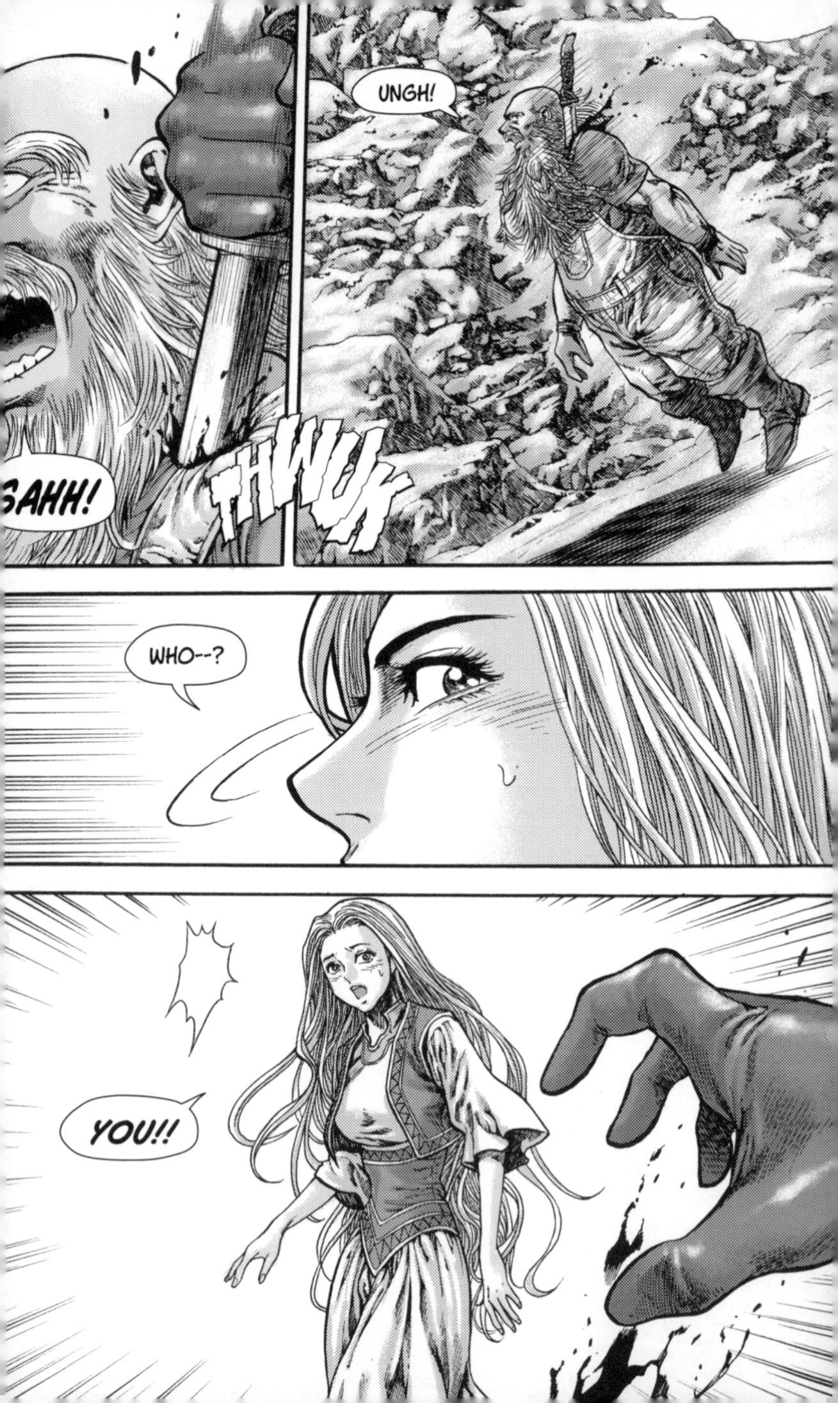
SAHH!
THWUK
UNGH!
WHO--?
YOU!!

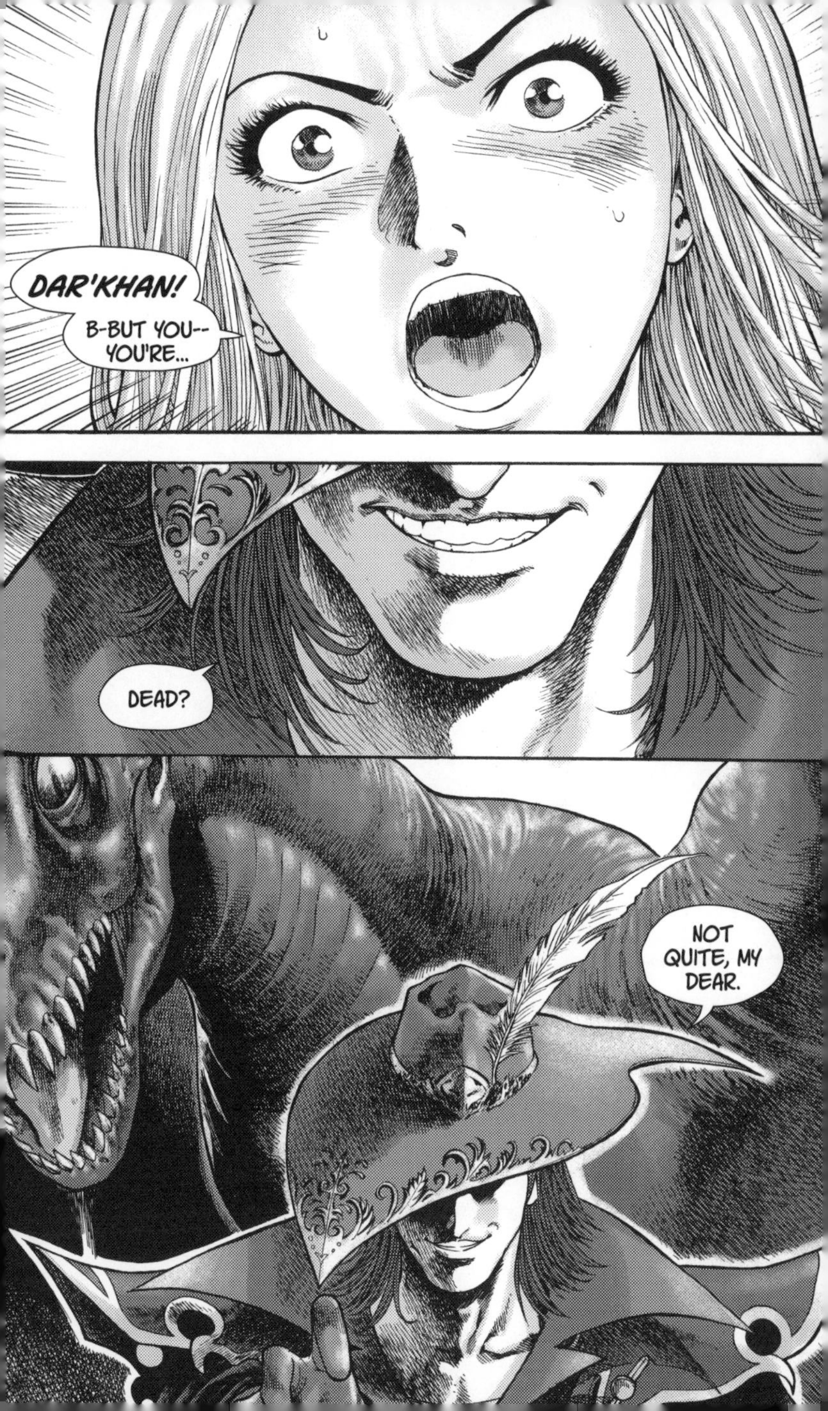
DAR'KHAN!
B-BUT YOU-- YOU'RE...
DEAD?
NOT QUITE, MY DEAR.

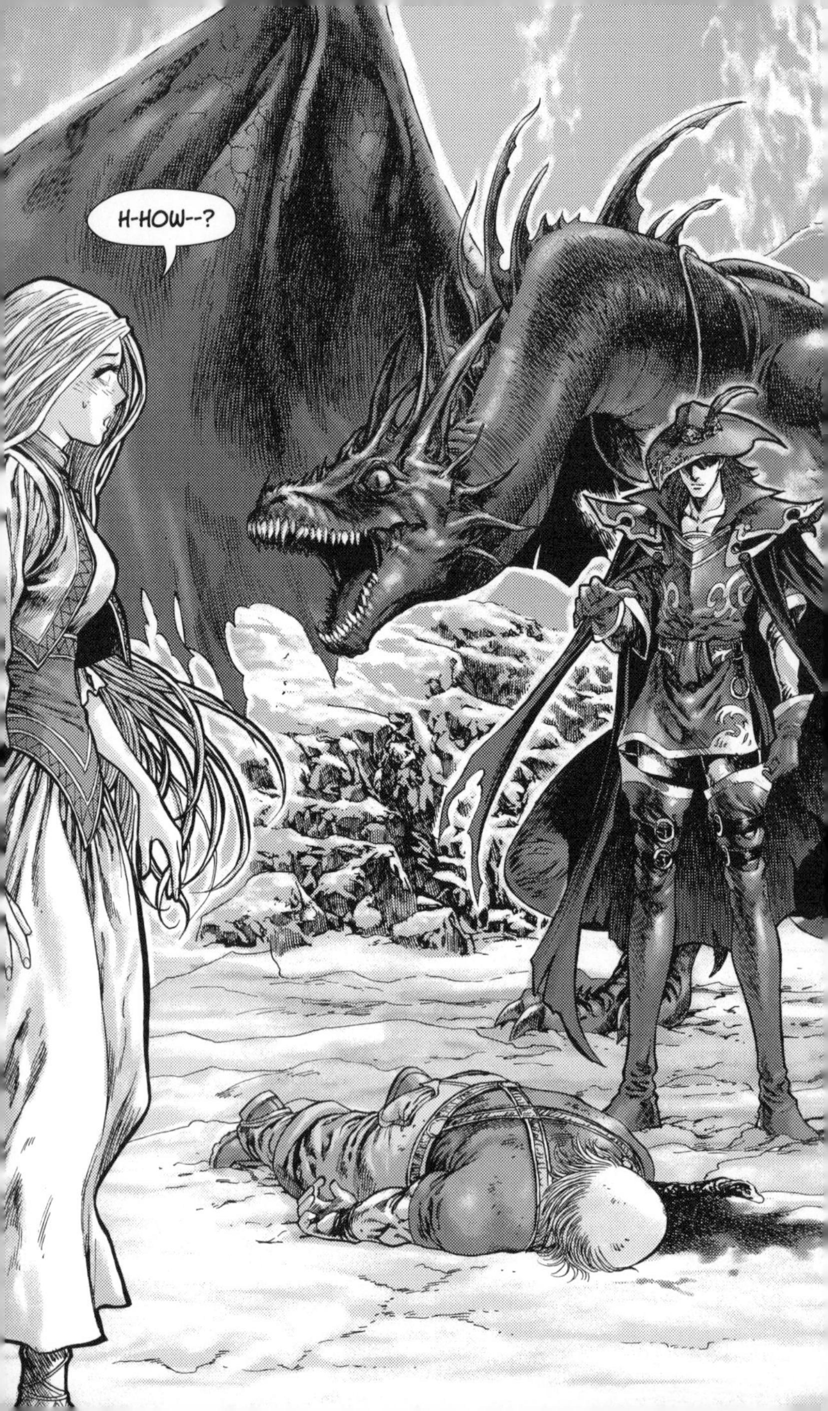
H-HOW--?

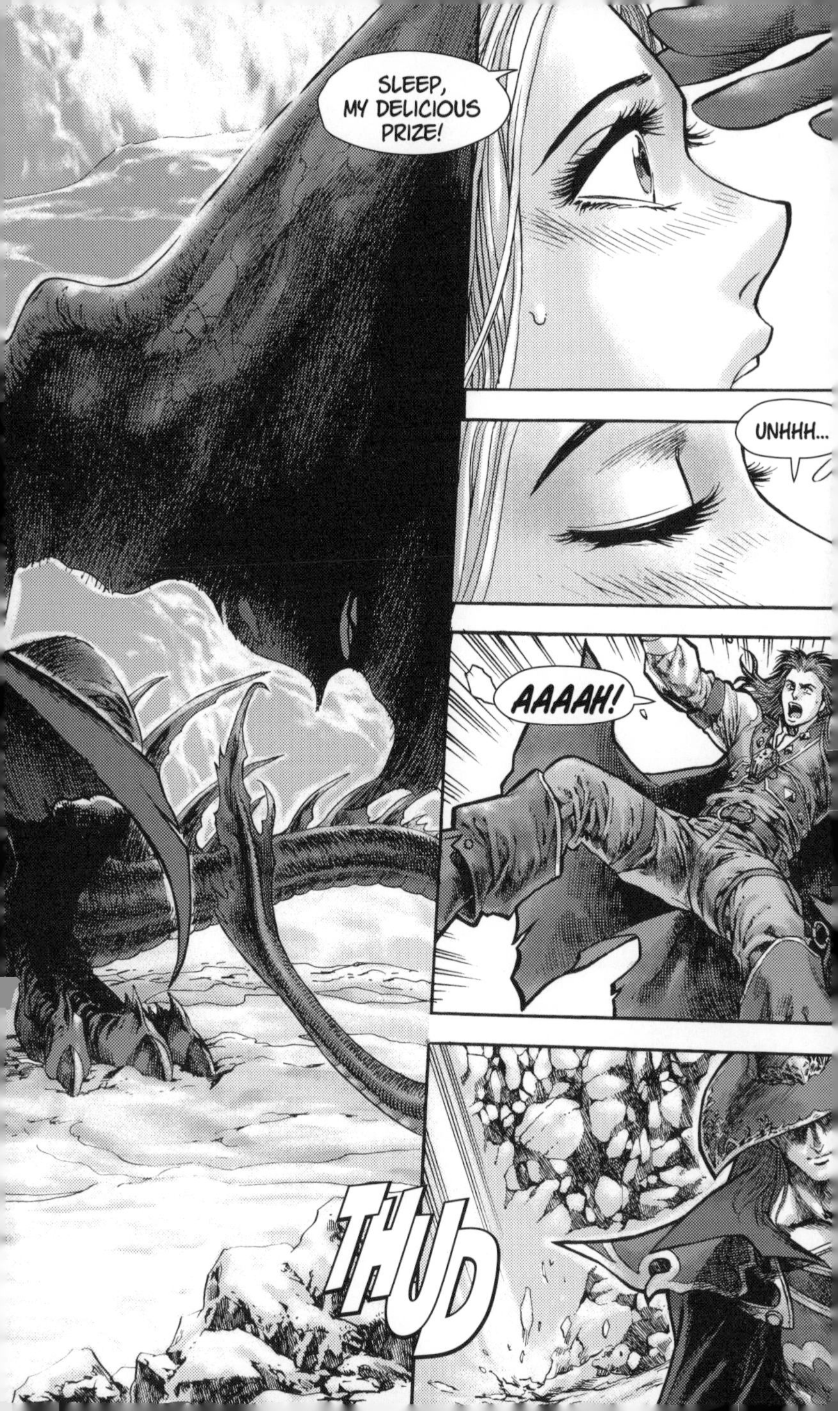
SLEEP, MY DELICIOUS PRIZE!
UNHHH...
AAAAH!
THUD

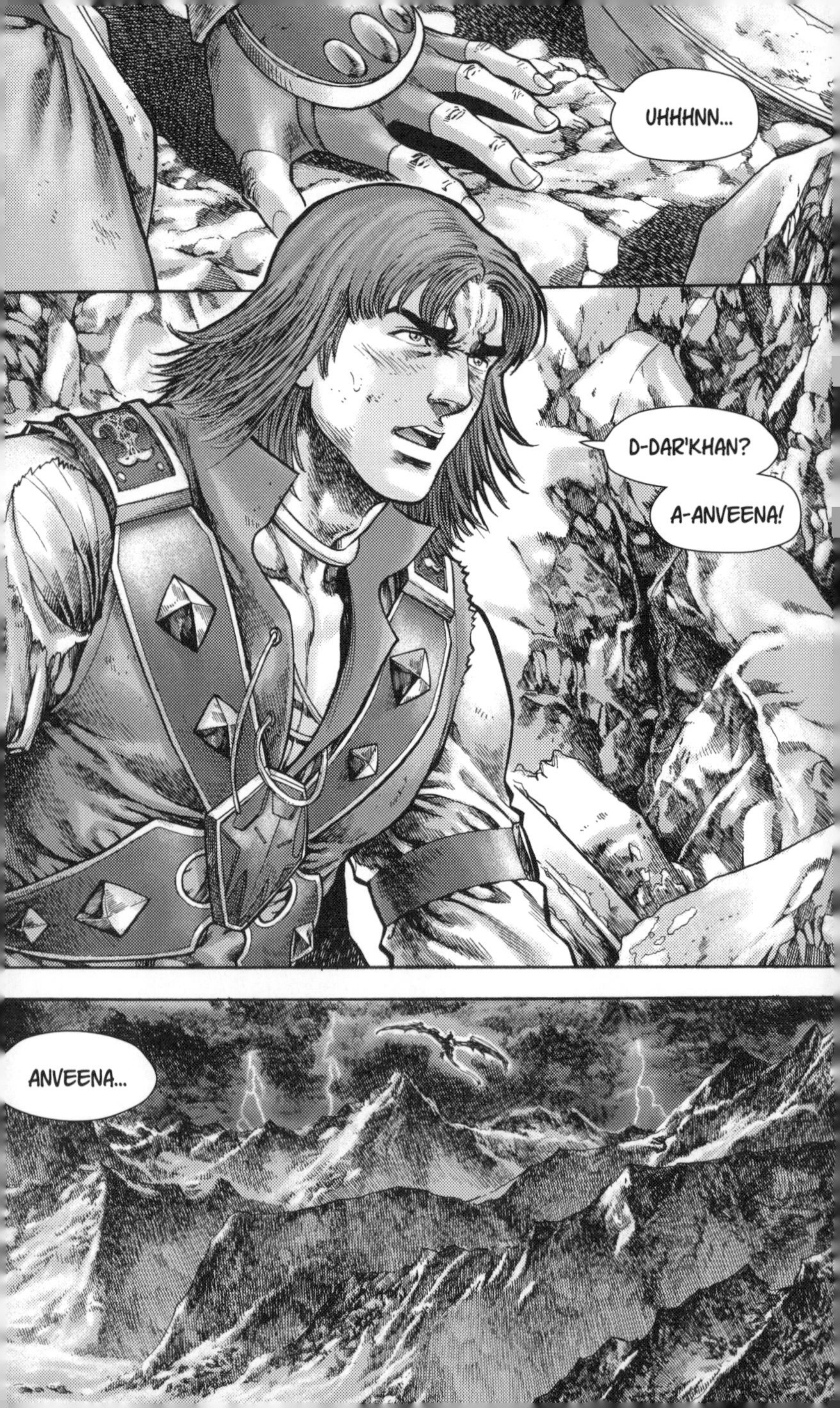
UHHHNN...
D-DAR'KHAN?
A-ANVEENA!
ANVEENA...

To be concluded in

Volume 3

GHOSTLANDS

Dar'Khan ventures to the desolate plaguelands where once stood the elven kingdom of Quel'Thalas . . . and the mighty Sunwell. The dark elf will stop at nothing to gain the power that was once almost his . . . but what role could Anveena play in his mad quest?

Kalec, Tyri, Jorad Mace, and Raac are hot on their trail, but there are other forces in the ruins of Quel'Thalas--including a certain dark banshee queen--they must contend with before they can hope to thwart Dar'Khan.

The mysteries of Raac, the Sunwell, and Kalec's quest will all be laid bare . . . and when all is revealed, nothing will be the same!

ABOUT THE CREATORS

Richard A. Knaak is the *New York Times* and *USA Today* bestselling author of some fifty novels and numerous shorter works. He has written for such well-known series as WORLD OF WARCRAFT, DIABLO, DRAGONLANCE, CONAN, and PATHFINDER and is the creator of the long-running, popular epic fantasy saga THE DRAGONREALM. He has also written comic, manga, and gaming material, and his works have been translated worldwide.

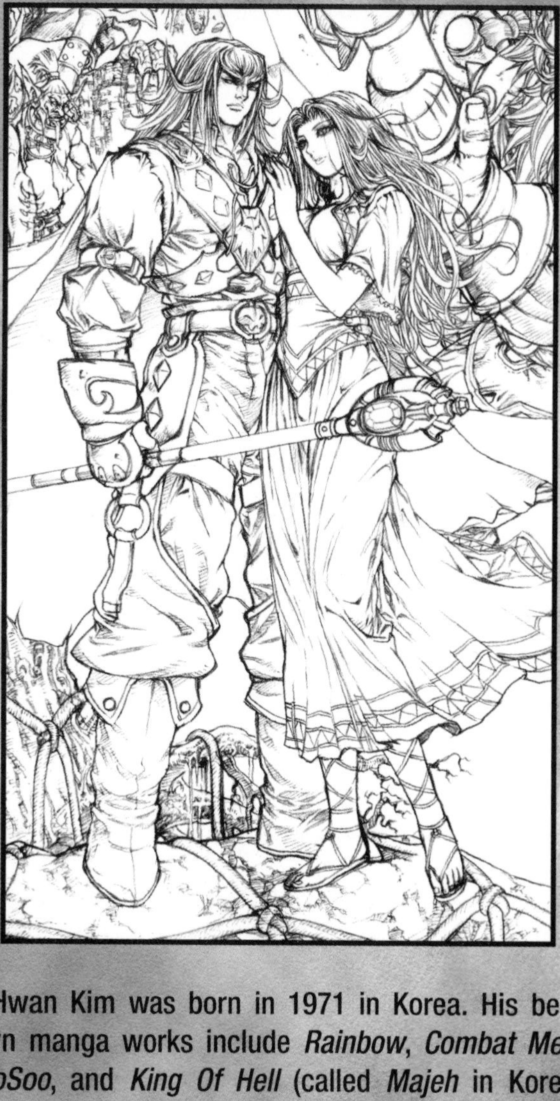

Jae-Hwan Kim was born in 1971 in Korea. His best-known manga works include *Rainbow*, *Combat Metal HeMoSoo*, and *King Of Hell* (called *Majeh* in Korea). Jae-Hwan currently lives and works in Thailand.